Disclosing Secrets

When, to Whom, and How Much to Reveal

M. Deborah Corley, Ph.D.

Jennifer Schneider, M.D., Ph.D.

Gentle Path
PRESS

GENTLE PATH PRESS
P.O. Box 3345
Wickenburg, AZ   95358
www.gentlepath.com
800-955-9853

Library of Congress Control Number: 2002105722

ISBN: 1-929-866-04-6

Authors' note:
The stories in this book are true; however, each has been edited for clarity. Names, locations, and other identifying information have been changed to protect confidentiality.

Publisher: Shari Jo Hehr
Marketing Director: Byron Oldham
Editor: Toni Zuccarini Ackley
Cover Design: Tammie Oldham
Interior Design: Kim Eoff

Books of Related Interest from Gentle Path Press

Open Hearts
Renewing Relationships with Recovery, Romance & Reality
By Patrick Carnes, Ph.D.
Debra Laaser
Mark Laaser, Ph.D.

Cybersex Unhooked
A Workbook for Breaking Free of Compulsive Online Sexual Behavior
By David Delmonico, Ph.D.
Elizabeth Griffin, M.A.
Joeseph Moriarity

Disclosing Secrets
When, to Whom and How Much to Reveal
A Gentle Path Workbook for Disclosing Sensitive Addiction Secrets
By Deborah Corley, Ph.D.
Jennifer Schneider, M.D., Ph.D.

Reclaiming Intimacy
Moving From Sexual Addiction to Healthy Sexuality
A Gentle Path Workbook for Continuing Recovery from Sexual Addiction
By Maureen Canning-Fulton, M.A.

AND PLEASE BE SURE TO VISIT OUR WEBSITES

www.gentlepath.com

www.sexhelp.com

This book is dedicated to our daughters
Jessica and Stevie. They have brought us great joy and pride. Each
shows compassion for others, strength, and courage in all they do.

Jennifer Schneider, **M.D**., **PhD**., practices internal medicine and addiction medicine in Tucson, Arizona. She is the author of ***Back from Betrayal***, ***Sex, Lies and Forgiveness***. She recently coauthored ***Cybersex Exposed*** and also coauthored a book for addicted clinicians, ***The Wounded Healer***, and is associate editor of the journal ***Sexual Addiction and Compulsivity***. She lives in Tucson, Arizona.

M. Deborah Corley, Ph.D. is a Clinical Associate in private practice at the Family Psychology Institute of Dallas and consultant. She is also co-owner and co-founder of Sante Center for Healing, a residential addiction treatment center near Dallas. Deb is the 1999 recipient of the Carnes Award for outstanding achievement in the field of sex addiction and received the 1999 Clinician's Most Valuable Article award by the American Foundation on Addiction Research for her work on disclosure. She is the part president of the Board of Directors for the National Council on Sexual Addiction and Compulsivity, and a clinical member of the American Association of Marriage and Family Therapist.

Table of Contents

CHAPTER THREE: Is Disclosure Right for You?

Introduction

This book is about the disclosure of secrets that have kept addiction and self-doubt alive. It is a guidebook for healing. It is about how to hold onto, repair, and grow a relationship after disclosure.

This book started as a book on disclosure for sex addicts and their partners, based on research we have done over the past several years and a combined 20 years of clinical and personal experience. With encouragement from our editor and readers, the book has evolved into a workbook on disclosure for any addict and/or partner, because all addicts keep secrets, not just sex addicts.

A lot of thought, care, and planning should go into any disclosure. The meaning of a disclosure is different for the addict than it is for the partner or other recipient of a disclosure. Behaviors that are illegal or put at risk the partner's health or the finances of a household or company make the timeliness of a disclosure even more important. Matters are complicated further by the number and age of children, the state of finances and health, years invested in a marriage, and in many cases for sex addicts, if other children are the result of sexual behavior outside the marriage. However, a disclosure indefinitely postponed or thoughtlessly carried out can be as destructive as the addictive behavior itself.

This book is written for men and women who are looking for help for themselves—for couples who are reeling from the effects of an unplanned and painful disclosure, for addicts who've been keeping secrets that they are now ready to disclose, for co-addicts who suspect that there are secrets that need to be shared, and for parents who want guidance on what to tell their children.

Several years ago, when we started our research on disclosure, the focus was around disclosing secrets about sexual behavior. The first question Jennifer wanted answered was, "Do partners of addicts actually leave?" Deb's first question was, "What is the meaning of disclosure to the person disclosing, and to the partner receiving the disclosure?" Obviously, because Deb is a therapist and facilitates disclosures with addicts and their partners every week, she was also interested in feedback about what worked best and what fueled the hurt feelings when working with disclosure. In our research we gained the answers to those questions and learned what was the most and least useful advice offered by any therapist involved with the disclosure as well. Some results of the research are located throughout this book. The rest of the results were published in 1998 in *Sexual Addiction and Compulsivity: The Journal of Treatment and Prevention* and in 1999 in the *Journal of Sex Education and Therapy* and can be found online at our Web sites at **www.jenniferschneider.com** or **www.makingadvances.com**.

Of the 200 people who donated their time and energy in completing the surveys of our original research, some were recovering from chemical dependency, food addiction, out-of-control spending, codependency, or Internet addiction; all were recovering from sex addiction problems. We'd like to thank them, as well as the countless numbers of individuals and couples who have shared their stories with us. What we learned from them about disclosing secrets is applicable to people recovering from *any* addiction. We believe that you, our readers, will find it useful no matter what your addiction history. In fact, people who are not addicts but want to disclose a secret in a healthy way, such as a child out of wedlock or childhood abuse, will also find this book vital.

We have taken great care to change specific information to protect individuals' anonymity. Despite our efforts to change identifying information, many stories are alike in many ways—so don't be surprised if you read something that sounds like your story or that of a friend. Addicts and their partners do lots of the same things.

Statistical research tells us that in most coupled relationships where the addiction is sexual, the addicts are male and the co-addicts/partners are female. That is not always the case, but for ease of presentation, we have used the pronouns *he* for addicts and *she* for co-addicts/partners in most instances in this book. At times we use she for the addict and he for the partner just to remind you that addiction is not gender biased. Both addicts and co-addicts are codependent in some way, so we don't often use that descriptor.

We mean for this book to help people in all types of relationships, not just those who are in a heterosexual marriage. We use the terms *relationship*, *coupleship*, and *marital relationship* to reflect a committed relationship that exists or is being formulated between two people. We try to make a distinction if we are talking about a parent–child relationship, patient–physician relationship, supervisor–employee relationship, or some other type of specific relationship.

If you have been in recovery for a while, you have undoubtedly had to disclose secrets, and/or have received disclosures from your spouse or partner. Perhaps you still bear some scars resulting from the way the disclosure occurred. You probably already have some spoken or unspoken rules about how much you plan to disclose in the future, or what you do or do not want to hear. You may well still be carrying secrets that have not yet been disclosed or have questions you feel have not been adequately answered. This book will provide you with a blueprint for further disclosures, and may help you understand more clearly what information is advisable to disclose, and how the process can be done constructively for both partners. The book will also tell you ways to use the disclosure to help your relationship heal.

If you are new to recovery, you are fortunate! With the help of this book you may be able to do it right the first time. You will certainly be able to negotiate the turbulent waters of disclosure in a more knowledgeable and informed way. You will have a greater awareness of the support you and/or your partner need, have guidelines for how much and when to disclose, and ways for discovering the value of disclosure for you and your partner.

This book is organized in three sections. The first section, Chapters One through Four, looks at the power of disclosure, examining a variety of situations where people have kept secrets and told lies, but are faced with a disclosure. This section also discusses why people chose to disclose, the wide range of reactions and consequences, including if partners leave after a disclosure. Additionally, this section addresses how to determine what type of disclosure is right for you.

The middle section of the book, Chapters Five through Eight, tells you how to go about doing a variety of types of disclosures. Chapter Five outlines our step-by-step approach to a formal disclosure. People ask if anything is private or if everything is a secret that is going to keep the family sick. Chapter Five addresses these issues as well. Most people wonder what (if anything) to tell the children—even adult children—and that information is located in Chapter Six. It is common for addicts to relapse, and dealing with the disclosure of a slip or relapse is a serious issue. Chapter Seven provides tips for what to do when there is a relapse, how to handle other disclosures when the addict remembers something else, boundary setting, testing for sexually transmitted diseases, and coping. Finally, Chapter Eight speaks to special issues that sometimes exist and decisions that need to be made about what to say at work, what to do if the media gets involved, or what to tell people in your faith community or the neighborhood. Here is where you will find information about what to share with others outside your immediate family.

The final section, Chapters Nine and Ten, tells you how to proceed after disclosure as well as how a therapist can best help you with disclosure. Chapter Nine addresses what to do next after a disclosure—formal or otherwise. Determining if a separation is in order, if reconciliation is possible, or if you are still ambivalent about the next step is discussed here. This chapter provides the nuts and bolts for your repair kit—the steps for healing and forgiveness. In every situation there is an opportunity to better oneself. It takes such courage that sometimes we miss the opportunity. One of the facts of life is that the opportunity to learn an important lesson will turn up again if we don't learn it the first time around. Ways to learn from the lessons are located here.

The final chapter is really for professionals who are helping couples work through the process of disclosure. Although we believe this book will help any addict with this process, disclosure often generates strong emotions that not everyone is able to manage. We strongly encourage you to seek the help of a trained professional to help you. If you are already working with someone, this chapter may be of help to them.

As this book evolved into one for all people in recovery, we preserved some of the material specific to sexual addiction—Appendix A: Frequently Asked Questions About Disclosing Sexual Secrets, Appendix B: Suggested Reading, and Appendix C: Recovery Resources. Appendix D contains statistics from our study we thought would be useful to those needing hard data to support our positions.

Excruciating as disclosure is, it's a process that can strengthen and even improve a relationship. Disclosing secrets is always difficult. With this book, the process can become an opportunity for healing. We hope you will take that opportunity now.

MDC and JPS

CHAPTER ONE: The Power of Disclosure
Why People Disclose

Jay, a 40-year-old salesman—and a long-time drinker—had had a string of affairs in his first marriage, which ended in divorce. He hoped to do better by Monica. He had joined Alcoholics Anonymous (AA) and had tried to stay sober, but within a year of their wedding he had already racked up two brief affairs and in both had returned to drinking. He rationalized that his problem "wasn't all that bad, he could control things" because he had only consumed alcohol during the short-term affairs. The crisis came after three years of marriage, when following an argument while they both were drinking, Sue, his latest affair partner, threatened to tell Monica about the relationship. Jay decided to disclose to Monica before she would hear the bad news from Sue. Monica was devastated. Knowing about Jay's history of infidelity in his first marriage and his past problems with drinking, she asked him about any other affairs during their three years together, and was distraught to learn that Sue was already number three in the series and that he had returned to drinking in all three.

Monica and Jay's marriage survived his affairs and his alcohol relapse with the help of addiction counseling, couples therapy, and Twelve-Step self-help meetings for sex addiction and co-addiction as well as AA. Years later, remembering the anger and pain she'd felt at learning of Jay's affairs, Monica recalled that the *single most important factor that made her willing to stay in the marriage* was Jay's decision to disclose his secret to her before she heard it from Sue. What this decision meant to Monica was that she and their marriage were important enough to Jay that he would tell her his secret. He was willing to risk losing her in order to save the marriage, and this was very powerful to Monica.

This book is about *secrets* kept by addicts and their partners (co-addicts). It is about the secrets parents, kids, friends, and others keep in hopes that if no one talks about the secret, it doesn't exist. This book is also about *lies*, which protect secrets; about *disclosure*, which is how people reveal secrets; and about *forgiveness*, which is how painful secrets, once revealed, get processed and ultimately lose their ability to wound.

Not all secrets are bad. Secrets can sometimes enhance intimacy and protect life. A partner who chooses to share something special and private about himself that no one else knows makes you feel special and can strengthen the bond between you. Sometimes, not telling a secret can protect life when violence is a real threat or when someone's health is fragile or if the person lacks the intellectual capacity or maturity to understand the information.

Most people keep secrets because they are afraid. Secrets are commanded by the fear that if the truth is known, something bad will happen. That's what happens with all addicts—they think that if anyone finds out the truth, something bad will happen.

Yet people do decide to disclose.

Why People Disclose

Sometimes people disclose because they feel so guilty that the guilt overwhelms them, so they tell. Others are forced to tell because some authority (such as the law, a boss, a friend, or a therapist) insists on it, and they figure it is better to do damage control than have the partner hear about their addiction from someone else such as the boss, the police, the health department, or the media. Sometimes people tell because they think it is the right thing to do—they are trying to be congruent with their values, and deep down, they value honesty over lying even if they haven't always told the truth. This is especially true for people who are in recovery and starting new relationships. They decide to tell because they want to start the new relationship on a foundation of honesty. By telling, the addict honors the new partner and knows that the new partner is making a choice based on truth and honesty.

Other people break under the intense scrutiny of a partner, therapist, employer, or the police and tell because they are tired of keeping the lie or don't see any other way out.

In cases in which a partner's health could be harmed with a sexually transmitted disease, or if a pregnancy is a possibility (especially if the pregnancy is from another relationship outside the marriage), people tell because they feel they owe it to their partners. Protecting their partner from a health risk is more important than are other consequences for telling.

Like Jay in the example above, some people tell because they got caught or someone else threatened to tell. Sometimes they feel they have no choice, or they tell out of obedience or because they hope this will be the end of the pain they are experiencing as a result of carrying the secret.

Others tell because they are members of a Twelve-Step program of recovery and believe that the recommendations of the program are right—believing that rigorous honesty is a requirement for sobriety. Yet sometimes the advice from the Twelve-Step program is a bit confusing, leaving the addict wondering whether to tell. Often the reactions of the partner are not what they expected. Take John's case:

John, a 33-year-old stockbroker with a three-year history of cocaine addiction, hit bottom after a particularly intense binge and went into treatment. As is true for many cocaine addicts, his sexual appetite had been sent into high gear by the drug, and for several months sexual activities with prostitutes had accompanied his cocaine use. John's wife, Ellen, knew he was going into treatment for cocaine, but she was unaware of the frequent cocaine-sex connection and had no idea he'd been seeing prostitutes.

At the treatment center, John's counselor, Larry, told him that recovery requires rigorous honesty. "We're only as sick as our secrets," he intoned, opening up the *Big Book of Alcoholics Anonymous* to page 58. There John read "Those who do not recover are people who cannot or will not completely give themselves to this simple program, usually men and women who are constitutionally incapable of being honest with themselves"—and with others, Larry added. Larry encouraged John to disclose he had had unprotected sex with the prostitutes and had put his wife's health in danger by then having sex with her. "Keeping such a big secret will poison your recovery," he cautioned John as he left him alone with the *Big Book*.

John remembered the time he'd come home late smelling of perfume. He had thought to cover the alcohol smell with a breath mint, but did not think about the perfume. Ellen had immediately noticed the unusual scent and confronted John. "Have you been with another woman?" she demanded.

John had learned that the best defense was a good offense: "No, of course not! You're supposed to be my best friend, not my interrogator! No wonder I don't like to come home! When you start acting nicer, I'll be more interested in spending time with you!"

Ellen immediately backed down: "I'm sorry, John, I don't know what got into me. I go crazy when I even *think* of you with another woman. I just couldn't stand it. If you ever had sex with someone else, I'd have no choice but to leave you. I couldn't bear it. It would be the end of our marriage."

John thought about Larry's words, and then Ellen's threat to leave if he ever had sex with someone else, so he felt he couldn't possibly tell Ellen about the prostitutes. He idly turned the pages of the *Big Book*, until suddenly the words on page 81 jumped out at him: "After a few years with an alcoholic, a wife gets worn out, resentful and uncommunicative. . . . The husband begins to feel lonely, sorry for himself. He commences to look around in the nightclubs, or their equivalent, for something besides liquor. Perhaps he is having a secret and exciting affair with 'the girl who understands.'" Boy that fit his story—there was no pressure with a prostitute. "The guy who wrote this knew what he was talking about!" John thought.

He read on,

> Whatever the situation, we usually have to do something about it. If we are sure our wife does not know, should we tell her? Not always, we think. If she knows in a general way that we have been wild, should we tell her in detail? Undoubtedly we should admit our fault. She may insist on knowing all the particulars. She will want to know who the woman is and where she is. We feel we ought to say to her that we have no right to involve another person. We are sorry for what we have done and, God willing, it shall not be repeated. More than that we cannot do.

This was more like it! The founders of AA were recommending *against* telling her anything more than she already knew! John began seriously reading the *Big Book,* looking for more support. He found it on page 124:

> We know of situations in which the alcoholic or his wife have had love affairs. In the first flush of spiritual experience they forgave each other and drew closer together. . .Then, under one provocation or another, the aggrieved one would unearth the old affair and angrily cast its ashes about… and they hurt a great deal… In most cases the alcoholic survived this ordeal without relapse, but not always. So we think that unless some good and useful purpose is to be served, past occurrences should not be discussed.

Although a bit confused by the *Big Book's* words, especially when he thought about what his counselor had said, John chose to say nothing to his wife to be on the safe side. After discharge from the treatment center, he joined Cocaine Anonymous (CA) and began working a Twelve-Step program. For two months he did well, until one night an old using buddy offered him some cocaine, just for "old time's sake." Suddenly he felt an urge to visit a prostitute, and justified it by telling himself that it was the lesser of two evils, not as risky as using cocaine. However, sitting in the hotel room with her, he felt an irresistible desire to snort cocaine, and suddenly recovery seemed very distant and unimportant. Three days and a lot of cocaine later, John realized he had a second problem. John couldn't stay clean unless he also stayed away from prostitutes, and it was hard for him to give them up. A friend at the CA meeting suggested he check out a Twelve-Step program for compulsive sexual behavior, so John began attending Sex Addicts Anonymous (SAA) meetings.

Once again faced with the problem of what to tell his wife, John appealed to the book *Hope and Recovery*, a Twelve-Step guide for sex addicts considered by many to be analogous to the *Big Book of AA* for alcoholics. The recovering addicts who authored *Hope and Recovery*, like the authors of the *Big Book*, advise waiting to tell the partner until one has first discussed it with the group, prayed about it, and felt it was the right time to do so. "Some of us found that it was helpful to have our sponsors with us when we told our partners about our addiction. And if our partners also happened to be in recovery, it was helpful to have their sponsors present too. . . . We wrote down exactly what we wanted to say to our partners and shared it with other addicts first." (p. 97).

Armed with this advice, John chose to wait to tell Ellen until he had some more SAA as well as CA recovery. He did not have a chance to tell her on his own schedule, however, because two months later Ellen found his copy of *Hope and Recovery,* as well as an SAA meeting schedule, in his car and insisted on a full explanation. By now, four months had elapsed since John had initially gone to the treatment center, and Ellen was extremely angry about having been kept in the dark for so long about his sexual acting out. During those four months, Ellen had continued being sexual with John, and her fear and anger about the possibility of exposure to HIV disease added fuel to the flame. She felt she could not forgive John for continuing to risk her life by having unprotected sex with her after being sexual with prostitutes. Overwhelmed by anger, despair, fear, and distrust, Ellen asked John to leave.

Addicts and Co-addicts Cannot Tolerate Emotional Distress

Daniel Goleman, in his book *Emotional Intelligence,* points out that people who are emotionally intelligent are able to identify their feelings and tolerate how they and the people around them feel. A person who is emotionally competent can identify not only how he or she is feeling, but can identify the feeling states of those around them and respond appropriately.

Unfortunately, addicts have poor emotional competence, as John demonstrates in the above example. Addicts' strategies for controlling their impulses involve using some substance or engaging in a harmful behavior or both in order to alter how they feel. John demonstrates this unhealthy strategy. However, unlike many people whose disclosure is precipitated by discovery of the affair or other secret, John had the opportunity to choose the timing and method of disclosure. Sadly, guided by his motivation to reduce his anxiety and shame rather than to do the right thing or be his authentic self, he found reasons to repeatedly delay his disclosure, until eventually the delay itself became the major problem. He was motivated by fear and rationalized that an early disclosure would result in something bad happening.

Exercise:

We learn how to show and manage feelings from our caretakers—that is usually our parents, or sometimes grandparents or others who took care of us when we were young. Generally, in addicted families feelings are either disapproved or dismissed. For example, a disapproving parent judges and criticizes a child's emotional expression, and the child is often punished for it. A disapproving parent believes negative emotions make people weak and demands that the child be obedient. This parent treats the child as if the child's feelings are unimportant and disengages from or ignores the child. The parent minimizes the child's feelings and downplays the events that led to the emotional state.

Think about your own family and what type of parents you had. Describe what you learned in your family of origin about feelings. How would a delay in disclosing impact your relationship with yourself and your mate?

_____

_____

_____

_____

_____

_____

Helpful Hints

If you feel anxious about a disclosure, there are ways you can improve your emotional intelligence that will help you deal with the emotional distress. Be your own emotional coach:

- Remind yourself of the type of parenting style you were raised with and determine what you would need if you were a child and feeling scared and anxious right now.

- Think about the negative emotional states you are having. Identify each state. Are you angry and scared? Are you anxious because you don't know how to take the next step? Empathize with yourself about how awful it feels and that it is normal to feel that way under the circumstances. You may find it helpful to talk with your sponsor or therapist about these feelings. This will also help reduce your distress and let you know if you are on target about how you are feeling. Often, if feelings have been discounted when you were a child, you are not sure what it is that you feel!

- Set limits for yourself while problem-solving that are consistent with recovering. Assure yourself that you can feel these feelings in recovery, but to try to "medicate" them will be an invitation to relapse. Again, this is why it is helpful to have another person to talk to about how you are feeling.

- Identify and clarify your goals. These might be something like staying in recovery, learning about self, being honest every day, feeling feelings, and self-soothing in healthy ways.

- Identify specific steps to reach your goals.

- Self-soothe in healthy ways. This might include deep breathing, visualizing a positive outcome, prayer, meditation, talking with others, taking a walk or exercising, reading, or listening to soothing music.

- Avoid negative self-talk.

Addiction and Honesty: The Impact of the Twelve-Step Philosophy of Disclosure

Addicts are told that honesty and accountability are important for recovery. The eighth of the Twelve Steps of Alcoholics Anonymous states, "We made a list of all persons we have harmed, and became willing to make amends to them all." The purpose of the eighth step is to identify individuals who have been harmed by the addict's behavior as well as assigning ownership of responsibility for the addict's behavior. By preparing to make amends, the addict begins the process of releasing guilt and wiping the slate clean in order to make a fresh start.

However, Step Nine cautions the addict who is about to reveal "all": "We made amends to such people wherever possible, except when doing so would injure them or others." Fear of hurting the partner and fear of the partner's response is a common reason for minimizing the disclosure. Sometimes it is difficult to sort out whether you are holding on to the secret because you believe your partner truly can't handle it, or because you are afraid of being left.

We think it is also important to look at the facts behind the life of the author of the *Big Book*, Bill Wilson—or as most people refer to him, Bill W. In his biography of Bill Wilson, author Francis Hartigan reports that Bill Wilson may have been sober from alcohol, but seems to have struggled with other addictive and compulsive behaviors all his life. He writes, "Bill was compulsive, given to emotional extremes. Even after he stopped drinking, he was still a heavy consumer of cigarettes and coffee. He had a sweet tooth, a large appetite for sex, a major enthusiasm for LSD." Hartigan goes on to say, "Judging from the guilt and remorse he suffered over his inability to control his sexual impulses, even his infidelities seem to be evidence not of a lack of standards but of a failure to live up to them."

In addition to his many sexual conquests, Bill also had a long-term affair with a woman named Helen Wynn, to whom he left part of the *Big Book* royalties. He felt both guilty about the affair and obligated to Helen as well as his wife Lois.

Not to discount all the work Bill Wilson did to start Alcoholics Anonymous, but one has to wonder what influence his "womanizing" had on his advice in the *Big Book* regarding telling one's partner about sexual infidelities. Perhaps Bill was afraid to tell Lois for fear that she would leave or that she had been put through so much already. He often underestimated Lois and her ability to cope.

Thinking your partner can't handle it is really slighting your partner. The results of our research overwhelmingly indicate that partners want to know. Addicts often lie in such a way as to make their partners feel crazy. By revealing the secrets through disclosure, the addict allows the partner to regain his or her sanity. Taking the approach that your partner can't handle it only further hurts your partner. If you are worried for your partner, then make sure you have thought through how you are going to tell and have a therapist available to help.

Different addicts have dealt with this dilemma in different ways: Bill Wilson chose to disclose the minimum, and continued having affairs for the rest of his life. Reportedly he never could hold onto good feelings about himself. Like Bill, some addicts disclose only non-sexual behaviors and never reveal affairs or sexual acting out even if they feel they aren't addicted to sex. Others tell everything, or all the information that their partner asks for. Still others reveal the basic behaviors but not the details. Each of these choices has different consequences for the addict and the partner. (In Chapter Five, we will provide specific information on how to disclose as well as samples of disclosures.)

Honesty—Not Just for Addicts

The Bible says that the truth will set you free (John 8:32). All religions value honesty as a character trait and expect honesty as a sign of a covenant. In most marriages the covenant of honesty is usually an expectation, even if not voiced.

For many addicts, admitting the truth, although extremely difficult, feels like freedom. This freedom is the power of disclosure. So many addicts are sick of living the double life that telling results in a reduction of guilt. Of course, this is dependent on the consequences of telling, but over time most addicts report that, despite the consequences, they are glad they told.

All couples who have a major secret between them face the decision of disclosure. When the secret is sexual, keeping it secret can be very destructive. Frank Pittman, in *Private Lies* (1989, p. 20), defines *infidelity* as "a breach of the trust, a betrayal of a relationship, a breaking of an agreement." However, infidelity involves much more than sex: The dishonesty about the infidelity involves loss of self-esteem, the value of the rule broken, and the energy of keeping the secret that is taken from the relationship. Pittman states that dishonesty may be a greater violation of the rules than the affair or misconduct, and acknowledges that more marriages end as a result of maintaining the secret than do in the wake of telling. He firmly supports rigorous honesty. He speculates that the partner may be angry, but will be angrier if the affair continues and the partner finds out later.

Although not all addicts are sex addicts or have been sexually unfaithful, they have been unfaithful in that the drug or addictive behavior becomes the primary relationship in their lives. It is as if the person has an affair with the drug. It becomes the most important thing in his or her life and the addict will put the drug or behavior before family, job, community, and all other meaningful relationships.

Emily Brown, in her book *Patterns of Infidelity*, advises that, in most circumstances, the unfaithful person must tell the partner if healing is to occur. When an affair remains secret, communication about other matters is gradually impaired. When the affair is with a drug, the same thing is true— all communication between the addict and partner or other important people is damaged.

Ms. Brown advises that behaviors from previous relationships or from long ago do not always have to be revealed. She agrees with our assessment that before actual rebuilding of the relationship can occur, time and support for the partner are necessary and that therapy sessions often take longer or are more frequent to help the partner express her or his anger and sadness about the infidelity.

Addict Exercise:

Complete this exercise to help you determine your reasons for being honest. In the top-left quadrant of the square below, list all the positive reasons you have for being completely honest about your addictive or inappropriate behaviors. Then, in the top-right quadrant, list all your negative reasons for being completely honest about your addictive behaviors. In the lower-left quadrant, list all the positive reasons for not disclosing or disclosing only a partial amount (what your mate already knows or is likely to find out). In the lower-right quadrant, list all the negative reasons for not disclosing or only partially disclosing. Now examine which of these options bests fits your recovery and your values as an authentic person.

Partner Exercise:

You may have already received some disclosure or suspect that the addict in your life is going to disclose more. It will be helpful for you to think about how you can make the most of the disclosure for healing by completing the following decision matrix box.

In your decision matrix box, in the upper-right quadrant, list the positive reasons for full disclosure to you. Then, in the upper-left quadrant, list the negative reasons for full disclosure to you. In the lower-right quadrant, list the positive reasons for not knowing (for example, you don't have to deal with the pain during a time when another crisis is going on). In the lower-left quadrant, list the negative reasons for not knowing. Now review your responses and determine what will be best for you. List ten ways you can use information shared in a disclosure to help yourself and your relationship. List ten ways you might misuse the information and ways to guard against that.

Telling Because of Health Risks

When a person is diagnosed with Hepatitis C (transmitted sexually or through dirty needles) or a sexually transmitted disease (STD) that is reportable to the health department, a representative will notify all parties who have potentially been exposed. Many people disclose because they realize that the partner will be notified or that it is necessary for the partner to get medical care.

Since 1980, however, a new negative consequence has loomed larger and larger—the risk of acquiring a potentially fatal disease (HIV). This possibility brings a new ethical dimension to the choice of whether to reveal to or keep secret from the partner such information. Because of this risk, more therapists are now insisting on disclosure of extramarital sexual behaviors or intravenous (IV) drug use to the partner. We have found that one of the actions that are most difficult for the partner to forgive is when the addict practices unsafe sex or uses unclean needles for IV drug use and continues to knowingly expose the partner to the risk of contracting a serious illness. Many partners consider this action to signify such lack of caring that they are never able to overcome it and choose instead to end the marriage.

Also of concern to therapists is when an addict engages in behaviors that put him and his family in danger. Purchasing drugs and sex from armed and potentially violent persons, and/or persons who engage in illegal behaviors (for example, drug dealers and prostitutes) not only brings the risk of Hepatitis C, HIV, and other STDs, it also brings the risk of potential violence into a household. Police raids and attacks from revenge-seeking spouses are possibilities when persons with unsavory lifestyles are brought into someone's life. Threats from such persons may precipitate disclosure by the addict in an attempt to forestall the potential violence.

On the other side of the coin, a potential health risk that can be the *result* of disclosure rather than a *reason* to disclose is domestic violence. This is especially true when it is the husband who is the recipient of disclosure of his wife's extramarital sexual activities or high-risk drug use rather than the other way around. The response of many men to sexual betrayal is extreme anger, which may be directed at the wife, at the affair partner, or both. In the survey reported in *Sex, Lies, and Forgiveness* (1999), several men reported experiencing a murderous rage in response to learning of their wives extramarital sexual activities. One man displaced his anger onto some furniture, which he chopped to pieces with an axe; another stalked the affair partner, and reported that it was a good thing he did not encounter him alone, or violence would have resulted.

Interestingly, we have found that partners who are themselves recovering addicts tend to be more tolerant upon receiving a sexual disclosure than do partners who are not addicts. We hypothesize that addicts feel guilty about their past behavior and therefore are more willing to tolerate it in their partners.

Both intense jealousy by the male and more tolerance by the female in couples faced with infidelity are reported in David Buss's research on jealousy (2000). Buss and other researchers have found that women are more tolerant of sexual affairs than emotional affairs whereas men are just the opposite.

Everyone, especially women who are considering disclosure of material that is likely to be very upsetting to the partner, needs to assess in advance the risk of sustaining physical violence as a result of the disclosure. If there are any concerns about safety, it is imperative to delay disclosure until it can be done in a safe place in the presence of a professional.

Addict Exercise:

Sometimes addicts are so "out-of-it" when they are using, they aren't even aware of all the ways they have put themselves, much less their partners, in harm's way. Examine your own behavior by completing the following:

List all the ways you have jeopardized your mate's and your health and well-being. Of these, identify the ones she most needs to know to make smart, informed decisions about her own health.

_____

_____

_____

_____

_____

Partner Exercise:

It is common for the partner of a sex addict or drug user to be exposed to health risks. Request proof from your partner that he has not acquired any STDs, including Hepatitis C. To be on the safe side, unless you have proof that your mate has not participated in sex with others, get yourself checked.

It is common to have strong feelings about having your health or life being put in harm's way. Write a letter to your mate about how you feel about being exposed to personal risk. In that letter, tell him other emotions you've experienced beyond anger. Indicate what he can do today to help you cope better with this information. Ask for time to read the letter to him. You may want to do this with a therapist for support.

Damage Control Disclosure: I'd Better Tell Before Someone Else Does

Robert, a gifted and creative computer programmer who'd been highly paid and highly valued at his company, had always enjoyed print pornography, but when he discovered the many sexual opportunities on the Internet, he was instantly hooked. Because he had a lot of unsupervised time at work, it was easy for Robert to spend an increasing amount of company time on his office computer engaged in viewing pornography, exchanging sexually focused emails with women, and eventually participating in real-time interactive sexual activities. Because Robert's behavior at home did not change, his wife, Laurie, was completely unaware of these activities. Laurie did notice that Robert's interest in sex with her had diminished, but he explained this on the basis that he was working long hours on a complex project at work, and was exhausted by the time he got home.

Unfortunately for Robert, his supervisor walked in on him one day while Robert was involved in online sex. Analysis of Robert's computer revealed thousands of stored pornographic images, hundreds of saved personal emails, and evidence of dozens of hours of company time spent in personal sexual activities. Robert's supervisor was already dissatisfied with Robert's diminishing productivity at work, and the incontrovertible evidence he now had of Robert's unauthorized activities gave him the excuse he needed to immediately fire Robert.

Robert was given two hours to pack his belongings. Before the first day was out, a dozen other programmers, including two who were good friends of Robert and Laurie, knew what had happened. Robert went home and told Laurie he'd been fired. "Why?" she asked, incredulous. Robert had to instantly decide how much to tell her. Realizing she was likely to hear it from others the next day, he chose to explain it to her himself first.

Public Service Announcement: A Warning about Cybersex.

Many addicts never venture onto the Internet, but let this be a warning. The Internet has addictive qualities that researchers do not yet fully understand. It is the rare addict that does not get hooked by something on the Net, no matter if it is gambling, spending out of control, chatting, or sharing non-stop emails. Addicts just have to be careful. Clearly, online sexual activities, whether it is chatting about sexual topics, viewing and/or downloading pornography, or viewing another via video streaming, is very addictive for a brain already "wired" for addiction.

It has been estimated that 70 percent of online sexual activities take place between 9 A.M. and 5 P.M., meaning they involve work hours and work computers. The number of addicts who download pornography at work or misuse the Internet has made many employers establish policies of intolerance for such behaviors. When you have just been fired for spending work time doing online sex, it is difficult to keep this from your spouse! It's especially difficult if you know that others in the company know the reason and are likely sooner or later to reveal it to her. You realize all too clearly that it's not a question of *whether* your mate will find out, but *when*. In such a setting, it is wiser to tell your mate yourself than to wait until she hears it from someone else; in this way, you have some possibility of presenting the information in the best possible light. Unfortunately, in the interest of "damage control," too many people omit the most hurtful or egregious details. Although such a choice may seem like the most comfortable one initially, our research has shown that it can cause great difficulty later on.

The strategy of "telling it first" is most likely to be used when public disclosure is imminent or legal action is involved, such as being arrested for illegal drug use or possession of a controlled substance; driving while under the influence or while intoxicated; sexual behavior such as soliciting a prostitute, exposing oneself, sex with a minor, or voyeurism; or having a patient lodge a complaint against a physician, dentist, or therapist for engaging in a sexual encounter. The arrest report becomes public record, and the news media frequently look at these records seeking sensational stories. Clearly the spouse will find out about the conduct. Nothing is to be gained by the addict's withholding the information from the partner. Indeed, therapists frequently tell addicts and others that it will be better for them if this information comes directly from them rather than from some other source. Nonetheless, it is common for addicts to minimize and excuse their conduct, and to omit acts of very significant misconduct, about which the spouse learns only later.

"I'll Do Anything to Save This Relationship"—Including Disclosure

Yet another motivation for disclosing sexual behaviors to the spouse or partner is a desire to salvage the relationship. When the spouse recognizes that this is the motivation of the disclosure, the disclosure can be the first step to rebuilding trust for the couple.

If you recall Jay and Monica, whose story began this chapter, Jay decided to come clean with Monica about his affair with Sue after Sue threatened to tell Monica herself. Jay weighed the risks and benefits of disclosure and decided he had a better chance to save the marriage if Monica heard the bad news directly from him rather than from his affair partner. Upon learning of the affair and his relapse on alcohol, Monica had a mixture of reactions, among them anger, hurt, and the painful realization that she would have to construct a new picture in her head of the reality of her recent relationship with Jay. A series of confusing events came to her mind, and she recognized that Jay's ongoing affair and his drinking might have contributed to the confusion.

For example, Monica remembered a recent excursion with Jay to the Great Smoky Mountains, a vacation she'd really looked forward to but which turned into an emotional disaster. Monica loved hiking and camping, and Jay, who was a city guy at heart, had agreed to spend a long weekend with Monica in the mountains. She felt particularly warm and loving to him at the start of that weekend, and kept telling him how much she loved him—but every attempt to get close to him physically or emotionally was rebuffed by Jay. In fact, he seemed to be going out of his way to be particularly cruel and unpleasant to her. Monica kept wondering all weekend what she had done wrong.

Now, having learned about the affair, Monica asked Jay about what had been going on for him at the time of the camping trip. Reluctantly, he told her he'd been at the height of his affair with Sue, wishing every second that he was with his lover rather than her. Every loving word or gesture by Monica increased Jay's guilt. He kept thinking, "If she only knew how I'm really feeling, she wouldn't think I'm such a caring wonderful husband, she'd realize I'm really worthless." By his uncaring behaviors all weekend, Jay was subconsciously trying to prove to Monica that he didn't deserve her love and positive regard.

Hearing the truth from Jay, painful though it was for her, helped Monica make sense of the recent events in their marriage and *validated for her that she wasn't crazy* and that her reactions to Jay had been normal. Jay was clearly unhappy to be grilled about these events, but his willingness to answer all her questions suggested to Monica, even in the midst of her anger and pain, that he was committed to their relationship and willing to experience great discomfort in order to try to save the marriage. The power of disclosure is that it gave Monica hope that they might somehow rebuild trust and restore their relationship.

In a group discussion of difficult disclosures, Megan, a 50-year-old artist with three years of recovery from sex addiction, recalled the hardest secret she had to reveal to her husband:

> When my daughter Stephanie was conceived, I was in the midst of one of my many affairs. I wasn't sure who was her father—my husband Milt or my affair partner, and I kept my doubts to myself. When Stephanie was 17, her high school biology class had a project in which they obtained the blood types of all the kids in the class. I already knew my own blood type and that of my husband, and when Stephanie told me her blood type, I knew for sure that Milt was not her father. I was still having affairs at the time, and I managed to put the new information out of my mind and not think too much about it for the next 10 years. But when Milt came for Family Week three years ago when I was being treated for my sex addiction, I knew I had to disclose this awful secret to him.

> Believe me, it was the scariest thing I'd ever done. Even though by then he knew about the many affairs and seemed committed to sticking by me, I was afraid that this would just be too much for him and that he'd leave me. But he said that as far as he was concerned, Stephanie had always been his daughter and still was. He was angry with me, and also got very depressed, but he worked through it. I also told Stephanie about it at that time. Fortunately, she was 27, an adult with two young children, and she took it

pretty well. She already knew about my sex addiction, and she understood that this was part of it. I'm very lucky—I no longer have the burden of this secret, and my husband and daughter have both forgiven me.

Exercise for Both Addict and Partner:

Think through your motivation for telling or being told. Here are some questions to help you think about this:

- What are my values about honesty and trustworthiness? How is my life being affected by not honoring those values?

- How do I want my life to be different?

- What would be some unhealthy reasons to disclose?

- What would be evidence that a disclosure is one that is based on healthy reasons?

- What have you heard from others about disclosure? How is that information influencing your action now?

- Would you want to know every detail or just general information?

- What wouldn't you want to know?

Now think about what you have learned in this chapter and what your values are about honesty and healthy reasons for disclosure. Look back at the example of John and Ellen earlier in this chapter. As you can see, John's situation was complicated by his attempt to do damage control about his relapse and to relieve his guilt.

Describe what you think went wrong here. Was John doing what was instructed in the *Big Book* or could he have had another agenda? What could he have done differently that might have eased the pain that he and Ellen went through in the first year of his recovery? Describe what you would have done to be helpful to Ellen. What situations in John's and Ellen's lives are similar to yours? How do you want your outcome to be different?

The next chapter will provide a background for understanding the problems couples have with secrets, especially when the behaviors have been repeated and compulsive. It is very tempting to hold on to those secrets and not reveal them. Yet the benefits of revealing them can be enormous for most people. The chapter also reviews traditional advice offered by some therapists, addiction counselors, and self-help groups about revealing secrets. This will pave the way for our proposal of a new way to handle disclosure of secrets.

References

Alcoholics Anonymous. New York: Alcoholics Anonymous World Services, Inc., 1953.

Brown, Emily. *Patterns of Infidelity.* New York: Brunner Mazel, 1991.

Buss, David. *The Dangerous Passion: Why Jealousy Is as Necessary as Love and Sex.* New York: Free Press, 2000.

Goleman, Daniel. *Emotional Intelligence.* New York: Bantam Books, 1994.

Hartigan, Francis. *Bill W. A Biography of Alcoholics Anonymous Cofounder Bill Wilson.* New York: St. Martin's Press, 2000.

Hope and Recovery: A Twelve Step Guide for Healing from Compulsive Sexual Behavior. Center City, Minn., 1987.

Pittman, Frank. *Private Lies. New York: WW Norton Co., 1989.*

Schneider, Jennifer and Burt Schneider *Sex, Lies, and Forgiveness: Couples Speak on Healing from Sex Addiction.* 2nd ed. Tucson, Ariz.: Recovery Resources Press, 1999.

CHAPTER TWO: Secrets and Lies

Lies Influence Relationships, and Relationships Influence Lies

Why do people lie—that seems pretty obvious doesn't it? They don't want to get in trouble. But it is not that simple for most. Some people speculate that addicts are born liars, but that is not true. We all learn to lie through an important developmental process in which lying serves a specific purpose.

In his book *Lies, Lies, Lies: The Psychology of Deceit* (1996), Charles Ford, MD sites several studies that demonstrate how children use lying. He summarizes:

> Lying is . . . an essential component in the process of developing autonomy and differentiating oneself from one's parents. The capacity to fool parents demonstrates to children that parents are not omnipotent . . . lying is reinforced (positively or negatively) by the degree to which the child is rewarded or punished for deceitful behavior. (p. 86)

As children become older, lying provides a way for them to learn that their parents can't totally control them. In this way, the child gains a sense of autonomy.

In another example, Ford explains that children use lying to help them in other ways beyond the developmental task of separating self from parents/others. This important distinction relates to the addict and co-addict experiences:

> If the child experiences repeated trauma (such as sexual abuse, physical abuse, or being raised in a family with an alcoholic parent), lying may become one way to cope with stress. Certainly, putting on a false face appears to be one coping mechanism learned when growing up in a family with alcoholism. (p. 86)

Clearly, lying serves an important developmental function as well as a means for coping. Unfortunately, without help most addicts and co-addicts fail to learn other ways to gain autonomy and independence in relationships or cope well with adversity or trauma.

Of course, there are other reasons people lie. As we mentioned in Chapter One, a major reason is to avoid punishment or to punish someone when you are angry. Fooling someone else makes you feel powerful or that you are a part of something. When someone doesn't feel they can ever live up to the expectations of others, that person might lie as a form of self-deception, to maintain their self-esteem, or to accommodate the other person's self-deception. A lie can resolve role conflict or help create a sense of identity. Many times people lie about how they feel to avoid acknowledging the pain they are in.

To keep a secret, you must tell a lie. A lie is a deliberate act in which you either misrepresent or conceal information. There are lies of omission and commission (deliberate lies). There are lies you tell yourself and lies that you tell others. There are lies that are justifiable—for example, to avoid offending someone or to prepare a surprise party for a friend—and there are lies that are toxic. Toxic lies are the lies addicts and co-addicts use to keep others from learning their truths.

As the addict, telling lies helps cover the shame and guilt of knowing that the behavior you have engaged in has harmed you and your partner. Although telling lies is painful, addicts believe that telling the truth will only make things worse. Lies appear to be the lesser of two evils. But the unfortunate result is that not only do you obsess about your drug or behavior of choice, you now also obsess about how to keep the secrets about your behavior from your partner, family, co-workers, and friends.

As the partner, you can sense or feel the anxiety created by the addict's need to keep you from finding out the secret. Although you may not be sure about what is going on, your gut reaction tells you there is something wrong. However, the more you ask, beg, nag, threaten, snoop, or doubt, the more the addict denies and the more you obsess about finding out what is wrong. You sometimes catch part of the lie, but the addict is so clever about covering one lie with another, you are never totally sure what is the truth. In an attempt to figure this out, you obsess about it for hours on end.

The obsessing crowds the heads of both the addict and the partner. It takes up valuable hours each day and night, causing loss of productivity by day, insomnia by night. Gradually it builds a wall between you and your mate as it erodes your self-confidence and faith in yourself.

This chapter illustrates several types of secrets guarded by various types of lies and how addicts and partners use and fear the secrets and lies that influence their relationships.

Crazy-Making Abusive Lying

In the old movie *Gaslight,* Ingrid Bergman plays Paula, a young, vulnerable woman who married a suave, romantic Gregory Anton (played by Charles Boyer). She is swept up by his romantic gestures and believes he is the answer to her loneliness. What she doesn't know is that he is obsessed with finding jewels that are supposed to be hidden in her home. Over time, the audience sees him change from being romantic to being cunning—he begins to mess with the gaslights in the house but tells her it is her imagination; the lights have remained the same. He slowly, insidiously drives her to the brink of insanity by changing her environment and then telling her she is seeing things, that she is mistaken, and finally that she is crazy. Because she has no proof to believe otherwise, she begins to doubt herself and believe him. Eventually she actually believes his lies and is convinced she is insane.

This is how lying and keeping secrets by an addict in a relationship makes the partner feel crazy. The addict usually begins the relationship by making promises of some kind either with a noble cause, as in *Gaslight,* or by being kind, compassionate, or attentive in ways the partner longs for. Sometimes the addict tells some pitiful story about his own life and how the partner has made it all better. In these situations the partner feels the intensity of this "sharing" and mistakes this feeling for intimacy and she feels unique.

Usually early on in the relationship, the addict validates the promises in some way that further gains the partner's confidence and feels like some unmet need during childhood is being met—so the partner gets hooked. Then the first betrayal happens. The addict does something that seems so out of character, so painful that the partner has difficulty believing that this really happened, but usually demands some explanation. The addict always has an explanation that seems plausible. It makes sense because the addict is careful to include some grain of truth in the explanation so he can demonstrate how "honest" he is being. However, the lies continue and the partner is exploited in a number of ways. But the addict rationalizes that the costs for lying are less than those of telling the truth, so he fools himself into believing there is no way out—so he tells more lies and the partner stops listening to her inner voice and starts to feel crazy.

This type of lying is very traumatic for the partner. It is a form of the worst kind of abuse.

Several Types of Secrets

Secrets that hurt relationships are as common and numerous as are people. Here are a few types of commonly kept secrets that are often triggers for addicts or codependents.

The Emotional Secret

Most addicts and co-addicts were raised in families with emotionally dismissing or disapproving parents. Disapproving parents disregard, ignore, or trivialize a child's negative emotions. Disapproving parents say, "Don't feel—all feelings require something of me that I don't have to give or don't know how to give, so don't feel. If you have a feeling, I will ignore it or tell you it isn't that important." Consequently these children grow up unable to identify the feelings they or others have, or discount their own feeling states.

Dismissing parents reprimand or punish children for emotional expressions. Similar to the disapproving parent, these parents also cannot tolerate the child having an emotional state that they can't control, so the child's response to emotional situations is shut down by threats or punishment. A common response would be, "You better stop that crying before I give you something to cry about!"

Research shows that children raised with these types of parents grow up having a hard time trusting their own judgment. This makes sense. If children are told that their feelings are wrong—that they really don't feel the way they say they feel—then they are likely to grow up believing there is something inherently wrong with them. Unfortunately, the result is someone who can't tolerate emotional distress in others or him or her self—common in addiction and codependent behaviors.

Take Martha who is married to Michael. Martha was raised in an alcoholic family and suffered from low self-esteem. Her father's rages during drinking left her and her siblings afraid to show any emotions. If he was raging, she did everything possible to disappear. She remembered once when her sister started to cry while her father was raging. Her father picked up her sister, slapped her hard across the face, and then shook her for what seemed like forever while yelling for her sister to stop crying. Martha quickly learned it wasn't safe to show any emotions around her father.

When her father wasn't drinking, Martha tried to be the best she could in hopes that she could prevent him from drinking and her mother from getting depressed. Hoping to somehow get her parents to stop their crazy behaviors, she did everything she could to be the "perfect" child. She tried out for school plays and was always given a part, but both parents were too busy to attend. She studied hard in school and was at the top of her class, yet neither of her parents attended her college graduation where she was valedictorian.

Martha felt that no matter what she did, it was not good enough to deserve their love. Working constantly to keep her feelings in check, she behaved kindly to everyone, no matter what they did to her. But before long, she noticed that the people she seemed to attract took advantage of her, asking her to do things that were beyond her capability or her wishes. She continually struggled with her feelings of resentment and frustration that others were taking advantage of her, but feared that if she said anything, they would abandon her. Sometimes, though, when the stress overwhelmed her, she would eat with a vengeance: ice cream, doughnuts, potato chips— whatever she could get her hands on, bingeing until she thought she'd burst. Then she'd feel so guilty for the feelings and for eating so much that she'd make herself throw up and then run several miles in a day or take laxatives to make sure she did not gain weight. She remembered how when she was a child, her mother complained that she was too fat. Her response was to try even harder to please everyone.

Martha was very surprised when Michael, a medical resident from the hospital where she worked part time, asked her out. She couldn't believe that this man, who was both good looking and came from a prominent Jewish family, would be interested in her.

Michael's background included a prominent family that looked good on the outside. However, Michael was raised by emotionally dismissing parents. Even though Michael was now over six feet tall and in excellent shape, as a child he was thin and shy. Often last to be chosen on the team, he was frequently taunted and sometimes picked on by the bullies at school. When he would come home crying, he was told that he needed to stop acting like a sissy, to stop crying and "be a man." His father was famous for telling him that there was something wrong with him because Michael cried when his dog was hit by a car—that it was just a dog. Michael was then told the story of his father's family's experience during the Holocaust and that Michael was just a spoiled baby trying to use tears to get his way instead of minding his father. Early in his life, Michael vowed never to cry or let himself feel anything again.

Like Martha, Michael set out to make his father proud of him—playing football in the homecoming game despite having a fractured collarbone, working two jobs to save money for college even though his family could easily afford the college tuition, and being in the top quarter of the students in medical school. Yet each time he talked to his father, he was told that he could have done better in some way. Michael felt totally inadequate, but vowed never to show it. Instead he covered it with working harder, being firm with those around him, and not giving in to his feelings.

Michael was drawn to Martha like a moth to a flame. People are commonly drawn to mates who they think will provide for them what they missed in childhood. Here was Martha, kind to all the patients, attentive to his stories—laughing and enthusiastic about everything. This clearly was a woman he wanted to marry. She was interested in his work and understanding of his work schedule. She seemed to have no problem rearranging her schedule to fit his so they could be together. She was pretty, smart, and a hard worker herself. She even agreed to raise their children in the Jewish faith. Surely this would please his father.

Martha saw Michael as a sensitive doctor, caring for others, kind and gentle. He did not drink much and was a hard worker—he would be able to provide for her and their children. He was committed to his faith and felt strongly that their children be raised the same way. Although her family was not very religious, she longed to belong to a religion and hoped that Michael's faith could be her own. As the wife of a doctor, perhaps her parents would finally think she had done well.

So Michael and Martha got married. But Michael soon found that his work schedule did not leave much time to be with Martha. After the children were born, she began to focus increasingly on them and complain more and more about why he wasn't home more. He didn't know why she could not see the stress he was under or hear the demands the hospital was making of him. It seemed the harder he worked to bring home a substantial paycheck, the more quickly she spent it and the less she was available to him. Over the years she had emotional outbursts during which she would begin to rage, criticizing him for what seemed like everything he did. When he tried to defend himself by saying she was never around when he was at home because she was always out spending the money he made, she would fly off the handle even more or leave in a hysterical fit and refuse to talk to him for days. This scared him so he would just leave the house. It was not long before work was the only place he felt valued. Unable to voice to Martha his fear that he was no longer important to her, he turned to work to make himself feel better. It was at work that a young female intern began to pay attention to him, commenting about what a wonderful doctor she thought he was and how grateful she was for all his help. It wasn't long before he was sharing with her his frustrations about the hospital, then about his marriage. This sharing led the intern to believe that there was intimacy between them and she invited him to her apartment for dinner, a nap, and eventually sex.

In the meantime, Martha grew increasingly resentful that she had given up everything of importance to her for him. She saw him working more and more, while being less and less available to her and the children. In the past he at least complained about the demands of work, but he no longer even shared that with her. All he did was demand that the family appear perfect in the community. Unable to talk about her fear that she was no longer important to him, she put all her energy into the children and her volunteer activities. She wanted to punish him for his rigidity and isolating behavior, but he would never listen to her unless she was totally out of control with her anger. Eventually she would just blow up and shut herself off from him. He would walk out of the house and she would eat to make herself feel better. Then she would put her fingers down her throat, vomiting to keep herself below the petite 95 pounds Michael said he liked.

What a painful existence for both Martha and Michael! Martha's eating disorder was out of control; Michael's work addiction had not been the solution and an affair with an intern was about to make things even worse. As you see, they both feared the same thing—that they were not important to the other person. If each had been able to talk about the pain they were in or hear the other, perhaps they would have been able to create solutions.

Keeping secrets about how they really feel emotionally is a component of all secret-keeping for both addicts and co-addicts. This type of secret is usually the one that people are least concerned about, but for most addicts and co-addicts it is a catalyst to engage in some behavior that is not good for them or the relationship. Stopping this type of secret-keeping is the key to obtaining emotional competence.

The Secret That Isn't a Secret—The Elephant in the Living Room

Sometimes secrets are known, but the unspoken (or sometimes even spoken) rule is to pretend they don't exist. Keep quiet, don't rock the boat, don't bring attention to the elephant in the living room. Then you don't have to face the situation. An example is what happens to children in families in which there is ongoing addiction or domestic violence. The children see Mom drunk or simply "not there," perhaps because she is using prescription drugs. Or they see Dad hit the older brother so hard that his nose and mouth bleed and then hear Dad tell him "this is for your own good." These children often pretend that nothing out of the ordinary is happening; they make it their job to do whatever it takes to keep the secret for fear matters will get worse if they tell. They don't invite friends over fearing that the friends will discover the truth about their family. They learn to discount any feelings, and to carry on conversations in which nothing important is ever discussed. They find ways to hide evidence, and frequently take on adult responsibilities far beyond their years. This type of secret-keeping influences both the day-to-day relationships within the family and external relationships.

The normal, healthy development of a child includes opportunities for the child to experience painful and confusing situations. What makes the difference is when a caring adult helps the child identify the feelings he or she is having, validates the feelings, and then helps the child figure out what to do and how to take steps to feel better. But in families where secrets are kept at all costs, children grow up unable to tolerate emotional discomfort. Boundaries are often overly controlling, and children have little emotional competence. Later on, such people usually attract someone with a complementary style of relating, so it is no surprise that many addicts choose as a partner an adult child of an addict or victim of some type of abuse. Such relationships are very likely to quickly include secrets: Each member of the couple lacks the skills to cope with addiction and co-addiction, and keeping secrets is already a part of how the couple relates.

Exercise:

Family secrets are often carried from generation to generation, especially in addicted families. It isn't that the family doesn't talk about or admit Uncle Johnny's alcoholism, but they are less likely to talk about the sexual abuse he experienced as a boy by an older male cousin. A family might talk about an older sister's weight problem, but go to great lengths to keep the secret that the grandfather is actually this woman's father. Identifying the secrets kept in your family will help you to see how you have been influenced by those secrets. Sometimes it is helpful to ask your parents or other relatives about the family's history and include a question about any family secrets they know about.

List the secrets that were kept or that you suspect were kept in your family of origin. Describe the extent your parent(s)/grandparent(s) went just to keep these secrets. How did you then begin to help keep those secrets for your parents? (If you are aware of secrets from your extended family, note those here, too.)

_____

_____

_____

_____

_____

_____

_____

_____

_____

_____

_____

_____

_____

_____

_____

Identify any secrets you think your children may witness about you and are now carrying along with you.

_____

_____

_____

_____

_____

_____

When it comes to secrets, what do you want to model to children as a parent in recovery? If you have no children, think about yourself as a child. If you think that part of your childhood still exists somewhere inside, how is the child part of you reacting to carrying the secrets from the past into a relationship filled with secrets now? What would you have to do today to help that "inner child" feel less responsible for carrying those old family secrets? What would be evidence that you have given up keeping secrets?

_____

_____

_____

_____

_____

_____

_____

_____

_____

_____

_____

_____

_____

_____

The Secret No One Else Knows

Not all secrets exist exclusively between two people. A person can hold onto a secret that no one else knows about. Think about the lesbian teenager who has never told anyone how she feels or thinks about her sexual orientation. The impact on her as an individual intensifies when her parents begin to pressure her during college to get married and give them grandchildren. If this young woman continues to maintain that solitary secret, and fakes attraction to the man she then marries in order to please her parents, not only is her life affected, but so is that of her husband and child.

John grew up in a strict Catholic family and was expected to marry and have children. Although he regularly dated girls and then women, he knew early in life that he was more attracted to males, but kept this secret. He had heard of "bath houses" and rest stops where sex with men was an easy commodity, and soon became a regular visitor to such places. Sometimes he even put himself in danger by having unprotected sex or sex with strangers who threatened him. On occasion he was beaten and robbed, but told no one and was not able to stop his behavior.

Being what he termed "the favored child," he felt he had to keep quiet about his homosexual behavior. He forced himself to be the best at his job and do what was expected of him not only by his parents but also by the church. He became friends with Jill, a woman who worked in his law firm, and asked her to go out with him. In fact, he felt close to her and soon he asked her to marry him, thinking she would solve the problem of his attraction to men. Of course, he did not tell her his secret. Initially he found sex pleasant with her, but later had to fantasize about other men to be sexual with her.

After the birth of their first son, instead of feeling happy about this event, he was overwhelmed with fear of not living up to the expectations his son might have of him. He sought relief for his anxiety through sex at a rest stop. Unfortunately, this time, the rest stop was a location for a police sting operation. He was arrested the night before his wife was to be released from the hospital. Knowing that she would find out because of the arrest, John felt he had to tell her, but did not know how.

Exercise:

Even though you may not have to deal with a homosexual's secrets, this kind of secret is similar to others. Think of the similarities and differences.

_____

_____

_____

_____

How are you like John or Jill, the woman he became friends with and then married? What might have been another way to handle this secret? What are all the possible responses Jill might have given?

_____

_____

_____

_____

_____

Fear-Based Secrets

At times someone in a family knows the secret but is sworn not to tell for fear that something bad will happen to him or the family. For example, a pre-teen catches his father having sex with someone other than his mother. The father implores the son to keep the secret, for to tell would only hurt his mother. This puts the child in an impossible loyalty conflict, for which there seems to be no way out. If the woman with whom his father is having sex happens to be the wife of a neighbor, this complicates the situation even further for the son.

The Secret Affair

In reality, an affair may be with another person, or a drug, or work, or food, or even spending money. In each example, one person is putting energy into a relationship with someone else or some*thing* else and that is interfering with the marital relationship. The most painful type of affair is with another person—it represents the betrayal of the spoken or unspoken commitment people make to each other when they agree to be in a relationship. Yes, people can be just as distracted when the "affair" is with food or work—but an affair with another person makes the betrayal feel more personal. It is common for the spouse to believe that the reason the partner looked elsewhere was because the spouse is somehow not good enough.

Richard was a judge in a mid-sized city. Despite his power in the judicial system, he felt insecure. Over the years he had gained a little weight, really did not like his work, and longed for a more fulfilling career. Richard made a good salary and his wife Rachel liked the money he had and the prestige of being the wife of a judge. Their children were enrolled in the finest private schools, they belonged to the country club, lived in a beautiful home, and drove the best cars, yet he felt he could never please her. He felt stuck. For years, just as he did with his own mother, he felt no matter what he did, it wasn't enough for his wife. Besides feeling inadequate with Rachel, he also felt she did not understand his need to be creative. For years he had been painting watercolors and at times was convinced he had some talent. But each time he thought of taking a stab at being a professional artist, his wife just laughed and told him to "get real."

For the past few months he had been taking an advanced watercolor course and was really enjoying himself, but had not told Rachel for fear she would disapprove. This was the first time he had been in a class in which he and the other students were encouraged to critique each other's work. To his surprise he had been given very enthusiastic feedback, especially from Tonya, a young woman who shared his love of art. Soon, they began to confide in each other after classes, talking first about their family history, then their disappointment in their respective marriages. Richard began to fantasize about Tonya when he made love to his wife or when he mastur-bated in the shower. Before long, Richard and Tonya had arranged an out-of-town watercolor workshop together. Richard lied to Rachel about the workshop and told her he would be out of town for business.

While he was on the trip his son broke his leg in a soccer game and Rachel phoned his hotel room to ask him to come home. Tonya answered the phone. They had just ordered dinner in the room after having had sex, so she assumed it was room service. She handed the phone to Richard. Not only was Rachel upset about their son's leg, she was furious about Tonya. He quickly returned home.

After the crisis of the broken leg subsided, Richard realized how much he did love his wife and children, and did not want to lose them. Yet, he thought he loved Tonya. Rachel confronted him about the "woman's voice" on the phone and demanded to know who she was. Richard minimized his feelings for Tonya but disclosed to Rachel that Tonya was a friend with whom he was only emotionally involved—that his being with her was really nothing and not to take it personally.

Rachel took it personally!

Often other people in the family know or get pulled into the affair. For example, in the movie *Moonstruck*, Cher's character, Loretta, sees her father, Cosmo, out at the opera with a woman with whom he is having an affair. She enters into the secret with her father rather than let the temperature get too hot by telling on him because she also has a secret—she is dating and having sex with her fiancé's brother!

As in *Moonstruck*, one lie is used to cover up another. But the guilt and tension is too much for Loretta and Cosmo to tolerate, so over the kitchen table a fight ensues where each tries to minimize their behavior. The emotions that led to the fight are actually generated by the secret. A person might also use other tactics to reduce the toxic pain of the secret, such as getting sick, over-focusing on the children, using drugs, or working more at the office. Sometimes this works like a thermostat within a relationship—when the temperature gets too hot the thermostat kicks on the "air conditioner" to cool things off, or if it is too cool, the heat get turned up. We all can think of ways we know how to "cool things off" or "heat things up" in our relationships.

One strategy used to attempt to keep the temperature in the relationship stable is by telling a lie and keeping secrets about the lie. For every lie that is told, another is told to cover the first one. Sometimes silence (lying by omission) is the lie. It doesn't take a rocket scientist to know that when one is spending significant amounts of time thinking about the lie, making up the lie, presenting the lie, making up another lie to secure the first one, worrying about whether there is evidence somewhere that will expose the lie, creating evidence to further cover the lie, acting some way to further secure the lie, reviewing the story with someone else asked to hold onto the lie, wondering if you need to bribe that person to keep the lie, and wondering if you need to buy your spouse something so she won't suspect the lie—there is not much time or energy left for anything else. You can see how secrets and lies can shape the behavior in a relationship.

Most people think addicts lie more than partners or that addicts lie to everybody and partners only lie to themselves. Examine below the reasons why addicts and partners lie and see what you think. Can you think of other reasons why you have lied?

Partners' Lies

Partners tell lies to others to cover up their shame about the addict's behavior. Yet, the partner lies to herself first to be able to lie to others. In her book *When Your Lover Is a Liar,* Susan Forward identifies six common lies women tell themselves. Co-addict partners use all of them—see which ones you have used.

He Would Never Lie to Me.

This is used by partners who are basically honest and believe that everyone else is too. This lie is particularly true of the naîve partner who is new to a relationship or marriage. They have little experience with betrayal, so often are not as aware that something is not right in the relationship as are partners who grew up in families in which betrayal was a norm.

The partner new to recovery may hear the addict profess at self-help meetings that he shares the value of honesty, but notices that at home, the addict is very different. The discrepancy between the public and the private is the "red flag" that all is not right in the relationship. Yet believing he would never lie to her, this partner may stay stuck in denial until very serious consequences happen.

Exercise for Partner:

Perhaps you grew up in a family that had some dysfunction—most families do, at least to some extent. In what ways did you experience betrayal while growing up? Perhaps the betrayal happened in your adulthood, or you only became aware of it as an adult. What effect did the betrayal have on you in your relationships today?

_____

_____

_____

_____

_____

Think about your current relationship. Identify a "red flag" or two you ignored. What is one that you are still ignoring? Did you believe that your mate would not lie to you?

_____

_____

_____

_____

_____

_____

Perhaps this is the type of lie you've been telling to yourself and keeping it secret. Who could you tell? How will it help you to tell?

_____

_____

_____

_____

Maybe He Lied to Other People [Women], but He Wouldn't Lie to Me.

This lie is common in situations in which the addict has been open about his previous addictive behavior or acting out. During the courtship stage, with the best of intentions, the addict kept a lid on his old addictive behaviors, but over time, they re-emerged. Despite seeing and hearing evidence that the addict has slipped or relapsed, the partner tells herself that he is different now. Because he trusted her enough to tell about the past, she tells herself that he won't lie now.

Partner Exercise:

In what ways has your addict spouse's history returned? What evidence do you ignore? If your current relationship started as a result of an affair, have you based the beginning of this love relationship on a foundation of a lie he told to a former wife or girlfriend whom he at one point professed to love? If he would lie to her, what makes you think he would not lie to you?

_____

_____

_____

_____

_____

_____

_____

_____

_____

_____

_____

_____

Yes, He Lies, but He Loves Me and That's All That Matters.

Some people are so desperate for love that they will submit to various forms of abuse in an effort to win or keep a relationship. When someone says "I love you" to a desperate person, the person interprets that to mean there is a relationship—a future—and that someone cares. We see this lie in partners of all types of addicts, who settle for less because they believe the relationship they have is better than none at all. More times than not, the partner using this type of lie hasn't a clue what love or friendship really is.

This lie is also the favorite of partners who begin an affair with a married addict and believe that somehow their relationship is special and that someday he will leave his wife for her. She believes his explanation that his wife doesn't want to have sex anymore, that he doesn't love the wife, and that the affair partner is the most important person in his life. She lies to herself and says it must be true. She waits for his call on weekends and holidays in case he can "get away" for a secret phone call or a few moments for quick sex or sexual talk. Her efforts to be always available to him result in her shutting herself off from her friends. She becomes progressively more isolated and dependent on the lover.

Partner Exercise:

In what ways does the type of relationship you have make you feel like a victim? When the addict leaves, describe how you feel. Do you feel stupid, crazy, fulfilled, or empowered by being in the relationship? How does the love demonstrated in the relationship nurture both of you?

_____

_____

_____

_____

_____

_____

_____

_____

Partner Exercise:

If you are involved with a person who is married to someone else, it may be useful for you to do this exercise. What promises has this person made to you? How has he lied to you or others? Did you find that you justified his lying? Do you tell others about how much he loves you in an attempt to get their support?

_____

_____

_____

_____

_____

_____

_____

Yes, He Lies, but He's a Victim of Circumstances.

Even if the addict was a victim, his victimizing you is not justified. Having empathy is important in any relationship, but no one has the right to hurt another to try to make themselves feel better. There are better ways to cope.

Partner Exercise:

In what ways do you find that you deny your needs because you feel so bad about what happened to your addict spouse in the past?

_____

_____

_____

_____

List four ways you get caught in memories of the past and wallow in that pain rather than stay in the present and focus on present-day solutions. What might you do instead?

_____

_____

_____

_____

Yes, He Lies, but I Can Fix Him.

Many addicts and co-addicts come from homes in which one or both parents were also addicted, forcing the child to take on adult or care-taking roles too early in life. It is no surprise that this lie is used often. Of course the partner has a secondary gain for being in the "fixing" mode—you have the illusion of control and the crisis keeps the relationship in enough chaos that you don't have to face the reality that there are real problems with the way both of you behave.

In a common scenario, the wife covers for the husband who is out drinking while she waits for him in her party dress. She tells the friend or family member on the phone that he isn't feeling well, so they won't be there.

Sometimes co-addicts feel they have to cover for him at work. They justify this lie by saying, "His boss won't understand that he just had a slip. It is okay that I lie to the boss for him—otherwise he will lose his job and what will happen to me and the kids?" Ultimately the co-addict thinks, "If I pretend all is well, then I don't have to face the fact that this marriage is a mess and I am stuck."

Partner Exercise:

Describe how you "fix things" for your mate. How do you cover for your mate? How do you feel about yourself and your relationship when you do this?

_____

_____

_____

_____

When he is emotionally in distress, how to you try to manage that for him. To get his attention, what do you have to do?

_____

_____

_____

_____

If you are already in recovery for codependency or coaddiction, how have you become the "probation officer" of his recovery? Do you keep asking about his progress? What advice have you been offering about how he can change or improve his situation? What are signs he has begun to ignore you or is reactive when you start this?

_____

_____

_____

_____

_____

_____

Yes, He Lies, but It's My Fault.

For those who care-take too much, the other side is taking on the blame for the addict's behavior. A favorite method addicts have for manipulating the situation is to try to convince you that his out of control behavior is your fault. Codependent partners get caught up in the cycle of trying to fix things, feeling that they did something wrong. Wake up! You can't make anyone lie. You can't force words to come from his mouth. You can't fix him no matter how hard you try to remedy the situation.

Partner Exercise:

Keep track during the day of how many times you ask yourself, "What did I do wrong?" or "What can I do to fix this?"

_____

_____

_____

_____

How often have you thought: "If I just try a little harder, take on a little more, be more available, he won't use again?"

Co-addicts use the last three lies more often than the others. How have you lied to yourself? How could you be more truthful about your situation?

_____

_____

_____

_____

_____

_____

_____

Partners also tell lies of omission. For example, you may feel angry and scared. When your spouse asks what is wrong, you say "nothing," not want-ing to rock the boat for fear that he will act out again. Or when others see you are not doing well, you falsely reassure them that everything is fine.

Maybe you have not been sleeping and go to the doctor for help. She asks you if you are having problems with your marriage and you report "not really," rather than telling her the evidence you have found about your spouse.

Partners also minimize the seriousness of the problem when shame is attached to the addictive behavior. This is common when an addict goes to treatment for cocaine and sex addiction. The partner often tells others only about the cocaine addiction.

Why Addicts Lie

Although most addicts lie to cover their tracks, the real fear is that if the partner knew the truth, there would be no way for her to forgive him. The addict fears the partner will leave. That fear of loss motivates the addict more than anything to lie.

Addicts are famous for lies of omission. Do you recognize this situation? Your partner senses something is up. You don't want to lie, so if she doesn't ask you specifically, you do not offer the information. Or perhaps you are worried that telling her the truth will hurt her so much, you can't possibly do it, so you deliberately leave out the most troubling part of what happened. Mostly, you don't want to further incriminate yourself! Perhaps you have been caught and are scared, but your partner does not know everything about what you have done. You tell part of the truth to reduce your guilt and to be able to say that you told the truth, but you fail to give your partner a valuable piece of information that will help her make a decision about her future.

But addicts also lie for different reasons. Check the heading below and see if any of these fit for you.

Withdrawal Is Scary and Painful

Withdrawal from any drug (even the ones that the brain makes for the sex or gambling addict) is painful and scary. Once the addict is entrenched in the addiction cycle, the brain continues to crave the neurotransmitter changes the addictive cycle has created. Stopping addictive behavior results in urges, cravings, and often unpleasant or painful withdrawal symptoms. Many addicts have no clue what to do to get the brain to stop calling out for more drugs. The addictive behavior has also been a reliable source of companionship, emotional pain relief, and glue that has held the addict together. Giving that up is also frightening and emotionally painful, even when the addict is highly motivated to stop using.

Addict Exercise:

Identify four "withdrawal" symptoms you have noted since abstaining from acting out. In what ways are you continuing to hold onto some type of acting out behavior that is keeping the withdrawal at bay?

_____

_____

_____

_____

Keeping the Mask Firmly Attached

All addicts portray an image that they think others want to see. To tell the truth means letting go of that safe identity. The real fear is that if she really knew what you were like, she'd leave you.

Addict Exercise:

Take out a paper bag or piece of paper. On one side draw the image that you allow your mate to see of you—the image that you want her to judge you by. Write a brief explanation of this mask you wear. Then turn the bag or paper over and draw the real you that you have been hiding. Write a brief explanation of this side of your mask. Now describe the person you want to be, the authentic you that you want to be with her. List three steps you will take daily that will help you be the authentic you.

_____

_____

_____

Fear of Loss

Loss of control: If I lose control something bad will happen to me. If I don't have control then you do. You already run my life; it would be impossible for me if you controlled it even more. I don't want to be dominated (engulfed/smothered).

Addict Exercise:

List ten ways you try to maintain control with your mate, at work, with friends, in your community. Describe what will happen to you if you lose control. How realistic is this fear?

Loss of opportunity: If you know, then how will I tolerate this pain without my "fix?"

Addict Exercise:

List the five most common ways you have talked yourself into using because the opportunity was there. What other options did you have?

_____

_____

_____

_____

_____

_____

_____

Loss of marriage, children: If you know the truth, there is no way that you could forgive me.

Loss of material things: If I tell the truth, I will lose the house, retirement, savings, cars, etc.

Addict Exercise:

How has the fear of loss impacted your decisions about keeping secrets and telling lies? How has it hurt you? What are you losing by continuing to lie?

_____

_____

_____

_____

_____

_____

_____

Fear of Emotions

Addicts report these thoughts: "If I tell you, the consequences will be too painful."

"I can't stand conflict. I don't know what to say when you confront me or when you are that angry. It reminds me too much of when my mom/dad got angry and I did not have an answer then either." "I cannot tolerate the pain of the past or what I think the future will bring." "I do care about her and don't want to see my partner hurt. Any way I do this, it will just kill her. She just can't take it."

Many addicts say they lie and resist disclosure because they don't want to hurt their partner. That stance shows little respect for your partner. Our research shows that over 90 percent of partners wanted to be told the truth. Despite the pain, they felt better about being told. It is future abuse of your spouse to keep the secret.

Addict Exercise:

Draw a picture of the pain you are medicating. What does it look like (color, shape, texture), sound like, feel like, smell like—even taste like? List five healthy ways to soothe that pain.

_____

_____

_____

_____

_____

_____

Denial

Most addicts have thought, "If I pretend that all is well, then I don't have to face the fact that I'm screwed up and have made this relationship a disaster." Denial is one of those things that either helps you or hurts you. Denial is a necessary part of grieving, protecting you from pain for a while. However, if you never face the pain, it gets worse and becomes the source of more trouble. To be in denial is to say that you don't have a problem or that you don't have to face the consequences of your behavior. Eventually you do—life becomes an out-of-control mess. To avoid the reality of your life is to avoid taking responsibility for your life. The only way to get better is to be accountable for your life, take responsibility, and move through the pain.

Addict Exercise:

Have you stayed stuck in denial so you don't have to face your problems? List ten ways you have been out of control and the denial statements you made that helped you rationalize your behavior.

_____

_____

_____

_____

_____

_____

_____

_____

_____

_____

_____

_____

_____

_____

At this point it is important for both the addict and the partner to think about the role secrets played in your family when you were growing up, as well as how secrets are influencing your current relationship with your spouse. Later, spend some time thinking about the influence the secrets have on your relationship with your children (if you have any), your friends, co-workers, and so on. The following exercise contains some questions you might find useful to guide you in this process.

Exercise for Both Addict and Partner:

Describe the types of secrets kept in your family of origin. In what ways did those secrets influence your life as a child, teen, and now as an adult? What did you learn there that you are now repeating in your current relationships?

_____

_____

_____

_____

_____

_____

_____

What belief do you have about yourself that influences your decision-making now?

_____

_____

What secrets are in your current relationship?

_____

_____

_____

_____

What skill do you need to do something different about it?

_____

_____

Now think about your authentic self. The kind of person you want to be. If you are a parent, the kind of parent you want to be.

What value do you have or want to have about keeping secrets that you want to implement in your life?

_____

_____

_____

_____

What do you want to model to your children?

_____

_____

_____

_____

_____

What is one thing you can do today to honor your authentic self while modeling healthy behavior to those around you? Share the answer to the last question with your mate.

_____

_____

_____

_____

_____

_____

_____

_____

_____

Disclosing a secret *sometimes* leads to favorable results, and *sometimes* results in devastating consequences. Finding out someone is keeping secrets throws the relationship into turmoil. Either way, the process of creating, keeping, telling, and hearing the secret alters the relationship in very important ways.

Many addicts say they lie and resist disclosure because they don't want to hurt their partner. That stance shows little respect for your partner. Our research shows that over 90% of partners wanted to be told the truth because they were made to feel crazy—like the reality they were seeing did not exist. Despite the pain, they felt better about being told. The next chapter discusses the consequences of telling: the good, bad and ugly.

References

Ford, Charles. *Lies, Lies, Lies: The Psychology of Deceit*. Washington, D.C.: The American Psychiatric Press, 1996.

Forward, Susan. *When Your Lover Is a Liar*. New York: Harper Collins, 1999.

CHAPTER THREE: Is Disclosure Right for You?

If, When, and How Much to Disclose

Disclosures come in all forms; some are done with integrity and some are done in the worst way possible. Obviously, if you are reading this book you are considering disclosure, have disclosed to someone, or have been disclosed to and are looking for ways to make things easier and better.

It is safe to say that all disclosures are painful and hard for the couple. Yet, most couples (over 90% in our study) report they are glad the disclosure happened. This high approval, and the fact that most couples did not split up after disclosure (see Chapter Four), led us to think that the couples who had disclosed had a better chance of saving their relationship than those who had not disclosed.

We have come to believe that the reason disclosure is necessary and encouraged by most couples in recovery is because shortly after disclosure both individuals feel some relief. When the disclosure is done with integrity, the partner often feels validated that her suspicions were correct and she isn't crazy. The addict feels a sense of freedom from the secret life and relief from the shame. This relief is immediate for some; for others it takes more time. But the reduction of anxiety and stress allows a period of time during which the couple can begin to heal.

The primary core of healing is forgiveness, but forgiveness cannot happen unless a disclosure is made. When the secret or lie remains undisclosed, it festers and grows into a bigger hurt. But who you tell, when you tell, what you tell, and how you tell are the keys to a successful, healing disclosure.

Forgiveness

If you want to work on your couple relationship and have it survive and grow, then your partner has to know about your problem. Awareness of your difficulty also gives your partner a better chance of identifying and dealing with her own problems.

Other people who need to know may include your children, other family members, select people at work, or best friends. Disclosing to these people is different in many ways than disclosing to your partner. This issue is discussed in sections of Chapters Six through Eight.

Whether the couple does well has to do with how committed each is to working on their own health and how differentiated or emotionally competent each becomes. (See Chapter 1.) Couples also do better when they are willing to work to change themselves. This is not easy; often people are so beaten down by the unhealthy relationship that staying stuck in anger and fear seems easier than working on self-improvement or forgiveness. At the point of disclosure, it is very difficult to know what you want or think or feel.

Fortunately, with time and work towards awareness, the anger and fear do lessen, recovery gets under way, and decisions can be made. Forgiveness is essential for peace of mind. Forgiving the wrongdoer is essential for the couple to heal; forgiving oneself is essential for the individual to heal. Because disclosure is often the first step to forgiveness, we want to digress here and summarize the steps to forgiveness.

Steps to Forgiveness

Karl Tomm, MD of the University of Calgary indicates there are two contrasting methods in which a person restores a sense of self worth after being hurt. The first, often used by the partner initially, is to diminish the worth of the other through retaliation or revenge. The second is to enhance self worth through competence and forgiveness (Tomm, 2002). We believe the second method is by far the better and healthier way to restore self worth. Having competence in managing your emotions is a must, but forgiveness is what enables you to manage resentment and anger in the wake of being wronged.

In his excellent book, *Forgive and Forget*, Lewis B. Smedes describes what forgiveness is *not*. First, forgiving is not forgetting. By forgiving someone the hurtful act, you do not forget. You need to forgive precisely because you remember what someone did; your memory keeps the pain alive long after the actual wrongdoing is past. Because forgiving is healing, it will make it easier to forget. But it is not necessary to forget in order to forgive. What forgiving will accomplish is to heal the pain of the past.

Forgiving is also not excusing. Excusing is appropriate when you believe the person was not to blame for the wrongdoing; you forgive because you believe the person *was* to blame. Excusing is easy but forgiving is hard.

Forgiving is also not condoning or tolerating. You can forgive someone without condoning what he did or being willing to tolerate similar actions in the future. You may forgive someone yet realize you cannot have that person in your life.

Forgiving is healing yourself of the painful memories of the past. When you have really forgiven someone, you can remember what the person did without re-experiencing the pain. This process can take years and involve several steps. According to Smedes, these steps are:

1. Recognize that a wrong has been done to you—that someone's behavior caused you a great deal of pain.

2. Recognize that you have strong feelings about the wrong that was done to you, and actually *feel* those feelings, which undoubtedly include anger and hate.

3. Share your strong feelings with others—ideally with the person who has hurt you, or else with a therapist, support group, or someone else.

4. Understand what may have led to the hurtful behavior—what the other person's motivations and background were, and how you may have contributed to the situation, for example by your own vulnerability.

5. Decide what to do with the relationship with the person who has hurt you.

The process of forgiving can be accelerated if the other person sincerely wishes to be forgiven, but it is possible even if the other person is unavailable or uninterested.

You forgive primarily to heal yourself, not for the other person.

An example of the process of forgiveness was described by Mariah Burton-Nelson in *The Unburdened Heart*, in which she describes her healing journey years after having been molested by her high school coach. Agreeing with Smedes, Burton-Nelson describes the first stage of forgiveness as awareness that a wrong has been done. She is quick to point out that the first defense against pain is denial. Denial is a close personal friend of every addict and co-addict. The addict uses denial to convince himself that he won't get caught, that it isn't so bad, or this one last time will be the last time he acts out. Likewise the co-addict uses denial to brush aside the evidence that something is going on, that things will get better, that if she just tries harder all will be OK. But without the awareness of what happened and how it affected everyone involved, it is difficult to know what you are forgiving the person for. The disclosure process allows clarity and validation of what happened and who was responsible for what. It is through these first events of talking and listening that healing can begin. Disclosure can bring an end to denial and thus a beginning to forgiveness.

Addict Exercise:

List all the people you have hurt with your addiction and the various ways you have hurt them. Be sure to include yourself in the list. How have you used denial to help you stay detached from the feelings you experience from hurting those people on the list?

_____

_____

_____

_____

_____

_____

_____

_____

_____

_____

_____

_____

_____

_____

Partner Exercise:

List all the ways addiction has impacted your life and the lives of those you love. Indicate in what way denial has played a part in the past. How have you minimized the behaviors you have seen or experienced as a result of the addiction that exists in your relationship? What meaning does disclosure have in your healing process?

_____

_____

_____

_____

_____

_____

_____

_____

_____

_____

_____

_____

_____

When to Tell

John, who'd been actively involved in addiction recovery for six months, desperately wanted his wife Jody to participate with him in recovery activities. He saw some of his program friends being supported emotionally by their spouses, speaking the language of recovery together, being able to let go of the shameful secrets they'd been keeping. But John was afraid to tell Jody about his past addictive activities, which he'd managed to keep secret for so long.

Finally he saw what seemed the perfect opportunity—a weekend workshop for couples recovering from addiction and co-addiction. He signed himself and Jody up, telling her it was a marriage enrichment program. During the two-hour drive to the retreat center where the program was to be held, John told his wife about the hundreds of lies he had been telling her, the hours he had spent at the race track, drinking and gambling, the hours spent on the computer at night when she thought he was asleep, the online risks he had taken, as well as about the young woman he met at the dog track who had offered him a blow-job for $20 after he had won. As he drove, he began crying as he told her what happened next: While he was in the restroom stall with his pants down around his ankles—never thinking he could ever do something like that—this woman stole the money he had won and the remainder of his paycheck. John hoped that over the weekend she would have help from the other couples and the facilitators in processing the disclosure, so he told her about everything he'd done.

When the couple arrived at the retreat center, Jody was in a state of shock. The two facilitators found themselves unexpectedly faced with a woman in crisis, in need of immediate one-on-one attention. Leaving the first group session to his associate, one of the facilitators ended up spending the entire evening counseling and supporting Jody. The following morning she was able to join the group and explain what had happened.

John had good intentions—to disclose to Jody in a setting where she would have support. But the manner in which he chose to do this put an unfair burden on the weekend facilitators, who had not planned for, and did not have the manpower for, one-on-one crisis counseling. It also put Jody in a difficult situation—reeling from the shock and the shame and self-blame that often results from the disclosure of infidelity, Jody was not yet ready to have 30 other people immediately hear about her situation. Given that John had the opportunity for a planned disclosure, it would have been better for him to plan with his therapist to bring Jody into therapy, assess her emotional state, and disclose to her in therapy.

Sara and Sam had been married for three years when Sam started attending Twelve-Step meetings for cocaine addiction. Sam had not mentioned to Sara that he was also addicted to sex and frequently sought out sexual encounters with prostitutes when he was using cocaine. During the Twelve-Step meetings, his sponsor and other group members encouraged Sam to tell Sara about the sexual encounters because she may have been exposed to a sexually transmitted disease as a result of his behavior. Sam feared that disclosure would mean the loss of his marriage and his son.

On more than one occasion Sam had had sex with Sara after having had unprotected sex with a prostitute when he was high. In fact, he had admitted to his sponsor that at times he had been so unaware of reality when he was using that it simply had not occurred to him to use a condom. His love for Sarah motivated Sam to disclose to her because he realized she needed to know that he might have exposed her to an STD, even HIV. Sam was determined to disclose but did not know how. His sponsor suggested that Sam tell his wife with the sponsor, a therapist, or perhaps the minister from his church. However, Sam was so consumed with shame and anxiety that he called Sara from a pay phone right after the Twelve-Step meeting. In the midst of panic and shame he told her, "Sara, I've been at my CA meeting and the guys tell me I really need to tell you that I, ah, ah, once, when I was really out of it using crack, I hired a prostitute and had sex with her. I don't remember if I used a rubber or not, so you should go get tested for AIDS right away." He was crying now and rambled on, "I'm sorry; I know you are really mad now, but please don't leave me or take Ryan. I love you both and can't live without you. I'd kill myself if you left me. Please tell me you won't leave. I'll do anything to make this up to you. Please, please, you are more important to me than anything."

Sara was stunned by what she heard. In shock she thought, "What does he mean? First the cocaine, now this! And AIDS! What is happening? What is wrong with me that he would have to have sex with a prostitute? When did this happen? My God, what am I going to do?"

The fact that Sam told her over the phone just made her confusion worse. She said, "I don't understand. What do you mean prostitute?" Then she began to scream and cry at the same time, "AIDS! How could you do this to me? Don't you love me? Was it because I wouldn't let you have anal sex with me? You told me you just had a little problem with cocaine and now you say crack! Why didn't you tell me before? Why would you lie to me like this? How could you do this to me?" As she began to sob, she slammed down the phone.

In the ideal world, disclosure takes place in the therapist's office, after the addict and partner have both been prepared in earlier therapy sessions to go through the initial stages of this process and have been advised how much to ask and how much to disclose. In Chapter Five, we will describe a formal disclosure from start to finish.

In the real world, however, the first disclosure often happens precipitously when someone actually gets caught red-handed. For example, a woman may walk in on her husband when he has just snorted a line of cocaine or perhaps when he's masturbating while "chatting" with someone online and demand an explanation. A man may observe his wife taking money from her mother's purse while her mother is in the restroom during dinner in a restaurant. Seeing a huge increase in the cost of automobile insurance due to a ticket for driving under the influence of alcohol may elicit questions from a partner. A man may have his credit card denied only to find when he gets home that his wife is in front of the computer, gambling online, and that their bank account is overdrawn and savings depleted. A man is arrested for possession of methamphetamines while soliciting a prostitute who happens to be an undercover police officer, and he calls his wife from jail. Such situations demand immediate disclosure.

Typically, the person on the spot will attempt "damage control" by revealing as little as possible, most often only what he thinks the partner already knows or is likely to find out.

Another type of precipitous disclosure occurs when the person holding the secret comes to believe he can no longer live with it, and dumps everything on an unprepared and unsuspecting partner. To make matters worse, the disclosure may happen over the phone or email, from a distance, rather than in person.

For example, Daniel, a physician who had had sexual relations with several patients, was admitted to a treatment center in another state. After a few days there he phoned his wife Lorelei. She reported,

> Daniel didn't have the guts to tell me face to face, so he told me over the phone. He was safely away at the treatment center surrounded by nurturing caring professionals and fellow addicts. I was in our bedroom painting furniture, surrounded by our five small children. Laundry needed to be done, dishes from supper were waiting on me. I had to talk to him as though nothing was happening to my heart. It was horrible! I felt so alone and desperate! But what could I do?

Lorelei continued,

> I never would have believed for a minute he would actually have sex with anyone outside our marriage. I would actually have bet money on it. I was absolutely shocked by the seriousness and extent of his addictions and the many years he'd been lying to me. There never would have been an easy way to disclose all this stuff, but I deserved better. He described all the times he'd had sex with other people, and then said he did it because I was too tired all the time to have sex. He just went on and on. I didn't even hear half of it. I was in so much shock. I should have been given the same supportive environment as my husband, surrounded by other people in my circumstances. If I had not had those kids to take care of, I'm not sure what I would have done to myself.

Years later, Lorelei still harbors resentment over the way this disclosure was carried out. This contaminated her ability to separate her anger at the acting out behaviors from her anger at the insensitivity of the disclosure.

Unexpected disclosures via letters are no better than phone calls. Georgia, a bright young attorney, shared her story with us:

My husband left me a letter on what I call "the morning from hell." I was in a hurry when I left the house because I was on my way to my doctor's office for a pregnancy test. I just picked up that letter and stuck it in my purse and off I went, anticipating, thinking about maybe being pregnant. I forgot about the letter until I opened my purse to get in the car. Reading that letter, alone, in the car in the parking lot after leaving the doctor's office, was devastating. Here I was, just having received information that I was pregnant! This should have been the happiest day of my life—instead I was shocked beyond belief. But I had so much shame about what he said he had done, I couldn't tell anyone. I was dazed. I truly believe God drove the car the 10 miles home because I didn't even see the road. I felt suicidal—even pictured killing him and then myself. I never thought myself capable of considering those actions. I felt betrayed by the person I trusted the most. I went into shock. I was numb. I lost the baby eight weeks later and to be honest, even today I still blame him.

Television talk shows are yet another venue for inappropriate disclosures of secrets, sometimes with devastating consequences. In a highly publicized case, host Jenny Jones, in a program taped in March 1995, had a 26-year-old guest, Jonathan Schmitz, who was told only that he had a secret admirer. The secret admirer turned out to be a young gay man, Scott Amedure. The surprised Schmitz, who reportedly had a psychiatric history, was so distressed at being the public object of a homosexual crush that days later he shot Amedure dead. Schmitz was eventually sentenced to 25–50 years in prison for second-degree murder. Jenny Jones was subsequently sued for her role in this murder.

The opening scene from the movie *Hope Floats* is another good example of how not to do a disclosure. The heroine, Birdee Calvert, is invited to be a guest on a popular "afternoon talk show" where her best friend is going to share a "secret" with her. Birdee thinks this is just a funny gag and goes along. What her best friend tells her is that she (the best friend) is having an affair with Birdee's husband Bill. Birdee is naturally devastated as her whole life falls apart.

There is a right and a wrong way to handle disclosures that result from suspicions or from incriminating evidence, and disclosures that are a complete surprise to the partner. Later in this chapter we will make recommendations regarding the timing and content of these disclosures.

Addict Exercise:

If you are concerned for your mate's well-being and have postponed telling her, what conditions do you think need to change in order for you to be ready to tell? What will be evidence that the time is right? How might you be making things worse?

_____

_____

_____

_____

_____

_____

_____

_____

Partner Exercise:

You may suspect that your addict mate is not disclosing but has been using or acting out. One way to improve your ability to process a disclosure is to create a support group with whom you can share this information. You may think that you could never tell friends about what you suspect, especially if it is true. However, you will be surprised how friends want to help. Write out what you'd like to say to a friend about how she could help you if you disclose to the friend.

_____

_____

_____

_____

_____

_____

_____

How Much to Tell

Unfortunately, most addicts' first attempts at disclosure come when incriminating evidence shows up and then the addict tells only what he thinks will generate the least painful immediate consequences. Children learn early on to lie to avoid pain, and, until people get pretty healthy, they continue to repeat this behavior as adults. For addicts, it is a way of life.

In our study of sex addicts and co-addicts who had experienced disclosure (Schneider, et al., 1998), addicts reported that disclosure brought relief, ended denial, and proved to be the gateway to recovery for the individual and the relationship. But it was not all positive. Disclosure also brought shame to the addict, pain to the partner, and fears about loss of the relationship for both.

Some addicts had revealed every single detail of their sexual acting out, and they suffered negative consequences for it. Several wished they had disclosed differently. This was particularly true for addicts in early recovery (whose partners, of course, were generally also in early recovery).

For example, Clark, 28, who'd been in recovery for 10 months when he completed the survey, wrote,

> I feel I offered too much information. To admit I was involved with another woman was one thing, but I truly wish I had never told her who the woman was. She became obsessed with trying to find this woman and search for proof that I was still seeing her. Some people cannot handle truth and honesty as well as others. You have to know your partner and what they can handle.

Eleven months after his disclosure, Ben, 31, related,

> I hope it wasn't just "dumping," but I felt cleaner, relieved. But I shouldn't have shared so much, it was hurtful to her. Now it's hard for her to have so much information. The knowledge doesn't help her and seems only to cause pain as dates roll around or if we drive past a particular place. She can't stop thinking about it.

Disclosure precipitates obsession for a period of time. Co-dependents by their nature easily become obsessed with the addict's behaviors. If that obsession becomes intrusive for the partner—she literally can't stop thinking about it months or even years after the disclosure—she needs professional help. The obsession is a sign that the disclosure has gone awry.

Partners often begin by demanding complete disclosure, which is a way for them to make sense of the past, to validate their suspicions and the reality they had experienced that had often been denied by the addict. Partners long to have a sense of control of the situation, to assess their risk of having been exposed to financial disaster, violence, and diseases. They want to evaluate the commitment of their partner to the future of the relationship: "If I didn't get information, I could not trust the relationship to go forward. I needed every question answered, or I would not have been able to trust and therefore stay in the marriage. I can deal with truths, but not half-truths."

However, sometimes things get worse before they get better. Disclosure often creates more problems than you think it will. When a disclosure happens the partner may also spontaneously disclose her own set of secrets. This creates one more layer of work that has to be handled by the couple and by each individual.

Finding out that someone has been arrested and can anticipate legal consequences will affect the family for decades because of reporting requirements, probation, and loss of financial assets. In some cases the existence of another family creates ripples that members of both families will feel for years to come.

One can never be 100% sure where disclosure will lead. Nonetheless, people insist that disclosure is the best way to find healing.

Reveal All Now, or Save the Worst for Later: The Pain of Staggered Disclosure

Staggered disclosure usually doesn't work for long and makes everyone more angry and less trustful. Disclosure is painful, and often precipitates a crisis in the couple's relationship. It is hard enough for someone to admit to being a drug addict, or gambling away a family's livelihood, or having food control one's life. But disclosure is even harder for sex addicts or addicts who have both a drug and sexual addiction, often with a long list of secret sexual activities in which they have engaged. This is made even worse by an equally long list of lies that were told to cover up the activities.

When considering the consequences of the disclosure, addicts fear that the partner will leave them. Our research showed that the majority of partners do threaten to leave should they learn of an affair (60% of partners, in our study). This is often the case for other types of addicts, too—the partner threatens to leave if the addict doesn't stop the behavior. Female addicts in particular may fear physical or sexual violence from their partners as a response to the disclosure. Both male and female addicts may worry that an angry spouse will use the information against them as a means of emotional blackmail or in a future battle for custody of the children.

It is tempting for an addict to attempt damage control by initially revealing only some of what he or she did. Often, only the least damaging information is revealed, or else only those activities that the person believes their partner already knows about. Then, at some future time, the addict discloses additional secrets, or the partner learns the whole truth independently. Unfortunately, this strategy turns out to be very short-sighted, and likely to increase t'he chances of an unfavorable outcome in the long run.

In our survey, 59% of addicts and 70% of partners reported that there had been more than one major disclosure. This was not always because the addict had deliberately withheld information. Some addicts did not initially remember all their actions, especially if their addictions included multiple episodes or different types of activities. In other cases, it was only after experiencing some time in recovery that the addict realized that certain behaviors were sufficiently important that they should have been disclosed.

The lesson here is that disclosure is more likely to be a process than a one-time event. Whatever the reason for the staggered disclosures, the process is particularly difficult for the person at the receiving end. It is especially destructive when the reason was a deliberate lie.

A recurrent theme among partners is the damage of staggered disclosure by the addict. When the addict claims at the time to reveal all the relevant facts but actually withheld the most difficult information for later disclosure, partners reported greater difficulty in restoring trust. One woman wrote:

There were several major disclosures over six months. I
was completely devastated. He continued to disclose half
truths—but only when his lies didn't make sense so that
he was backed to the wall. This only increased my pain
and anger and made the whole situation worse. Each new
disclosure was like reliving the initial pain all over again.
Part of that was not being told. I felt lied to and didn't
trust any of the relationship. All I wanted was the truth. I
wish the truth had been disclosed all at once and not in
bits and pieces.

Another woman wrote of her feelings after her husband lost his job
because of sexual misconduct:

He had to tell me something because he was fired, and
people in his profession are seldom fired for any reason
other than gross malpractice or sexual misconduct. He
told me he had sexually touched a subordinate at work.
He said it was invited, which turned out not to be true.
His revelations continued to dribble out over weeks as I
continued to ask for information. Each new piece of
information felt like a scab being ripped off.

A similar strategy, with tragic results, was used by a physician who had
sex with several patients and was asked to appear before the licensing
board (Schneider, 1994). Initially, he told his wife that a single patient had
complained to the board, but that it was all a misunderstanding. Convinced
of his innocence, his wife insisted on accompanying him to the hearing to
support him. It turned out that several of his victims were present and told
their stories, in a very credible manner:

What she heard was a litany of behaviors that shocked
and stunned not only the Board, but also the local press
that was in attendance. She said she didn't care about the
other allegations, just the last one. She asked me if I'd had
sex with that woman. I had to tell her the truth. I will
never forget the look that came across her face. It was the
look of ultimate pain that comes with betrayal, a shattered

dream, a broken promise, and a broken heart. She walked out of the room and out of my life, never again to love me as a wife. I'd lost not only my career, but also my wife and daughter.

Sexually exploitative professionals and other public figures often initially try to minimize their misconduct, not only to licensing boards and assessment teams, but also to their spouses. When a wife who has publicly supported her husband because she believed in his innocence eventually learns that he continued to lie to her about the allegations after they were made public, her public humiliation and sense of betrayal are compounded, and the healing is that much more difficult.

Recipients of disclosure need to remember, however, that disclosure is always a process, not a one-time event. The reason is not always that the addict is deliberately holding back some damaging facts to protect himself or to avoid unpleasant consequences. Other reasons for not having immediately disclosed "everything" include:

- The addict has acted out in so many different ways or with so many different people, or has told so many lies, that she genuinely does not recall some of them until a later time.

- The addict was in such an altered state at the time of some of the episodes of acting out—especially when associated with drinking or drug use—that she simply does not remember particular events.

- The addict, although remembering all the details of his acting out, does not initially consider particular events or actions significant enough to bother disclosing. With increased recovery, the addict realizes the need for disclosing additional history.

- Disclosure of certain actions may be so damaging to the partner or to family relations (for example, an affair with the wife's sister, purchasing and using drugs with a brother who is a minor, driving under the influence with children in the car), or may entail significant risk of violence to the addict (for example, a female addict married to a man who has a history of physically abusing her), that a therapist recommends not disclosing these facts initially, until the partner or family member has received counseling and preparation.

- Certain episodes of acting out occurred only *after* the initial disclosure. That is, they represented slips or relapses of the addiction. (This is the most problematic situation, in that it is likely to cause the most damage to the process of rebuilding trust.)

- The addict may be so frightened that what he or she has disclosed may truly be all they were capable of at the time.

For example, Sam had revealed his worst behavior, but had kept to himself some other forms of sexual acting out in which he had indulged. When Sam heard that staggered disclosure is to be avoided in favor of full disclosure of all the elements of a person's sexual acting out, his eyes filled with tears and he told his therapy group,

> I was so scared to tell my wife about my voyeurism, I could barely manage to get through it. I thought I would die right there! There's no way I could possibly have told her about the other stuff. You have to realize that sometimes a partial disclosure is all you can do!

Sam's point is well taken: A partial disclosure is better than no disclosure at all, and sometimes it takes all the courage an addict has to explain to his partner *some* of what he has done. The spouse who later gets upset at hearing an additional disclosure may find it helpful to recognize that the addict may have been doing his best at the time.

One of the most important things we have learned from talking with partners of sex addicts is that staggered disclosures are very destructive to the relationship. The spouse may spend weeks or months after the initial disclosure learning to trust again, only to have the rug pulled out from beneath her or him by learning of additional secrets and lies that had not previously been revealed. In fact, often new lies had been generated to cover up the old ones, such as "I've told you everything," or "This time I'm telling you the truth." It is our belief that what is most helpful for the restoration of the relationship is for addicts initially to disclose at least the broad outlines of *all* their significant compulsive activities, rather than holding back some damaging material.

To summarize, because early on, the partner tends to want to know "everything," sometimes with negative consequences, we recommend that the partner discuss with a counselor or therapist what details are really important to know and what the likely effect will be on the partner.

Should I Tell "All the Gory Details?"

In our survey, disclosure of various details often turned out to be "devastating" and "traumatic" and left recipients with unpleasant memories and associations that were difficult to ignore. Lara, who persuaded her husband to tell her "everything," regretted it: "I created a lot of pain for myself by asking questions about details and gathering information. I have a lot of negative memories to overcome; this ranges from songs on the radio to dates, places, and situations; there are numerous triggers."

In later recovery, partners typically reported that they recognized that knowledge is not necessarily power, that no matter how much information they had they were still unable to control the addict. Instead, they developed guidelines for themselves about what information they wanted (typically more general information such as health risks, financial consequences affecting them, and level of commitment to recovery and the relationship) and what they did not want (such as details of what the high was like, sexual activities, locations, and numbers of partners).

Another partner spoke about the difficulty of hearing all the details:

> I think it's best for the addict to work through it with a knowledgeable therapist, then disclose the nature of the problem and have the partner determine what level of detail they are comfortable with. For me, I didn't want any more detail, because it tormented me. Others feel they want to now everything. Not me. The bottom line I needed to know was whether he was exposing himself to disease, and then not protecting me. The actual details of who, where, and when were extremely distracting to me and caused me to lose ground. I'd make some progress, then think about one of those details and spiral down.

It can be very helpful for partners to have a therapist encourage them to consider carefully what information they seek rather than ask for "everything." If you feel you need all the information you can squeeze out of the addict, ask yourself why. Could it be that you still believe that if you know everything, you can control the situation and prevent further acting out? More time in recovery may persuade you that this is not true. Or do you feel that having more answers will empower you and help you recover from the previous imbalance in the relationship (he kept the secrets; he decided how much you should know)?

One helpful therapy technique is to write down every question to which you want an answer, then agree to give the list to your therapist or sponsor to put away for an agreed-upon time period, say two months. At the end of that time you will review the list and decide which questions you still want answers to. Your spouse agrees that at that time he will answer any of the questions that remain on the list. You may be surprised by how differently you will feel about detailed information after two or three months. The therapist can assist in monitoring the intent of the disclosure: Moving toward greater intimacy is a positive intent; to obtain ammunition to punish, control, or manipulate the partner is a poor intent.

Private Information vs. Secret Information

In the recovering community "rigorous honesty" is virtually a dogma, and people get the idea that if you keep any kind of information from your partner you are lying and thus on the verge of a relapse. An omission about anything becomes the catalyst for suspicion and recriminations. It is important to separate out what information is private and what is secret.

Anita had been involved with several men over the past year. Alcohol, cocaine, and having sex with men at conferences had been part of her ritual for many years. Yet when she found out she was pregnant, she knew she had to stop if she had any hope of sanity for herself or her marriage. Because her husband had had a vasectomy, she knew that the pregnancy could not possibly be his, and because of potential problems with the fetus due to her drug use, she opted to have an abortion. When she was preparing her disclosure with her therapist, she said, "I'm so confused about what to do. My peers in SLAA tell me that I am keeping secrets and harming my recovery, but I just don't think it will help our situation for me to tell him about this abortion. It was a private decision between me and my God, and not a part of our relationship. Still, I don't even know who the father was! I just don't want to screw up my recovery. Should I tell?"

In this case, Anita has done well to evaluate how it might help or further complicate the situation to tell her husband. She is correct in her assumption that the decision legally is hers to make and is a private matter. If she is convinced that telling would help her stay sober, she can make the decision to tell information that is private. Had her husband been the father, although the decision remains hers legally, he would have had the right to know to at least voice his opinion, allowing him to grieve the loss and/or support her in the decision, or experience any emotions that might arise about the pregnancy and drug use. Either way, she is faced with the consequences of her decision.

How about in the case of Marty, married to Suzy, who had gotten Sandy, his secretary, pregnant during a two-year affair with her? Would he be keeping a secret if he did not tell Suzy that Sandy reported having an abortion shortly after the affair ended? Is it a secret or private? Would it be different if Suzy and Marty had been trying to get pregnant for several years with no success?

In this case, Suzy had a right to know because Marty's actions could result in legal consequences (sexual harassment) since Sandy was an employee. Also, she might still be pregnant and waiting until a later date to sue him for child support and medical care. This would directly impact Suzy. To make matters worse, Sandy's best friend, who ran the local newspaper, saw Marty come out of the Motel 6 with Sandy and photographed them together. No amount of back-pedaling on Marty's part could save him from Suzy if the story about a sexual harassment suit showed up in bold color on the front page of the local paper. In order for Suzy to make decisions about staying, boundary setting, what to do if the media got involved, and what to tell the children and family members, Marty would be wise to disclose before someone else does.

It is sometimes hard to know what is private and what is a secret. What is private does not interfere with someone else's physical or emotional health or cut us off from the resources we need to solve problems. A secret prevents one person (or both) from making truly informed decisions.

Secrets sometimes become private information once they are shared with the appropriate people. So it is important to decide who else needs to know the information. It is not appropriate for the addict to tell everyone his First Step or for the spouse to tell all her friends and relatives specific information contained in a disclosure. Decide who needs to know before making the private moment between you and your spouse a public display of pain without boundaries—that is one good reason to do disclosure with a therapist who knows something about addiction and lots about couples.

The Therapist and Secret-Keeping

Whether or not to disclose a secret is a decision that therapists, as well as clients, need to make. The therapist's decision can significantly impact the effectiveness of the therapy. Some therapists would continue working with the couple while keeping the secret, hoping that they can still assist the couple to improve their relationship. Some therapists insist that secrets be shared and will refer you to someone else if you choose not to disclose. If you are seeking a counselor or therapist to work on relationship as well as addiction problems that include secrets, ask the therapist about his or her training and experiences. Also ask the therapist about his or her experience with addiction and the policy for insisting on disclosure if he or she sees the clients individually. How will this affect your ability to maintain recovery or trust the therapist? This should help you decide if this therapist is right for you.

The final chapter in this book is for therapists. If you have a good relationship with a therapist, you probably want to stay with him or her. You may want to share this chapter with your therapist.

Suggestions for Addicts Regarding Disclosure

Obviously, not all partners are in an emotionally safe place to hear a disclosure—but most can handle it if you have been thoughtful about the disclosure. Not all partners *want* to hear it all. But for your partner's sake and your own do not leave a letter or make a phone call—have the integrity to tell what you have done in person after doing adequate preparation.

Sometimes, it is more beneficial for the addict to get honest with "himself, God and one other" before he gets honest with his partner. In our work with hundreds of addicts, the relief that comes with finally getting honest with someone you trust about all your secrets—from all your acting out (hence the value of the 4th and 5th steps in the Program of AA (CA, OA, SLA, SAA, etc.) is what brings the relief. The truth will set you free!

But don't wait forever. Assess your situation. If you have already been caught but have many more secrets, take a couple of weeks or so to prepare the information. If you think someone is about to tell your spouse, then use interim disclosure with the knowledge that if you open Pandora's box, your spouse will want to look in more and more; in such a case, the help of a therapist may be in order.

The next chapter speaks more directly to the consequences of disclosure.

Interim Disclosure

We recommend a planned, thoughtful, full disclosure as early as possible. In cases where you as an addict are not prepared for a full disclosure, but know that it is quite likely your partner will find out about some of your addictive behavior, then an interim disclosure is in order. Interim disclosure is disclosing the information that you know your partner will find out. Be prepared that your partner may not accept the interim and press you for more detail. Have a set time in which you will strive to have your formal disclosure ready and set an appointment with her for that time and date.

Tell her you are preparing an amends letter that includes more specific information and at that reading you will answer any questions she may have about your behavior. Invite her to start a list of questions and her own letter about how this makes her feel. Acknowledge her frustration over not getting everything today, and admit you are telling her this because you want her to hear it from you rather than someone else. Request that she talk with someone in Al-Anon or other recovery groups about how she is feeling. Indicate that you are sorry for the behavior you have engaged in and will keep her posted about what you are doing for your recovery. Assure her that you are committed to the relationship and that you are sorry for the harm you have caused. Stay sober, and keep your appointment with her.

References

Brown, Emily M. *Patterns of Infidelity and Their Treatment.* New York: Brunner/Mazel, 1991.

Burton-Nelson, Mariah. *The Unburdened Heart.* San Francisco: Harper, 2000.

Glass, Shirley P. and T. L. Wright. "Justifications for extramarital relationships: The association between attitudes, behaviors, and gender." *The Journal of Sex Research* 29 (3): 361–387, 1992.

Herman, Judith. *Trauma and Recovery: The Aftermath of Violence—from Domestic Abuse to Political Terror.* New York: Basic Books, 1992.

Schneider, Jennifer. "Sex addiction: Controversy within mainstream addiction medicine, diagnosis based on DSM-III-R, and physician case histories." *Sexual Addiction and Compulsivity* 1:17–45, 1994.

Schneider, Jennifer, M. Deborah Corley, and Richard R. Irons. "Surviving disclosure of infidelity: Results of an international survey of 164 recovering sex addicts and partners." *Sexual Addiction and Compulsivity* 5: 189–217, 1998.

Schneider, Jennifer, Richard Irons, and M. Deborah Corley. "Disclosure of extramarital sexual activities by sexually exploitative professionals and other persons with addictive or compulsive sexual disorders." Journal of *Sex Education and Therapy* 24: 277–287, 1999.

Smedes, Lewis B., *Forgive and Forget: Healing the Hurts We Don't Deserve.* New York: Pocket Books, Simon and Schuster, 1984.

Tomm, Karl, *Deconstructing Shame and Guilt: Opening Space for Forgiveness and Reconciliation.* Texas Association of Marriage and Family Therapist Annual Conference, January 2002.

CHAPTER FOUR: Consequences of Disclosure

Everyone thought that Lyndon and Loretta were the ideal couple. Married for 18 years, they were both successful health-care professionals and the parents of three high-achieving children. What Loretta didn't know, however, was that Lyndon had a secret life, consisting of a series of affairs with women he'd met at the hospital and at conferences and a growing addiction to Fentanyl, a potent narcotic pain killer. Lyndon related:

> I was tired of living a double life. The lying, the sneaking around, the false reassurances to my wife whenever she questioned me"—I hated the person I had become. Finally I went to see a counselor, who recommended I join Sex Addicts Anonymous. The counselor told me I had to tell my wife if I was going to recover and that I would be wise to see a lawyer in case the situation at work created a legal problem. The guys in SAA were very supportive and that gave me some hope. However, some of the SAA members advised me to wait a year before disclosing to my wife to get some clarity, something from the *AA Big Book* supporting that position. But I loved my wife and hated that I had betrayed her. There had been so many times it had been on my lips that when my wife looked at me one day and said, "Lyndon—I'm so worried about you. You are losing weight and you are so unhappy

and tormented," I broke down and told her the truth. I had not intended to, but the feeling was bigger than me.

Loretta reported:

> I felt suicidal when he told me. What would happen to our careers? What did this mean about our marriage? Would he lose his ability to prescribe or do surgery because of his actions? What would happen to our children if the media got this information? I was beside myself. I pictured killing him and then myself. I had never thought myself capable of considering those actions. If it had not been for the children, I don't know what I would have done. I felt betrayed by the person I trusted the most. I went into shock. I was numb. Right then and there I decided the marriage was over. I removed my wedding ring and wrote him a letter telling him I was leaving and taking the children. Then I slept in a separate room because I was afraid of what I might do since all the children were out of town.

The next day, Loretta went to see a therapist who understood addictions. The therapist advised Loretta to take some time before making any decision about her marriage. Together they agreed to spend six months clarifying Loretta's feelings, exploring her abandonment issues, and helping Loretta understand the extent of Lyndon's commitment to the marriage and learn more about how the addiction impacted her and their marriage. By the end of the six months she and Lyndon were attending a couples support group and had decided to stay together.

Cary and Cynthia had a difficult marriage but had managed to stay together for 12 years. Part of the reason they were able to get through difficult times was because both Cary and Cynthia had been in recovery from alcoholism for four years. Despite his sobriety from alcohol, Cary had not been able to manage his anger and frustrations when they fought or when he lost his job. A few years ago he had turned to prostitutes, rationalizing to himself that if Cynthia wouldn't have sex with him, he deserved to get some relief. However, over time he had progressed from occasional use of prostitutes to frequent use of massage parlors and adult book stores where he could receive oral sex from anonymous partners. He knew he had to do something about this problem when the bookstore he frequented was raided by the police just as he was driving into the parking lot. Cary's fears of giving Cynthia a sexually transmitted disease, maybe even HIV, led him to seek help for his addiction and ultimately to disclose to Cynthia. "I felt a great deal of shame, and was afraid that Cynthia would leave me. But I knew I had to tell her anyway."

Cynthia reported:

> I felt as if I had been deceived, betrayed, taken as a fool, victimized. I thought I was a "loser" for being with him because he had done these things with men. Then I had to take a hard look at myself. I hadn't been there for him—that isn't an excuse for his actions. But I hadn't been there for him because I was involved in an affair myself. It would have been easy for me to blame him— but who was I kidding! Myself! I wasn't any more sober than he was. It was so clear that I also needed more work on my recovery too.

Cynthia and Cary both renewed their commitment to recovery and began marital therapy shortly after disclosure. Both agreed that disclosure opened the door to healing their marriage and got them back on track with recovery.

Mary and Bill had been married for 15 years and had two school-aged children. Mary was a very pretty, enthusiastic, and bright woman, with no college education. Yet it seemed that no matter what she embarked upon in her career, she was successful. Bill, on the other hand, had a college degree and had been in the same job, working his way up the corporate ladder at a painfully slow pace, with only one promotion during their 15 years of marriage. To others this marriage seemed perfect. However, Mary had not been content with Bill from almost the day they were married. She was disappointed that Bill was not able to progress more quickly in his job and she longed for excitement. Bill was just boring.

Mary had begun having sexual affairs in high school, when her biology teacher had approached her during her junior year. The attention, perceived status, and risk made this liaison exciting and set a pattern for her for years to come—older men and risk taking. For all the years of their marriage she had had numerous affairs, all with older men in risky situations. Over time, despite efforts to curb her behavior during the past several years, the risk taking became greater and greater.

It all came to an end when Mary and a board member of the not-for-profit agency for whom she worked were caught in the parking lot of an adult video shop engaging in oral sex on the hood of her car. Both were arrested for indecent exposure, and the call from the police station to Bill changed both his and Mary's lives. Not only was the arrest shaming and expensive, the news media made this story front page news for several days. Their children, neighbors, and relatives all were witnesses of the handcuffed professionals being shoved into the police car. Bill chose to escape with the children to his parents' home in another state, leaving Mary behind. As further revelations about Mary's past appeared in the local press, Bill decided to relocate permanently, and the couple eventually divorced.

Even though the media coverage, an overnight stay in jail, and loss of her husband and children had been horrible for Mary, the disclosure via the media had been the catalyst that gave Mary the push she needed to get into serious recovery:

> It was clear that I was on a pathway to destruction. If this had not happened, I would have picked the wrong guy in some bar and found myself beaten, raped, or even dead in some hotel room or back alley. This has been a hard road. I lost everything that I thought was important—Bill and for a while my children, my career, my so-called friends. But I found myself. It is still one day at a time, but I am sober. I have another job, some real friends, a chance to be a better Mom. I finally like myself. If this had not happened, I wouldn't be here today. I am sad for those who were hurt by my actions. But I am so grateful for my recovery.

Cynthia and Cary, and Loretta and Lyndon are two couples whose relationships survived and got better through disclosure. Other couples, such as Bill and Mary, do not reunite, but despite their divorce Mary was glad the disclosure forced her to get into recovery. No matter what the reason for the disclosure, it is a process rather than a one-time event. The first step is to identify and face the fears that come with disclosure.

Preparing to Manage Emotions

Emotions run rampant before, during, and after a disclosure. It is common for people to report combinations of feelings, ranging from relief and hope to rage and despair. Of course the addict has been planning and rehearsing what he will say in his head or with his sponsor, a friend, or a therapist. Prior to the disclosure he feels nervousness, fear, and anxiety. Most addicts hope that telling will in some way help, but fear a whole host of losses and do not want to suffer the consequences.

Joe, a 43-year-old electrician and father of two children, recalled,

> I had so much shame, I did not know how I was going to get through it. My self-worth had hit bottom and I felt like a worthless piece of shit. I was so depressed; often suicidal, but did not even have the guts to do that. I was scared she would never believe me again or worse yet, she would leave and take the kids. I couldn't blame her if she did. I felt like such a failure, like scum, horrified that I hurt her so much.

Exercise:

No matter whether you are the addict or the partner, you will have a variety of emotions throughout the disclosure process. Identifying those emotional states and then managing them is your task. Of course you may be angry or sad, fearful or full of shame, but knowing how you feel and then managing those feelings can make all the difference in how you are able to get through disclosure anytime during your relationship.

One way to learn about emotional states is to keep a journal of your thoughts. Finding the time to record and analyze all your feelings may be difficult, so we recommend doing one thoughts-feelings worksheet daily on a situation that caused you to experience a strong emotion. You may complete this journal now. You will find a blank journal in the back of the book that you may copy for your daily use.

Thoughts-Feelings Journal   Date: _____

1. Event or Situation

What happened? Who was there? When and where?

_____

_____

_____

_____

_____

Partner Example: I was going through Jack's pockets in the laundry room and found a receipt from a restaurant from last week. He did not tell me that he went to any restaurant.

Addict Example: Jill found a receipt from a restaurant and confronted me about lying to her.

2. Thoughts

What thoughts were going through your head just before the event, during the event, and immediately after the event? Circle the thoughts that may be related to your core beliefs about yourself.

_____

_____

_____

_____

_____

Partner Example: Damn him! He lied to me again! Just when I thought recovery was going somewhere. I am sure he was with that woman from work again—and probably drinking again—he must have relapsed. What am I going to do? What a jerk! How did I get into this mess? I wonder what else he is doing that I don't know about. I better check all his pockets and the credit card bill one more time.

Addict Example: I can't believe her—she is snooping and jumping to conclusions just like she always does. Why do I have to tell her everything? That lunch was just with my secretary but she will never believe me and I sure don't want to have to tell my secretary all about this.

3. Emotions

   What emotions or feelings did you feel? Underline the strongest two feelings. Circle feelings that are triggers for you to want to act out.

   _____

   _____

   _____

   Partner Example: Anger, rage, fear

   Addict Example: Fear, anger, shame

4. Body Sensations

   Often the body gives us a signal that something is going on before we are really aware that we may be in a bad place. Listen to your body. Describe any body sensations you felt during the process. What does your body do when you get angry or sad? How does it tell you that you are having a strong emotional feeling or reaction?

   _____

   _____

   _____

   _____

   _____

   Partner Example: Head and shoulders tense up; stomach begins to get tight; head begins to hurt

   Addict Example: Tighten jaw and grit teeth as she yells; heart begins to race; face gets flushed

5. What I Did Well

When we've gotten into a highly emotional situation that we mismanaged, we think we made a mess of everything. This section is to remind you that you did do something right (usually). Think about what part of the situation you handled well or did not make worse. Note those items here.

_____

_____

_____

_____

_____

_____

Partner Example: Despite feeling angry, I did not rage at Jack. Prayed for guidance on how to handle this. Tried to take deep breaths before we talked after the initial flare-up. Agreed to a time-out to self-repair. Figured out that I over-reacted based on my fear. Talked about it later.

Addict Example: Took deep breaths while Jill was losing it. Let her yell, tried not to get into defensive mode. Agreed that she has a right to be mad but that I had not acted out with anyone. Asked for a time-out until we both were more calm.

6. How I Made Things Worse

In this section, list the ways you made the situation worse.

_____

_____

_____

_____

_____

Partner Example: Jumped to conclusions, catastrophized about the situation before I found out the facts. Yelled at Jack. Doubted myself and our efforts at recovery. Obsessed about the past instead of staying in the present. Used old blaming statements to make him feel bad (I felt worse).

Addict Example: Got defensive immediately and started blaming her for going through my things. Stopped listening and started planning my retaliation plan. Started trying to manipulate her.

7. Thinking Errors

Look at your thoughts from Section 2. Are any of those thoughts thinking errors? Actively search for information or evidence that contradicts the thoughts or supports the thoughts.

_____

_____

_____

_____

_____

Partner Example: I did not have proof that he lied, just a receipt. It could have been business. It would be impossible for him to tell me every single thing he does daily—I have to ask for information when I want it. He isn't a jerk. Evidence is that he has told me several times when he has been triggered and what he did to shore up his recovery efforts. That has made me feel more confident. This wasn't a mess—until I made it one.

Addict Example: It was suspicious and she has every right not to trust me given my long history of lying. I don't have to tell her everything, but it is helpful to keep her informed of things I'm doing that might appear suspicious. I also don't have to tell my secretary, but I might be wise to give her some information so it would be easier to call Jill during those lunches to verify who I am with and why.

8. Plan of Action

This is what you plan to do to help this situation and plan for next time.

_____

_____

_____

_____

Partner Example: Apologize for reacting instead of responding and calling him names. Ask that he tell me about his day on a regular basis. When I find something, ask him to tell me about it rather than jump to conclusions. If I am still fearful, tell him what he can do to help me feel more confident, like call his secretary to verify he was with her. Discuss my reaction with my COSA (Co-Sex Addict) group.

Addict Example: Apologize for not telling her before about the lunch and for yelling at her. Discuss this with my therapist to make certain I am not "fooling" myself. Plan not to have lunch alone with any women, even my secretary, unless it is necessary and on those cases to call Jill and tell her.

Learning to manage your emotional states will help no matter where you are in the process of disclosure or recovery. It is a great tool to have and if you practice using the thoughts-feelings journal every day, you will find you are better able to quickly find and correct thinking errors so you don't waste time obsessing over things you can do nothing about.

Positive Outcomes of Disclosure

If disclosure had only the negative consequences reported later in this chapter, it is unlikely that couples who have been through this experience would recommend disclosure to other couples. In our survey we asked addicts and co-addict partners if they thought disclosure was the right thing to do. We asked them to think both retrospectively about how they felt at the time of the disclosure and how they felt about it when they completed the survey, which was weeks to years afterwards. Thinking back to the time of the disclosure, over 80 percent of the partners and more than 60 percent of the addicts reported they felt at the time that it was the right thing to do. The next statistic is even more impressive. At the time of the survey, that number had risen significantly. **Of the partners, 93 percent felt it had been the right thing to do. And a whopping 96 percent of the addicts felt disclosure was the right thing to do!** Despite all the pain and loss, enough good had to come out of the process for people to feel so strongly that it was the right thing to do and the majority said they would recommend disclosure to other couples. Sydney, writing two years after his original disclosure, said, "In some ways the disclosure was selfish. I couldn't stand the pain of the double life. This is who I really am. I had been so manipulative she had no idea the depth of my emptiness or my compulsive use of men to fill that void. This was a real chance to stop my out-of-control behavior because I could not continue on the course my life was taking if I wanted to live."

Jessica, who had been through a painful disclosure, reflected, "While it hurt, I did feel relief because now I knew I wasn't going crazy. My instincts were accurate: he had lied. For about two years I had suspected something. I can now understand the past; it helped me understand why he acted the way he did. I felt relieved to finally know the truth. Now I could make choices based on the truth, not some lies."

Echoing a common theme reported by partners, Lydia, aged 38, re-called, "The disclosure let me know he cared about me enough to share that difficult information. It meant he wanted to be honest with me. I saw it as an opportunity to seek help. This might be a beginning."

Although the above responses reflect the feelings of hope, the relief of finally gaining clarity about the past, and the recognition by some that living a double life was more destructive than disclosure, we will not gloss over the intense feelings people have during this process. Just as the majority of addicts and partners recommended disclosure, they also reported that each went through what seemed like the worst nightmare of their lives. Mary, 42, had a typical mixed reaction: "I felt like I'd been stabbed right through the heart; the pain took my breath away. I didn't feel that I could breathe or would live. At the same time, it made all the pieces fall into place. I knew I hadn't been crazy. By validating my suspicions, I felt better in a way."

During the process, anxiety is usually so high, your mouth is dry; it is hard to gauge what your partner is thinking or feeling—everything important to you is on the line and you know it. Depending on your partner's response, how you feel afterward varies, but most addicts feel some immediate relief and believe it is the right thing to do despite the consequences. George, a 51-year-old manager, told us, "The whole truth only helps. Honesty is essential in a healthy relationship and recovery. It was very cleansing and seemed to take away some of the power of the addiction as it always thrived on secrets and lies. Had I not told the truth, I would have stayed on a destructive course for longer—perhaps until I destroyed everything. Because I have been honest now I have nothing to hide."

Positive Aspects of Disclosure for Addicts and Partners

Both addicts and partners experience significant positive aspects of disclosure. For addicts, these include:

- Honesty

- End to denial

- Hope for the future of the relationship

- A chance for the partner to get to know the addict better

- A new start for the addict, whether in the same relationship or not

According to Eldon, "I was tired of living a double life. I did not have to keep on living with low self-esteem if I was willing to find help. I found out my partner really loved me and was willing to help me solve my problems with this addiction."

Peter recognized, "It meant that I had to admit to myself and my wife that I was gay. My marriage of 17 years ended, but it was not really an adverse consequence. It was the right thing for both of us. We survived it and remained friends."

Partners also experience significant positive outcomes from disclosure. These include:

- Clarity about the situation

- Validation that they are not crazy

- Hope for the future of the relationship

- Finally having the information necessary to decide about one's future

Misty, a 45-year-old accountant who'd been married for 23 years, was one of many women whose husbands had covered up their behavior by casting doubts on their wives' emotional state, telling her she was imagining things. Despite her pain, Misty felt that the disclosure was very helpful to her: "I needed to know what kinds of risks I was taking. Knowing he could relapse with men and prostitutes let me know how to protect myself from STDs. I also had suspicions about when he was active in his addiction in the past. By finding out that I was accurate in my hunches about his behavior, I learned I can trust myself and I'm not crazy, or at least I wasn't making things up or overly suspicious. It started us off on a footing of greater honesty."

Adverse Consequences of the Disclosure

As we stated earlier, we will be honest about the intense pain both addicts and partners reported as part of the disclosure process. As with all pain, it is a chance to grow and learn.

Disclosure of secrets is a traumatic experience for both partners.

Knowing you have been lied to is bound to cause pain; knowing you have lied repeatedly to the person you love causes guilt and shame. When the secret activities have been sexual, the pain and the sense of betrayal are more acute. Both partners are often forced to seriously consider the likelihood that the relationship will not survive the disclosure. Adding insult to injury, there are cases in which an arrest has been made, financial security lost, or a life-threatening or incurable disease transmitted. Sometimes addicts have another totally separate life, with another family, and children who see the addict as a father and for whom the addict has financial responsibility. If there are legal consequences with law enforcement or the Internal Revenue Service, or if the addict has lost his or her job, the addict and partner are plunged further into fear.

The anger or resentment the partner feels because of this threat is sometimes insurmountable. In addition, the core fear of abandonment that many partners of addicts feel is often triggered by the disclosure. You can expect that disclosure will be a traumatic experience, that the family will change, and that the consequences of the addict's behaviors often last for years.

Adverse Consequences for the Addict

Addicts who disclose their secret life to their partners can expect to experience some of the following adverse consequences:

- Worsening of the couple relationship

- Guilt and shame

- Anger and sometimes rage from the partner

- Loss of trust by the partner

- Cutting off of the sexual relationship

- Damage to other relationships, such as with children or friends

- Legal consequences

- Loss of job

Steven, 36, who had been in recovery from nicotine, alcohol, and benzodiazepines for five years, relapsed when a friend showed him some pornography on the Internet and how to enter a sexual chat room. He was immediately drawn to the excitement of the instant responses of the chat rooms and before long found himself smoking again in front of the computer. After several Internet affairs and one offline, skin-to-skin encounter, during which he resumed drinking, he returned to AA where his old sponsor told him he needed to disclose. But the disclosure brought consequences Steven had not expected: "There were fights before but now she had the ammunition she needed to keep me in line. She didn't trust me anymore. The doubt about what I might have done or might do in the future was debilitating—she tried to control my behavior to prevent my acting out. She was continually accusing me of affairs, acting out, etc. that I haven't committed. It was a nightmare."

After admitting her affairs to her husband, 37-year old Suzy told us, "My husband wanted to 'reclaim' me sexually. I felt so guilty that I let him consume me sexually for weeks. Then I became disgusted and started shutting him out. He then became vigilant about my behavior, thoughts, and actions for several months. He started to judge me and try to manage my program. Now when he is feeling insecure or mad, he brings up my history and throws up certain situations or individuals to me. I don't know what to say; I just feel worse, guiltier."

Other addicts complained that their partner was monitoring their every movement, or constantly reminding them of past transgressions, or withholding sex as punishment.

Initially after disclosure, adverse consequences for both addicts and partners that usually disappear after a period of time include sleep loss and obsessive thinking, loss of appetite, stomach pain, diarrhea, sometimes vomiting, and weight loss. Worry and lack of concentration interfere with work performance and day-to-day tasks. It is as though someone close to you died and the grief process crashes over you like a tidal wave. Not being able to focus makes everything harder. Depression makes decision-making difficult; making mistakes is common. Car accidents are commonly reported.

It is not uncommon for an addict to lose his or her job as a result of acting out in the work site or as a result of public exposure of some illegal acting out behavior. Sometimes illegal behaviors lead to formal charges against the addict, huge legal costs, and even incarceration.

The financial consequences can also be immense. Therapy and treatment are expensive; legal costs are even more costly. If job loss is a consequence, then financial problems are even greater. Often acting out has been associated with spending money—on pornography, prostitutes, drugs, and alcohol. Some addicts have led such a double life that they have another household set up, some even have other children to support. But the truth of the matter is, *even without disclosure most addicts experience these consequences.*

Adverse Consequences for the Co-addict/Partner

For the co-addict partner, the feelings are so intense, you think your head or heart will explode. There is a combination of anger, grief, confusion, pain, fear, and sometimes revulsion. The obsession that invaded your brain takes a new turn. Before, you might have suspected something, but now the obsession turns to worrying about how you missed it, what is wrong with you that this happened, and what will happen in the future. Theresa, a 43-year-old cashier and mother of three, reported,

> I couldn't believe what I was hearing. This was the man that I thought I could trust. This was my life, blowing up in front of me. I had never doubted myself any more than I did at that moment. What was wrong with me that something like this could happen? And how did I miss something this big? Then afterward, I lost my relationship with my family when they found out. I would have flashbacks of him telling and I couldn't stop the hurt, the loneliness, the isolation I felt. I couldn't tell anyone for the longest time. I couldn't sleep. I felt so old and tired, worn out. Not only couldn't I trust him with drugs and alcohol and money, now if he used—it meant he would be using crank in some hotel, wearing my clothes, and masturbating to some porn on the cable TV. God. . . . How the hell do you get beyond that?

Among the adverse consequences you can expect as a result of disclosure are:

- A worsening of the couple relationship

- Depression and even suicidal thoughts

- Attempts to compensate for the pain with acting-out behaviors such as drug use and sex

- Loss of self-esteem

- Decreased ability to concentrate or to function at work

- Feelings of shame and guilt

- Distrust of everyone

- Anger and rage

- Fear of abandonment

- Physical illness

- Lack of sexual desire

Some partners reported becoming depressed, distracted, even suicidal. According to Phil, whose wife had starting having sex with other men when using crystal methamphetamine, supposedly to lose weight, "I couldn't concentrate. I got into two car accidents and did things like putting milk in the cupboard and cereal in the refrigerator. I was afraid I would drive off a particular bridge and was afraid I would hurt myself with a kitchen knife."

Millie's husband told her a project at work required him to stay late for several months. In reality, he was spending hours every evening in cybersex activities in his office. He exchanged and downloaded S & M pornographic pictures on his work computer, engaged in real-time online sex involving bondage and domination, and occasionally had real-life sexual assignations with women he'd "met" online. After learning of her husband's double life, Millie said, "I felt total distrust in myself, in him, in the relationship. I felt betrayed, confused, afraid, stunned that the person I loved and trusted most in the world had lied about who he was, and that I had lived through some vast and sinister cover-up."

Other partners described their insecurity and loss of self-esteem at feeling unable to compete with sexual partners, the power of drugs, or the seduction of gambling or high-risk spending. Often co-addict partners have to have time away to think and let the anger subside. Sometimes there is a feeling of being suffocated by the presence of the addict.

Marie, whose husband had spent hundreds of hours on the Internet experimenting with multiple types of unusual sexual practices, including the viewing of teen pornography and engaging in sex with minors, explained, "I was so devastated and repulsed by him. I didn't want him to touch me; I hated him and wanted him to leave. I loathed him and wanted him dead. The betrayal on all levels was just more than I could take."

Samantha's spouse of 20 years disclosed a long history of unprotected sex with prostitutes while using cocaine. For years they had struggled to make ends meet. Time and time again she had had to explain to her children that there was no money for new school clothes or toys at Christmas. This information brought back all the sadness from those times of deprivation, "I'd been victimized and I took it personally. He could have killed me with HIV. It was like someone had taken a shotgun and blasted me all over, the pain was unbearable and I couldn't stand to be around him. I was embarrassed and humiliated. I couldn't bare to think what to tell the kids— how do I explain to them that they mean so little to their father that he would spend money we did not have just to please himself. I hate him and myself for being with him."

Constant confusion is common for the co-addict partner who can't decide if she wants him there or not: "I didn't trust him and I couldn't find the pride that I once felt. I'd get reminded of something, some lie he had told, and the feelings would start all over again. I'd want him out of my sight. 'Just get out, get out!' I'd yell. Sometimes I thought I just want to cut my losses and give up on him, get on with my life. Then he would be gone a while and we'd go out and before I knew it he was back in my house again."

Some couples experience several separations and reconciliations: "Sometimes I thought I was going crazy. He would move out for three or four months and then back in to figure out what HE wanted. I suffered abandonment each time and waited for him to make up his mind. Neither of us had enough recovery to deal with it."

Some co-addicts use alcohol and other drugs to "soften the blow." This can be a time of high risk for relapse by partners who are also addicts. Some co-addict partners have more sex with the addict because of their fear of losing him or to prove they can keep up. Others get involved in a revenge affair, sometimes disclosing and other times keeping their own secret. Too often co-addicts report that they end up in a liaison with someone they have turned to for help such as a work colleague, a friend of the addict, and in some cases even the attorney, physician, or therapist from whom they are seeking professional services. A rebound affair was reported by several partners. After the first rush of intensity, this did not prove to be a constructive solution to the couple's problems: It complicated their efforts to put the relationship back together, caused additional distrust, and often resulted in depression for one or both partners.

Friends frequently choose sides and, depending on how much is disclosed to them, can share information that should be private with people who do not need to know. Family members often side with the co-addict spouse and are incensed when she doesn't leave, so they sever the relationship. This is yet another disruption and often very painful for the co-addict and the children. If acting out behaviors are illegal, sometimes children are removed from the home—an extremely traumatizing event for children that compounds the pain of the betrayal.

Although the emotional pain seems to be the worst consequence of disclosure, there are many others. All addicts worry that they will lose the relationship, and the fear that the partner will leave is a huge deterrent to disclosure by the addict. But do partners actually leave?

Do Partners Leave As a Result of Telling?

Threats to leave are a common, easily understood reaction to the shock of learning that your partner has betrayed you with another person. About 70 percent of partners have some suspicions about the addict's behavior long before the addict admits the secrets. Some partners confront their significant other; others keep quiet either because they convince themselves it was their imagination, because they want to avoid confrontation at all costs, or else because they feel it's all their fault. Norma reported, "I had a few suspicions, just a feeling. I tried to ignore it and look at the good in our relationship. Finally I brought my feelings to him and said I felt suspicious. I proceeded to tell him that it must be just me, that I might need to get help. He let me take all the guilt and blame on myself, though he was the one using."

Those who do confront are sometimes met with active resistance. Sylvia, now divorced, wrote, "I was very naive and out of touch. A part of me knew that he was doing weird stuff and he even told me in subtle ways about it, but I wanted to minimize it all. When I told him about my fears, he would get extremely violent and throw things and break things and refuse to talk to me."

John related, "When I told Betty about my suspicions, she threw a fit. She accused me of not trusting her, said that if I wasn't satisfied I was free to move out, and stormed out of the house, leaving me with the four kids. She didn't return until next morning. I didn't say a word about it after that."

Lorelei, the wife of a physician mentioned in Chapter Three who had multiple affairs, said, "I had suspicions because he would not answer his pages and would come home late, sometimes reeking of cigarette smoke and alcohol. He would blatantly deny doing anything wrong. He'd be insulted that I questioned him and would often manipulate the scene and argue that I was pathetic and paranoid. Sometimes I would back down and actually apologize for accusing him. Then I would feel a terrible guilt."

Confrontation and denial are a recurrent theme in the relationships of addicts and their partners. This results in a pattern of dishonesty by the addict and distrust by the spouse, which subsequently makes it difficult for the partner to forgive the addict and for the couple to restore trust in their relationship.

In many cases, suspicions about secret activities result in threats to leave even before any disclosure is made. About 40 percent of partners make such threats, which understandably gives pause to men and women who are considering disclosing their secrets.

Threats to Leave After Disclosure and Outcomes

Receiving a disclosure can be painful, terrifying, hurtful, anger-provoking, and possibly the worst thing a person has ever experienced. Although some partners immediately close ranks with the addict and promise support, a majority (60 percent in our study) threaten to leave or to end the marriage or committed relationship. However, a large majority of partners (72 percent in our study) do not act on this threat. Among those who do separate, about half eventually reunite. Our findings should provide a large ray of hope for those of you who are struggling with a decision about disclosure of secrets: Even if your partner threatens to end the relationship, chances are good that you can work it through. In later chapters we will describe the steps that you can take to make it more likely that your relationship will survive.

Below we describe the different choices made by those who threaten to leave and their partners.

Separation or Divorce

"Our whole marriage has been one big lie."

"I was told by the treatment center staff not to make drastic changes now. He's now in a half-way house as per my decision."

"I said he needed to move out if he couldn't make a definite commitment to our relationship. He asked for time. It took five months and lots of support to get him out. We are separated."

"After my disclosure we separated initially for comfort and remain separate so I can learn to care for myself in healthy ways."

Separation and Now Reunited

"I stayed at first to give him a chance. After a year I asked for a period of separation which lasted three months. It successfully got me to focus on myself."

"I asked my husband to leave only after the third disclosure that the affair had not ended even though I was told that it was all over. We remained separated two years before reconciliation."

"My husband left the house; I told him I wanted him out of my life completely. We are now back together."

"We separated for three months [after my disclosure] but my good work and intentions and behavior have been the basis of reconciliation."

Worked through It/Went to Therapy/Twelve-Step

Partners stated,

"I told my husband unless he was willing to get counseling I could not stay in the marriage. He agreed to do whatever was needed to seek recovery."

"I told my husband he had to quit the job where this other woman also worked, and he did."

"We both went to therapy and put the relationship back together."

"I gave him my bottom line—three meetings a week of a Twelve-Step program and calling his sponsor every day. If he stopped the program I would leave."

"I said I would work together with him to try to salvage our relationship, and gave a commitment first for three months, then six months, then a year. It has been over a year since disclosure and we are happier."

Addicts wrote,

"Both of us got into Twelve-Step groups, we got into marital therapy, I got into individual therapy, and about six months later she got into individual therapy."

"He said he'd try our relationship again *only* if I went the full 28 days at the treatment center—I went and we are still together and in a better relationship than we ever had."

"She threatened with an ultimatum unless I got help, so I went to counseling."

Considered Leaving but Did Not Follow Through

Partners of addicts are often people who are struggling with their own codependency issues. Many come from dysfunctional families in which their own childhood needs for nurturing were not met. They may believe that love must be earned by giving. They may have been initially attracted to the addict because this was a person who seemed to carry childhood wounds, who needed to be helped, or whose family background was familiar.

Many partners of addicts have childhood wounds that result in a great fear of abandonment. Life without the addict may seem like a fate worse than death. Although they may threaten to leave as a result of receiving a painful disclosure, some partners are unable to take effective action because of their own fears. They may conclude that living with the pain is better than living alone, or may decide to give the addict "another chance." Some rationalize their lack of action; others simply postpone making a real decision:

"I felt he wanted the marriage and the thought of losing me would put an end to this 'nonsense.'"

"I threatened an end to the relationship if it ever happened again. He promised it would never happen again, but it did. I stayed with him."

"He often said, 'If this is too painful for you, I'll just leave, okay?' So I was careful not to get too upset."

"I elected to make my decisions slowly because I had two children and a dying father. I am still dealing with possible separation and divorce."

"I left home for one week twice but would always allow him to talk me into coming home."

"I always threatened to leave. However, I always knew that I never would. Threats don't work when you don't follow through."

The addict's perspectives included:

"She considered leaving, but she chose to wait and see how she felt and what I did."

"Well, she said it but she didn't leave."

"She stayed, but was very angry and continued to be suspicious."

"She stayed, but we didn't have sex for a while."

"She didn't follow through but she told me many times she would divorce me immediately if it ever happened again."

Threats Before and After Disclosure

Partners who threaten to leave when they only suspect infidelity might be expected to threaten to leave once their suspicions are confirmed. Interestingly, however, about a quarter of partners who threaten to leave on the basis of suspicions *before* disclosure do not make the same threat following disclosure. The reasons given by two women were:

"I was so happy he was finally in recovery that I felt we could make it as a couple."

"I stayed because of the serious level of his addictions—I believe he is *so* sick. I could not think of breaking up our relationship as long as he is 100 percent committed to a serious recovery program."

Conclusions

Disclosure of secrets, especially painful secrets involving sexual activity with others, usually precipitates a crisis in the couple's relationship and an initial worsening of the relationship. Both partners experience a series of adverse consequences. In addition to possible legal, health, and job consequences, the addict typically feels guilt and shame, anger at the partner, resentment that the partner no longer trusts the addict and may now keep him (or her) on a short leash. The addict often has to go through a period where the partner is not interested in a sexual relationship.

Partners who have been on the receiving end of a disclosure typically experience depression and even suicidal thoughts, fear of abandonment, loss of self-esteem, decreased ability to concentrate or to function at work, distrust of the addict and perhaps of everyone, anger, lack of sexual desire, physical illness, and at times, attempts to compensate for the pain with acting-out behaviors such as misuse of food, drug use, and sex. As part of their distress and anger, many partners react to the disclosure by threatening to leave. Fear of this possibility can prevent addicts from disclosing secrets, even if they wish to disclose as part of their own recovery process.

The good news, as we learned from many couples that have been through this process, is that most people who threaten to leave don't do so. Even when the couple does separate, the chances are good that they will reunite if each is committed to their individual recovery from their addiction and co-addiction. Disclosure can lay the groundwork for a new relationship, based on honesty and greater intimacy.

In later chapters we will describe how counselors can facilitate disclosure, what couples who have been through the process recommend to other couples, how much to disclose and when, and what tools of recovery are helpful for rebuilding trust and restoring the relationship. To prepare, we'd like to ask you to think about the following questions as they apply to your own life:

- What do you fear the most about telling? Being told?

- What sources of strength do you have to get you through this time?

- Who can you call to support you during this time?

- What skills do you need to improve on to handle the disclosure?

The next chapter gives steps for a formal disclosure.

References

Schneider, J.P., Corley, M.D., and Irons, R.R. Surviving disclosure of infidelity: Results of an international survey of 164 recovering sex addicts and their partners. *Sexual Addiction and Compulsivity* 5:189–217, 1998.

CHAPTER FIVE: The Formal Disclosure
How to Do It Right

Most initial disclosures are not planned. They are prompted either by *external* events such as a spouse's suspicions or discovery, or by being confronted by an employer, neighbor, or the police because of some illegal behavior: or else by intense *internal* emotions that can no longer be tolerated. Depending on the specific circumstances, the secret-holder's personality, his current emotional state, and his fears of the outcome, he may disgorge the entire story, replete with details; alternatively, he may attempt damage control by revealing as little as possible.

In Ricardo's case, he had denied his wife's suspicions of this affair and others and had given great thought about how to keep the situation secret as long as possible. When the time came, disclosure did not come off as he thought. As he put it, "The first disclosure was not pretty, but at least I told Kristy. The second disclosure was not too pretty either, but the truth that came out of it was beautiful for me. Without that truth, we could not have survived what happened."

Ricardo never thought his life would come to this. He had fulfilled his childhood dream of being a pilot and now worked for a major airline. Everything he had planned had fallen into place. He had a wonderful career doing exactly what he loved to do, had a terrific teenaged daughter and he was married to a beautiful woman. Yet, after hitting forty, he had noticed that life just wasn't as fun or fulfilling anymore—no matter what he tried. This changed at his twenty-year class reunion.

It was at the reunion that he reconnected with Irene, an old girlfriend who was just a little more than interested in him. Her interest made him suddenly feel young again. She was a gorgeous, successful business woman who was not shy about inviting him to be sexual with her to see "if it was as good as it used to be!"

Being a pilot, he could arrange to fly anywhere and, conveniently, his schedule allowed for a particularly long layover where Irene lived. He had had numerous casual affairs without Kristy's knowledge, so he had no problem calling Irene at the first opportunity. She was thrilled and anxious to see him. Soon they were seeing each other two or three times per month and calling each other daily. They soon believed it was "true love" and often told each other that they were "soul mates" and had a "perfect" relationship. They were always glad to see each other, never fought, and the sex seemed to Ricardo just like his fantasies in the pornography he regularly viewed when away from home. Even though they both drank excessively during the times they were together, Irene seemed sexually insatiable, always playful, enthusiastic, and willing to try anything.

This affair went on for almost three years. Ricardo spent thousands of dollars on plane tickets for Irene to meet him in various places, for the long-distance phone calls, and for many gifts. He was always careful to buy his wife the same gift so when Kristy found receipts and questioned him about the money he had taken from his savings account, he concocted various excuses, like buying parts for the Chevy he was refurbishing in the garage.

Soon Irene and Ricardo began to fantasize about him leaving Kristy for a life together. Ricardo did love Irene but did not know how he could leave his wife and the fifteen years of history they had together; yet he did not know what to say to her or to Irene about his ambivalence. In an attempt to make Irene more secure so she'd back off some on her demands, he began to talk as if he would leave Kristy sometime in the future. However, he took no action. The more time he spent with Irene, the more time she wanted. Meanwhile, back at home his wife and daughter were complaining about how distracted he had become and about the time he spent locked in his garage (phoning Irene) when he was home. Ricardo was not sure what to do. There was just not enough to go around.

Ricardo's life really fell apart when he agreed to meet Irene for a "quickie" at an airport in a city she was visiting for business. She was so sexually excited when she saw him that she insisted they go to the rental car in the parking garage. Having little time and loving the thrill of the risk involved in being in a car in such a public place, Ricardo felt wildly excited just hearing her talk about her desire to give him oral sex. About the time she began, he closed his eyes as he leaned back to enjoy this interlude between flights. They were so involved that neither Ricardo nor Irene noticed the police officer who had approached the car. When the officer knocked on the window and asked, "Is everything okay in there?" Irene quickly raised her head and completely exposed Ricardo. The officer demanded they both immediately get out of the car, hands up. He then informed Ricardo and Irene that they were both in serious trouble, that it was against the law to expose oneself in a public place. Ricardo could see his career and family pass before his face. He begged the officer not to arrest him, immediately inventing the story that he was an Air Force reservist about to leave the country on assignment and enjoying a last few minutes with his girlfriend. The officer escorted Ricardo and Irene into the terminal, charged him with public indecency, and then left them with airport security. Ricardo missed his flight, so it was not long before his whole crew knew what had happened. Ricardo was suspended until an investigation could be completed.

Irene was beside herself. Ricardo told her he would call as soon as he could. Fearful of losing his job, his wife, and his daughter, Ricardo decided he had to end the affair with Irene. Upon arriving home, he called Irene and told her he loved her but he had to end the affair. Irene was hysterical and reminded him of their plans to be together. She suggested that this might be just the opportunity to end his marriage. Ricardo told Irene that it had been a wake-up call and that he realized he loved his wife and couldn't see her anymore. Irene couldn't accept this, and kept calling, even to his home.

Unsure of what to do, Ricardo feigned illness for the next several days in order to justify his absence from work. He did not want to hurt Kristy but wasn't sure what to say. A week after the incident, he received a certified letter from Irene containing documentation that she was pregnant and threatening to sue him unless he left Kristy and married her. Ricardo knew that his life was out of control and he had to tell Kristy.

That night over dinner in a restaurant, surrounded by many people and after drinking three glasses of wine to bolster his courage, Ricardo began by announcing to Kristy he had something horrible to tell her. Alarmed, fearing he had some serious health condition, she put her wine down and stared at him with tears in her eyes. Ricardo said, "Kristy, I have been really horrible. I had an affair with Irene from the class reunion and it is over now. But the situation is really a mess. I haven't been sick, just avoiding telling you that I got suspended because we were caught with her giving me oral sex in a car at the airport—all of the crew knows. She wanted me to leave you and marry her. Really she trapped me with sex and now she is claiming she is pregnant and that I am the father. I have talked to our attorney and he is advising me to go to this place for treatment, thinking that I drank so much during this affair that I might have a drinking problem that impaired my thinking. Anyway, I have to leave tomorrow morning. I knew I had to tell you before I left. I love you, not her, and I am sorry for messing up our lives."

Kristy was so shocked by Ricardo's words that she threw her wine on him and stormed out of the restaurant, after telling him he need not come home. She refused to talk to him during the first three weeks he was in treatment. It was their attorney who helped her see that avoiding him and the situation wouldn't change things. She agreed to talk to him and to attend family therapy at the treatment center.

In treatment, Ricardo followed the steps outlined in this chapter to present a formal disclosure to Kristy. She was able to process the disclosure with therapists and with him. It was here that Kristy realized much had been going on in her life and marriage that she had not paid attention to. When she returned from the family session, she joined a support group and began her own therapy. Upon Ricardo's return, they both attended individual and couple's therapy. Realizing that other couples also faced similar tragic circumstances, they found the strength and support to sustain them during the challenging months to resolve the problems resulting from Ricardo's actions.

Ricardo and Kristy have now been married almost 25 years. Their daughter has completed school and is training to be a pilot herself. They provide financial support for the baby born to Ricardo and Irene and enjoy having him as part of their family during various holidays and each summer. They both agree that the second disclosure helped them start from an honest place in their marriage. With that beginning, lots of faith in a Higher Power, therapy, and their friends they made it this far. (See Ricardo's second disclosure in the box on page 107)

Ricardo's Second Disclosure

(This letter was read during a family session while Ricardo
was in treatment.)

Dear Kristy,

I know I have disclosed some of the "facts" to you but I did not do a very good job. I am sorry about the way I told you those things. Once again, I was selfish and did not consider the impact on you. Now, I want you to know the truth about everything and am willing to answer any questions you have now or in the future.

First, I tell you these things with a heavy heart. I know you always thought we had a good marriage. What happened and is happening is not fair to you or our daughter. What I did was wrong and I am sorry you are suffering the consequences for what I did. It isn't fair and I can't expect you to forgive me.

I want you to know, you did not do anything to cause what has happened. I made the choices I made because of the way I was thinking. That is not your fault; it is mine. You are a good woman, a good wife, and a good mother. I do not blame you or anyone else for what has happened. I am responsible.

I have learned lots about myself since I came to treatment. One of the things is that I am a liar. I have lied to boost myself up. I did not want to admit and sure did not want anyone, especially you, to know how insecure I felt. I have been a liar for so long, I don't know when I started and haven't always known when I was telling a lie. It is important that you know I do know now and am remembering how much I lied to you. I lied about how I was feeling, I lied about money, where I was, the people I was with. I told lies that suggested that you were at fault, or stupid for suspecting me. Remember when you asked me about the perfume you smelled on my uniform so often and I said you were paranoid, that it was just perfume from sitting next to a flight attendant on the bus. I was wrong to have lied and I am sorry for all the times I made you question yourself. It must have made you feel crazy at times. You were not crazy or stupid or foolish then and you are not now.

You were right to suspect me. I have had several affairs since we have been married. As well as I can remember, the affairs started after I got that "ass-chewing" from one of the dads at Shari's soccer game. I felt like everyone on that field thought I was a fool and just couldn't get it out of my mind. Instead of going to you to talk about it, I picked up a flight attendant who had been telling me all about her marital problems for weeks. Most of the women have been flight attendants. I have not been with anyone you are friends with or know other than Irene and I think you only met her briefly at the class reunion. That is where I hooked up with her and started seeing her shortly thereafter.

I have spent thousands of dollars that should have gone for things for you and Shari. I have put my career in jeopardy and by doing so have put your future and Shari's future in jeopardy. I was horrible to do so and I am sorry. Our attorney tells me my supervisor is seeing my time in treatment as favorable, but I will not know the outcome of the suspension until I am finished with treatment. I am sorry for placing you in this position. I know you must be worried about what to do next.

The most difficult thing for me to admit is that I have had unprotected sex with many of these women. Not only have I exposed you to sexually transmitted diseases, there is a baby on the way who will be my financial responsibility. I have had an HIV test and it has come back negative, but if you have not had one yet, you should.

I would not blame you if you wanted a divorce. I do not want that, but I would understand how you may feel like you can never trust me again.

I hope my honesty here and my behaviors from this point forward will help you see that I am serious about our marriage. I want to be your best friend. I know you thought we were, but I wasn't. I understand that honesty is the major quality of a best friend. That is where I have to start—not just for you and our marriage, but for my own sanity.

I can't expect you to forgive me but I am hoping that you will give me a chance to re-establish a new, healthier relationship with you. I love you and Shari with all my heart.

Love, Ricardo

Not all disclosures end happily, but as we've said before, the majority of couples interviewed agreed they were glad they disclosed. This was true even if the relationship ended. Ideally, disclosure allows people to make decisions based on accurate information instead of lies.

It is important to point out that disclosures do change everything and in the beginning change creates stress. The family dynamics change. Sometimes, like in Ricardo and Kristy's case, another child is involved and therefore another family. Career is involved. Finances are affected. People at work or in the neighborhood often find out and unimagined consequences can result. So be prepared for changes.

How and What to Tell

In Chapter Three we discussed the steps to forgiveness, and explained that forgiveness is primarily for *you*, for your peace of mind, not for the person who hurt you. Even if the person who harmed you is unwilling or unable to make amends and ask for forgiveness, it is possible, and can be helpful, to forgive him. But it is certainly easier to forgive, and you are far more likely to continue a relationship with the person, if he takes responsibility for his actions, seeks forgiveness, and makes amends.

Most therapists agree that a sign of recovery for an addict is when he is able to take full responsibility for what he has done. Judith Herman, author of *Trauma and Recovery: The Aftermath of Violence—From Domestic Abuse to Political Terror*, states "true forgiveness cannot be granted until the perpetrator has sought and earned it though confession, repentance, and restitution." (p. 190) In *The Unburdened Heart*, Mariah Burton-Nelson agrees that forgiveness requires confession and restitution, but adds that if reconciliation of an intimate relationship is desired, then remorse is also necessary.

Confession is disclosing while taking full responsibility for what you have done. It is tempting to confess by phone or via a letter sent through the mail. It takes more courage to confess face-to-face, to directly confront the other person's expression of pain or anger or grief—but that is the more effective and desirable way to do it. Preparing by first writing a letter is a good idea: A letter or written work helps you stay on track. It is okay to write a letter *that you read aloud* to your partner and then give to her. Reading your work also provides a starting and stopping place so that interrupting and getting off track is not as easy.

Taking responsibility for one's actions and demonstrating remorse make a disclosure more effective than just dumping on a partner. This is the first step of restitution, a process that will be described further in Chapter Nine. In the following example, Dan is a person who was willing to admit what he had done, but had trouble taking responsibility:

Dan, married for 10 years, had for years alternated between excessive use of alcohol and gambling. Eventually he settled on a combination of heavy cigarette smoking while masturbating to pornography. Dan had gone to treatment twice before for his compulsive sexual activities. After each treatment he would act contrite, but he never did fully disclose to Delia the range of his acting out behaviors. Eventually, the behavior would return. Dan and Delia had already been separated once for six months following one of his binge uses and treatment. His persistent efforts to woo her back and his declarations of evidence that he was attending Twelve-Step meetings eventually persuaded Delia to give the marriage another try.

A year after their reconciliation, Dan bought a computer and discovered the Internet. He immediately relapsed to nicotine and alcohol combined with his new online sexual activities. He began emailing women he met in chat rooms on the computer while he drank and smoked. Caught in fantasy, he eventually became infatuated with a young woman who lived 2,000 miles away, and flew across the country to meet her. This time Delia filed for divorce. After a month of romance, the bloom wore off the rose, and he begged Delia to let him return. He said he was sorry, he'd do anything to make it up to her, and he suggested that they go see a therapist for a session in which Delia could tell him all the ways he had hurt her, while he would listen without defending himself. Delia declined; she had already told him dozens of times over the years how his behavior was affecting her. What she wanted was to hear *him* describe how he had hurt her and express remorse, and this he said he couldn't do. They divorced.

Addicts, being willing to listen to your partner tell you how the lies and secrets affected her is valuable, but even more impacting is for *you* to tell *her* how you believe you hurt her and affected her life. Your ability to validate her reality through your understanding of what you did to her, and then your willingness to say you were wrong and you are sorry are huge steps in demonstrating remorse. This is so important that it is useful to have a therapist guide you, but not everyone has access to therapists with experience in disclosure with addicts and co-addicts. A helpful alternative is to have a sponsor or other support person facilitate the disclosure. It is critical for your partner to have support afterward, and it is likely she may not want that support to come from you. Offer anyway and have a backup. If the disclosure is to your children, respect age-appropriate boundaries, and plan to disclose to them in ways that are meaningful for their developmental stage. (Disclosing to children will be discussed in the next chapter.)

Finally, you honor your own courage in being willing to disclose, and your partner's courage in being willing to listen. The willingness by both of you to participate in this process is in itself a hopeful sign for the future of your relationship.

Sometimes, it is helpful to determine how both of you are feeling so that you can be clear how the addiction is influencing you and your relationship. You may want to complete the exercise below to gain more clarity and information. If you score high on either anger or fear, you may want to seek help from a therapist to form a plan for managing your emotions.

Exercise:

Using the scale below, assess your level of anger and fear. Zero means you have no anger or fear or are neutral, and 10 means you have the most fear or anger that you have ever had.

	Level	Level	Level	Level	Level	Level
Partner Anger	0	2	4	6	8	10
Addict Anger	0	2	4	6	8	10
Partner Fear	0	2	4	6	8	10
Addict Fear	0	2	4	6	8	10

If either of you scores more than 6, you need help working through your anger or fear. Discuss this with your group or therapist. Addict, is your fear about potential loss or about hurting your partner? Does your partner want to end the relationship or is she just ambivalent? Partner, do you want to end the relationship, or are you ambivalent? Do you want to punish your mate or yourself? How will that help the situation?

Are you both ready to walk through disclosure?

For the Addict: Eight Steps to Disclosing with Integrity

Here are the steps for the secret holder to take in order to prepare and deliver a full disclosure in the form of an amends letter:

1. Get honest with yourself. As the Fourth Step of AA says, "make a searching and fearless moral inventory of ourselves." Making that inventory of how you have harmed another person and yourself with your behaviors helps raise your awareness about the extent of the damage. At the same time, recognize that those behaviors do not reflect your authentic self. Making a comprehensive inventory is not easy. You need to review your relationship from its beginning to the present, and list how you have been dishonest about how you feel about situations; how your feelings were displaced onto your family—for example, you were mean to your spouse and the kids because you were angry at your mother and perhaps the boss; how you failed to set boundaries at work and became so stressed out that you made bad decisions about your health and family finances; and how you have not honored or respected your partner or yourself. Include everything, not just addictive misconduct. This usually takes some time, but it's important to take the time to do it. It also often brings up much guilt, shame, and pain. Sometimes when you are reviewing addictive behaviors or feeling shame you may be triggered to act out so as to escape from your feelings. To prevent a slip or relapse, first prepare a safety plan with your sponsor. Have several people on a call list who can be there for you when you are having a rough time, or ask another peer to be around when you are working on your list.

2. With that information in mind, write an "amends" or "I apologize" letter. **This letter is not to be sent or read to your partner**—it is a draft from which to be accountable with your higher power and/or your therapist or sponsor or someone you trust. In this letter be as detailed as you can about your behaviors that have been hurtful to others and yourself. Take full responsibility for what you have done. Do not blame others or try to excuse your behavior.

3. Once you've finished writing the letter, read it aloud to your therapist or ask a group of trusted recovering friends to hear it and then describe to you their reactions. This feedback is often hard to hear, but rather than defend yourself, tolerate your negative feelings by telling yourself that this is part of the process and that you have something to learn. Even if you disagree with what someone is saying, there is probably a bit of truth in what stings the most. Others can point out when you are minimizing your behavior. If they know you well enough, they may realize when you probably are omitting important information. Listen to them carefully and non-defensively. If they tell you that you need to redo the letter then do so and go back for a second reading. Stop only when they say you are ready to actually write your amends letter to read in person to your partner.

4. Now write the letter as if you are going to read it to your spouse. You should state the goal of the letter in the very beginning. For example:

> My goal in this letter is to be accountable for what I have done that has hurt you and the children/family/business. This letter is written with all the honesty I can manage today [because if you are an addict of many years, you probably can't remember everything you have done]. Because of my actions, you may have been put in harm's way, and you deserve to have this information so you can make an informed decision about the future. [If she stays because she thinks she knows everything, but you continue to lie, then she is not staying of her own free will!]

We recommend that you DO NOT report all the "gory" details of your addictive behavior in this letter. For example, rather than telling the number of times you had sex, or the positions, or how good it was or wasn't, or the names of all the people you had sex with during your 10-year marriage, it is more useful to focus on the values you once had or wished you had. Admit that you broke the promises you made in your marital vows by having a number of affairs (or whatever the behavior has been) during your marriage.

More importantly, admit you lied to her about the behaviors and be honest if you may have exposed her to health risks. (If you have had an HIV test, bring the results with you when you are to read the letter and indicate that you have been tested and that you were wrong to subject her to this danger as much as you were wrong to have lied and engaged in the behaviors.) Tell her that you have not given specific details because you do not know how much she wants to hear, but *are willing to answer any questions about your past behaviors* as long as it is with the therapist or in an atmosphere where you both can get guidance about how to process and manage the information. Your intention is not to do further harm by disclosing.

You can also let her know what you have learned about yourself since you've gotten into therapy or recovery without blaming anyone else for your behavior. This is your opportunity to state that you have also hurt yourself because you have missed the opportunities to honestly love and be loved by her and your children. Reiterate that no matter what you have learned, *you* are responsible for your actions. If your intention is to stop these behaviors, say so here, but acknowledge that you understand there is no reason for her to believe you at this point. Again repeat that your actions have been wrong and hurtful and that you are sorry.

Once this letter is done, repeat the process outlined in Step Three. With feedback edit this letter to your partner until those helping you with this task tell you the letter is appropriate to share.

5. Arrange with your therapist or sponsor to have two hours available to present the letter to your partner. Ask your partner to join you for a session with the therapist. If she agrees, arrange with a friend to be on "standby" should your wife want you out of sight for a while. The friend needs to be someone who knows or can know about the disclosure and is willing not to know details beforehand but to be with your partner to be supportive.

6. Practice, pray, or ask others for help and guidance during this time.

7. Often partners already know about some of the behavior, but not all. They may have written you a letter describing their anger and feelings about what they already know or about the impact of your behavior on them. You may want to address information your partner provides in her letter in your disclosure. With the guidance of your therapist, read the letter to your partner. If you are with a sponsor, or by yourself, it is important that you preface the letter by stating that the information you will share may be hard to hear, but you feel it important to tell her. Have tissue available and some drinking water for both of you. Let yourself feel your feelings, and let your partner have and express her feelings, no matter how uncomfortable this may be for you. Regardless of her reaction, hang in there. If she calls you names, agree that you were wrong and she has every right to feel the way she does. Trust that you will do okay if you remain authentic.

8. Once reading the letter is complete, the therapist or sponsor should ask your partner if she has any questions or wants to say anything to you. Respond to those questions and again repeat that you are willing to answer any questions she may have in the future but you want the help of the therapist or sponsor/recovering couple.

   The therapist or sponsor then should ask if your partner is ready to accept the letter and the amends contained in it. Whether she says no or yes, ask what she needs now to help the situation. Then wait. Respond according to her request.

For the Partner: What to Expect If Your Mate Goes into Treatment

If your spouse has been "discovered" or has partially disclosed and has gone to treatment, most treatment centers have a "family week" that you will be asked to attend. You will probably listen to lectures or see videotapes that teach you about addiction and co-addiction or codependent behaviors. This can be very useful because you get a chance to see that your behavior plays a role in the addiction. It's not that you have *caused* the addict's behavior—he's responsible for his own actions. It just means that you are in a "dance" with him. His behavior triggers thoughts in you that result in actions. For example, you sense that he is lying about where he has been and you start to nag him about it. Then he gets angry and frightened and reacts by telling you that you are crazy or mistaken. He acts in some way that he has learned over time will make you think perhaps you are wrong or will lose him, so you change your behavior. Or the "dance" gets so full of anger and fear that one or both of you leave in order to create distance. In that leaving, the addict and sometimes the co-addict then acts out. The addict acts out by using his addictive behavior. You may act out by over-functioning with the kids or on your job or in the household, or perhaps by eating too much, or exercising and restricting food, maybe spending money, or even using drugs or having an affair. Either in an individual session with a therapist or in a group of other family members, you will have an opportunity to talk about how you are doing. In addition, you may receive written assignments.

Most often, if the treatment center knows the "full story" of his addiction, they will have encouraged him (in some cases, demanded) to disclose to you what his behaviors were during his acting out. Ideally you will be asked how much information you want.

Steps to Preparing to Hear a Disclosure

Once some disclosure has happened at discovery, the partner generally doubts everything, is sure that the addict is not being honest, and doesn't want to ever believe the addict again for fear of being hurt. That is normal; it will take a while again to believe the addict (usually one to three years). When the addiction is sex, most partners think they want to hear all the details—who was involved, for how long, where, what they did, how many times, was it at home, whether the sex was protected or unprotected, what the other person looked like, what they said, and on and on. No matter what the addict says, you will probably embellish his horrible secrets with even worse betrayals. We recommend that the addict give general information and specifics about how your health may be compromised, but then let you be the guide about what details you want to know. You still have to determine how the information will help you.

Exercise for Partner:

This is the hard part for you. Although you may want to hear every single detail, you must ask yourself, "What is my goal? What do I want to do with this information? Use it to see how my health and relationship are affected? Or see what information I can get to measure my self worth. Perhaps my goal is to get enough information to see if I can determine when he is acting out again so I can protect myself."

Our experience is that minute details generally serve only to make you feel worse about yourself, and will cause you to spend hours and hours obsessing about the details rather than how you got into this "dance" in the first place. List your goals for wanting the information here.

_____

_____

_____

_____

_____

_____

_____

_____

It is also useful to have a set of questions that you want the addict to answer. This helps you get your needs met and gives him a place from which to start. Here are some examples of helpful questions you might ask the addict:

- Are you seriously involved in a recovery program or in therapy?

- Are you committed to working on our relationship and repairing the damage? What does working on the relationship mean you are willing to do?

- When in our relationship did these activities begin and how long have they been going on?

- Have you engaged in drug use or sexual activities that may have put me at a health risk? What risky activities did you engage in, and when?

- Have you cut off all contact with using friends/sexual partners? If not, what are the obstacles to this happening, and what are your plans for overcoming these obstacles? (Ask that the addict write a note to the affair partner that makes it clear that the affair is over and that he is committed to working on the relationship. Ask to see it before he sends it. Or ask that he make a phone call with you or the therapist in the room when he calls.)

- Have you been using or sexually involved with any people that I know? If so, with whom?

- What significant lies have you told me to cover up your activities?

- Can you think of arguments we had in which you blamed me when the real issue was your acting out?

We recommend you make #1 listed below your goal:

1. Make a commitment to yourself to use the disclosure as a way to start the healing process for yourself. You can decide if you want to work on the relationship after you have heard what the addict has to say. Part of working on yourself is acknowledging where you have not been honest with the addict about how you feel and what you really fear.

2. Acknowledge that knowing only part of the truth hurts and that being in limbo contributes to the confusion, fear, and anger.

3. Write a letter of anger about what you do know. Identify all the ways the addict's behavior has had an impact on you.

4. Write a boundaries letter about how you want things to be different. Review the letter with your therapist or sponsor, and then read it to your partner.

5. Formulate any questions you have, and what types of information you want to know.

6. Identify where you have made threats that represent your fear that you are not good enough and that you seek validation primarily through your spouse.

The Timing and Extent of Formal Disclosure

In our survey, we asked addicts and partners for their recommendations regarding optimal timing of a formal disclosure. The results varied, often based on their personal experience. After two years of recovery from co-sexual addiction, one woman advised:

> Do it soon, and in the safety of a supportive environment, such as a therapist's office. Be fearlessly honest, but not detailed. Be willing to share without regard to consequences that might affect honesty. Try to understand your partner's feelings without judging them or closing down. Realize you are valuable and lovable, regardless of what anyone says or does. Look at being honest as a gift you give yourself. You can say, "That's who I really am." Give others the choice to decide to like you or not, to be with you or not.

We agree this is good advice.

The next hardest disclosure is with children. Sometimes it is even harder than disclosure to your partner. Although it is difficult, disclosure to children is very important. How to do it depends on each child's circumstances and needs. The next chapter discusses how to disclose to children.

References

Burton-Nelson, Mariah. *The Unburdened Heart.* San Francisco: Harper, 2000.

Herman, Judith. *Trauma and Recovery: The Aftermath of Violence— From Domestic Abuse to Political Terror.* New York: Basic Books, 1992.

CHAPTER SIX: What to Tell the Kids

My Dad and Mom asked me to talk to them. My Dad said he had done some things wrong and needed to talk to me about that. He read me a letter and said he was a sex addict. We had talked about addiction at school and sex addiction was mentioned but I really didn't know what that was. He told me he'd lied to Mom and to us kids and that he was wrong to do that. He had gotten involved with other women and spent lots of time looking at pornography like people drink or use drugs, instead of figuring out how to solve his problems. He says that is why he goes to meetings, so he can learn to solve his problems. He apologized for leaving his porn where I could see it and said that it was a bad thing to look at pictures of women and make them into objects. Things like that. He said he was sorry that he had been gone all the time and that he hadn't made it to my baseball games or track meets.

I guess what I remember most is that he said he was sorry, that it was wrong to lie and that he loved me and he would try to do better. I believe him.

—15-year-old son after apology letter was read to him in a disclosure session with his parents and the therapist.

Disclosure to children is probably one of the most anxiety-provoking situations for families with addiction. When the secrets begin to come out and disclosures take place between the addict and partner, children know something is happening and want reassurance.

This chapter describes the atmosphere in addicted families and discusses some of the consequences for children living in a household with addiction. We also outline a process for disclosure to children over time and offer concrete examples of ways to discuss certain topics. The most important part of this chapter is about honoring your values and parenting well.

Generally, small children do not need disclosure or explanation about addiction. An apology for not being around is appropriate, but mostly they need good parenting. Because we believe there is some genetic predisposition for addiction, discussing your addiction with older children is appropriate and disclosure is one way to do this. Obviously, when younger children get older, that is a time to talk about sex addiction or any other addictive behavior. But because you are an addict, their risk for addiction is higher, so they have an increased need to know.

Atmosphere and Consequences of Living in Addicted Families

People who suffer from all varieties of addiction are consumed with planning, obtaining, using, or recovering from the use of their drug of choice and then trying to cover up all the lies and secrets, shame and pain. This behavior ignites the emotional distress of the co-addict. The co-addict partner is just as obsessed with discovering evidence and catching the addict, or reeling with anger and putting up emotional walls to stay detached, or pursuing with clingy behaviors. These behaviors contribute to the emotional distress of the addict. Both parents mismanage the emotional states that keep them trapped in addictive and codependent behaviors and intense shame. The addict and often the co-addict are unavailable for the children emotionally and, at times, physically.

To compensate for their own insecurities and to reduce anxiety, addicted parents may engage in several different types of behaviors with their children. Parents can be over-controlling, establishing rigid rules for children that are confusing and unrealistic. Parents may use destructive criticism of the child to cover their own pain and shame. This shame sets up a family system with rigidly defined boundaries in which secrets are expected to be kept, rejection is common, people are self-focused, maturity is rarely modeled and underdeveloped, and everyone—parents and children—lacks a sense of security. One 14-year-old girl complained to the therapist, "I'm not sure my parents even know I am alive. They made me come here, but they don't care, they are just trying to look good. I wish they'd just grow up and be normal or something."

Children get drawn into the discord between parents and may attempt to solve parental problems by overachieving and being the "perfect" child, by not rocking the boat in hopes of keeping the peace. Some kids take the opposite route—they are rebellious or engage in problematic behaviors to draw attention away from the parents' problems. An 18-year-old boy, in treatment for cocaine addiction, related, "No matter what I did, it wasn't enough. I used to make the best grades, was captain of the swim team, even won a medal at a debate a couple of years ago. They didn't even notice, but let me make one B and shit hits the fan. So I figured what's the use. I'd just get high and see what they thought about that! That's when my cocaine use first started."

It is common for addicts to have more than one significant relationship or marriage while they're using. Most single addicts, especially relationship addicts, become involved in serial relationships. Anxious for their children to accept their new partner, they bring this new person in the home soon after meeting him or her. If one or both members of the new couple are acting out sexually, the home environment is quickly sexualized. The couple talks openly about the sexual desire for each other, touch each other in sexually explicit ways, or have little regard for the sexual sounds that can be overheard by children even through closed bedroom doors.

Sometimes the new partner is very attentive to the child. This can be very confusing for the child because of loyalty to the addict's former mate. The child may try to please the parent and becomes attached to the new partner, and then experiences another loss when the parent moves on to yet another new partner. According to the 15-year-old daughter of a female relationship addict,

> At first, when my Mom would bring home some new guy, I'd think maybe she would settle down, be home more. I'd try to be nice to him, even like him, you know? About the time I was really getting to think he'd be like a second Dad, it would be over and she'd get involved with another guy. They'd be over at our house screwing like rabbits even before the other guy was gone. Finally, I just gave up. Why even try? Mom's a beautiful lady and some really nice guys have liked her, but she's . . . well, I am just sick of trying."

Co-addicts and addicts may make a child a confidant or even a surrogate spouse. These young people are given information and attention that are confusing and frequently far more sexualized or sophisticated than they can understand. Children hear and see the accusations and denials, the frightening fights, and the loud silence of stonewalling. Sometimes they see parents hit one another when anger gets mismanaged. Sometimes kids get hit as well. A 15-year-old girl, the oldest of three siblings, said,

> My Mother was out of control. She used to bring us in and sit us on the couch, tell each of us exactly what my Dad did in his sex addiction. My little brother was only four at the time. She was yelling what a bastard Dad was, standing right over Jimmy yelling "YOUR FATHER F—K'S WHORES! What do you think about him now? He's not so wonderful is he?" I felt like telling her to just shut up and get the hell out, but she'd hit me or Jimmy. Then she started making my little brother sleep with her so Dad wouldn't.

Children may witness or find evidence of the drug use, gambling, or sexual acting out and are coerced to keep secrets about the addict's behavior with threats that to tell will result in the family breaking up or Dad going to jail. Sometimes a child finds an Internet pornography file or emails from a sexual chat room and is faced with confronting the parent, telling the other parent, or holding onto the secret over time. When teens reach puberty, this secret-keeping can turn into intense rage and some teens even threaten to blackmail the addict parent. According to a 13-year-old girl,

> My Dad is so f—king weird. I can't stand him. He thought no one knew what he was doing. Like I taught him how to use the damn computer. How'd he think I wouldn't know—it was so easy. I could go in any time and read everything he said to that woman and what she said to him. I just got so sick of it. Like one day when I was really pissed at him, he was trying to act all cool you know, and I just told him he was a fag and sick and that I was going to tell Mom. He freaked out man! I could have gotten him to do anything for me then, but I hate his guts and I told Mom."

As discussed in previous chapters, some addicts act out in illegal ways and the disclosures happen through other sources such as police, attorneys, the wife of an affair partner, or the media. The list is long and the potential for children to hear about the addictive behavior from other sources is greater than you might expect. Therefore, disclosure from you as the primary source is helpful to your relationship with the child. It is the first step in helping your children deal with the adverse consequences of other people's judgments and behaviors and their disappointment in you.

> My Dad beat up this drug dealer who was with a prostitute and he was arrested. That's how my Mom found out that he was a sex addict and a drug addict. Then he talked to me and my sister. That went okay. I was really mad at first, but my Dad seemed so changed after he went to treatment that it was good. It really prepared us for what was about to happen. He's a big shot in our town—or at least he was until this happened. When he went to court, the newspapers and TV stations got word of his deal and they printed this trash about him in the paper—it was

even on the TV news. My folks knew it was going to happen and we all got together and decided what we were going to say to people. The news media got the old "no comment" line like you see on TV, but with friends it was hard. At first I was really embarrassed but then some of my friends were really cool and supported me against some other freaks at school. It isn't such a big deal now. I am proud about how we all got through it.

—17-year-old son of an addict who was also a federal judge

Contrary to what the media would have you believe, most children within a sexually addicted family are not overtly sexually abused. However, some are exposed to the sex addict's behaviors and use the behaviors as the seeds of their own sexual unfolding. Some adolescents and young adults find themselves caught up in sexual acting out in similar ways as the parent.

My Dad tried to tell me and tried to protect me, but I already had the "bug." I had seen the pornography he tried to hide and years before had discovered masturbation to stop thinking about my parents fighting or to go to sleep. Now I've started to drink to cover up my shame about not being able to handle this even though my Dad told me about his habit.

—20-year-old son of a sex addict who had disclosed his addiction when the son was 15

Addicts and co-addicts who use drugs sometimes use drugs in front of their children. Despite strict laws prohibiting adults from providing minors with illegal substances, some parents in addicted families even offer their kids drugs. It is common for addicts to reveal that their own parents smoked marijuana with them or gave them alcohol at a very young age. This modeling can send a very mixed message about the inappropriateness and hazards of drugs use by minors.

I didn't have a chance. Momma and Daddy were both drunks and pot heads. I can remember being really little and when the beer got warm they'd give me the can to finish. Their friends would come over and smoke joint after joint in front of me. One guy even showed me how to inhale. Everyone thought that was so funny. By the time I was 12 I was stealing their stash and it wasn't long before I was out buying my own. The only way I could afford my habit was to sell. Now they are sorry while I am stuck here in this hell hole. Sorry is a little late.

—16-year-old doing time in a juvenile detention center

It is common for children in homes with eating disorders or out-of-control spending or gambling to watch an adult engage in destructive behavior. They often see the consequences and feel helpless to change things despite valiant efforts to do so.

My mother was wasting away right before my eyes. She wouldn't eat hardly anything and then go exercise for a couple of hours. I thought at first she looked pretty good, then I started to notice the dark circles under her eyes. One day after she had gone to the dentist for a toothache, I heard my Dad trying to talk her into getting some help. Later he told me that she had been throwing up after eating and her stomach acid ate all the enamel off her teeth. Pretty weird huh? I have friends who do that kind of stuff but how can my mother?"

—14-year-old daughter of mother with eating disorder

My Dad always seemed lucky at cards and brought home lots of cash from the horse races. What I didn't know though was that he lost lots more, he just didn't bother to tell us. He used my college money to gamble with and lost. My grandmother gave me that money and it wasn't his. Mom told me that he had been betting on the horses on the Internet and now we have to pay back what he lost. Things are bad between them. If they just wouldn't fight maybe this would work out somehow. I hate it when they fight.

—17-year-old daughter of gambling addict

Any type of addictive behavior in a household is destructive to children, but making children the object of sexual acting out is one of the most problematic. Using a child as an object of sexual addiction is damaging for the child in more ways than just being exposed to adult sexual behaviors. Fear of abandonment or pain combined with the special attention of the parent makes this the perfect double bind for the child. While they fear the pain, they crave the attention and long to be special to the parent. It is common for adult survivors to describe how they feared and dreaded the sexual encounter with a parent, but at the same time how seductive was the pleasure of the attention and being told "you're special."

I'd stare at the door and hope it wouldn't open. When it did and he came over, I knew what to do, what he wanted. I hated the way he smelled, and can remember these sounds he'd make; when the sounds would start, I'd just go somewhere else [in my head] until I'd hear him say, "You're my girl, my best girl. I love you the most because you're special." As much as I hate him for what he did to me, I am ashamed to say I longed to see that look on his face the next day when he'd smile that smile—it was the only time I've ever felt like somebody. Later he told me he was addicted to me. I don't know what that means.

—20-year-old after leaving home, remembers abuse happening between ages 11 and 13

Because children are dependent on us, they feel they have few choices but to participate, often blaming themselves for what has happened. If they witness the abuse of another child, the guilt and pain are even more debilitating and long lasting.

When children's boundaries have been violated, especially by sexual abuse, they don't have a sense of boundaries for anything. They often take on "protecting" someone else because they feel powerless to protect themselves. They don't sense that their bodies are their own or that they have any say about what happens. They then become easy prey for someone else who has boundary issues themselves. It's not surprising that we see young people pairing up with unsuitable partners with whom they essentially repeat what happened to them in their family of origin. That's why we see people getting into one abusive relationship after another, (See *The Betrayal Bond,* by Patrick Carnes, Ph.D., for more information about how abuse regenerates itself.)

The effects on children raised in addicted families are not well researched but the effects of sexual abuse and living in chemically addicted families have been documented. These families are what Merle Fossum and Marilyn Mason, in *Facing Shame: Families in Recovery,* call shame-bound families. Their description provides an excellent overview of the dynamics of such families:

> . . . A shame-bound family is a family with a self-sustain-
> ing, multigenerational system of interaction among a cast
> of characters who are (or were in their lifetime) loyal to a
> set of rules and injunctions demanding control, perfec-
> tionism, blame and denial. The pattern inhibits or defeats
> the development of authentic intimate relationships,
> promotes secrets and vague personal boundaries, uncon-
> sciously instills shame in the family members, as well as
> chaos in their lives and binds them to perpetuate the
> shame in themselves and their kin. It does so regardless of
> the good intentions, wishes, and love which may also be a
> part of the system. (Fossum & Mason, Page 8)

In all cases of sexual abuse, the addict must be accountable for his actions, so some form of disclosure and acknowledgment is important for the child and the addict to heal. This is true even if the child is an adult by the time the addict gets enough recovery to take responsibility.

Exercise:

List ten or more ways your child has been exposed to addiction.

_____

_____

_____

_____

_____

_____

_____

_____

_____

_____

_____

Describe the impact you think this may have had on your child or evidence you already see of how this has impacted your child.

_____

_____

_____

_____

_____

_____

_____

_____

_____

_____

In what ways has your child been used to reduce your stress and anxiety about the problem?

_____

_____

_____

_____

_____

_____

_____

_____

How, What, and How Much Do We Tell

How, what, and how much to tell becomes the challenge. And how can we be both accountable and good parents? There are no exact formulas; there are no perfect answers for how you tell kids or what you tell. We are going to recommend a process instead of telling you all the "right" things to say. We will give you some concrete examples, but this disclosure has to fit the context of your situation.

First and foremost, your job as a good parent is to make your love visible by providing structure, guidance, protection, and nurturing in healthy ways. This is a difficult task since most addicts had little or no modeling from their parents on these topics. If this is true for you, you may need to do some homework. Figuring this out starts with a foundation—a foundation made up of your values.

It also means getting rid of faulty core beliefs. That takes time and requires taking active steps to change how you think, which changes how you feel, and in turn increases your chances of changing what you do. Remember the core beliefs as outlined in _Out of the Shadows_ by Patrick Carnes:

- I am basically a bad, unworthy person.

- No one would love me as I am.

- My needs are never going to be met if I have to depend on others.

- Sex is my most important need.

Exercise:

Describe how each of these core beliefs has influenced your value system:

_____

_____

_____

_____

_____

Perhaps you are not sure what your values are or you may want to change or "improve" your values. Here are a few questions to get you started.

- Where did you get your values? Parents? Other family members? Teachers? Preachers/rabbis/leaders in the faith community you were raised in?

_____

_____

_____

_____

_____

_____

- Which values that you learned in childhood can serve you well now?

_____

_____

_____

_____

_____

- Are there values you learned that are not respectful of your personal growth or recovery? What faulty beliefs were generated from those messages?

  _____

  _____

  _____

  _____

  _____

- How would you change or adapt both the beliefs and values to better suit you as a strong person in recovery who is also a responsible parent?

  _____

  _____

  _____

  _____

  _____

- Review your values with your partner/co-parent. Together list the values you want to guide you in creating structure, guidance, protection, and nurturing for your children (and yourselves!).

  It will be helpful for you to list statements that counter or refute those core beliefs above. Let this new set of values help you develop those counterstatements.

  _____

  _____

  _____

  _____

  _____

  _____

  _____

  _____

Your values and core beliefs that reflect those values can make everything easier if you actually follow them. It is much easier to disclose by admitting that you violated a value and that you had a faulty belief. For example, think about your behavior in the past. What were the values that guided that behavior? What values do you want to guide you now?

Here is a sample of what might be said just about honesty and being faithful to a teenager during disclosure:

> When I was growing up, I heard a lot about being honest and faithful in relationships. Yet, I did not *see* much of that, and my own experience led me to think I could get away with lying and feel powerful if I had lots of girlfriends. But I was mostly lying to myself. When I think about it, I was lonely and was faking it and that is what I have been doing for a long time. For years I have been telling lies to Mom, to you, and to myself—and that has hurt everyone. Because I have lied, Mom doesn't trust me and she has every right to be mad. What I did was wrong—lying to her and to you was wrong and I am sorry that I have lied.
>
> Lying is easier to talk about than being unfaithful because I am ashamed of what I have done. When I should have been with your Mom and you, I chose to find some other women to be with when I felt mad, or sad, or lonely, and some of the time I had sex with them. This was very hurtful to your Mom, to our relationship, and to the family—including you. It will take your Mom a long time to start trusting me again and she has every right to be mad at me. You did not do anything to make me do this. None of this is your fault or Mom's. I made wrong choices myself.

For a younger child, you might say:

> Your Mom and I have been fighting because I have been telling lies to her. Because I have lied, Mom doesn't trust me and she has every right to be mad. What I did was wrong—lying to her was wrong. Sometimes I even lied to you about working when I was off doing stuff with people I should not have been with. When I should have

been with your Mom and you, I chose to find some other people to be with when I felt mad, or sad, or lonely. Sometimes I would drink and do things that were dangerous and then lie to Mom about what I was doing when she was worried about me. Now I go to meetings at night to learn better ways to make decisions when I am feeling sad, or mad. What I did was very hurtful to your Mom and to our family—including you. It will take your Mom a long time to start trusting me again and she has every right to be mad at me. You did not do anything wrong. Neither did Mommy. I was the one who did things that were wrong. I am sorry I hurt her and that I have not been around much to spend time with you. I love you.

There is something very empowering about being honest.

Exercise:

Let's look at how this fits our previous discussions of parenting in terms of structure, guidance, protection, and nurturing. Think about marriage or a committed relationship. List your values about being in a marriage. Below write the messages you want to send to your children to *guide* them about marriage and commitment in what you say and do.

_____

_____

_____

_____

_____

_____

_____

_____

_____

_____

_____

It is common to feel guilty about what you have done in your addiction and to try to overcompensate by letting children run all over you. This is especially true when they reach their teen years and will use your addiction history to manipulate you. But your job as a parent is to provide *structure* to *protect* your child. Sometimes you have to be firm and say,

> I can see that you don't think it is fair that you are not allowed to date now, and that you think that because I was irresponsible when I was in my addiction, I should let you do dangerous things now. But I was irresponsible and hurt others and myself. The rule in our house is that children do not drive cars or date until they are 16 because we value your life. Since it is our job to protect you the best we can, and the odds are greater that you will get hurt if you date at this early age, you will have to wait to date until you are older and have more experience with life. Since you are 14 and have acted pretty mature at times, we agree that we will talk about when you can go with a group to an event without us, but for now—no dating. I see that you are angry and that is normal when someone is hoping to do something special and it has to be postponed. It is okay to be angry and we have talked about ways to deal with anger in the past. I have every confidence you will get beyond the anger and decide how you want to be with your friends in ways that fit our values and rules.

Certainly some 14 year olds will ignore this and do it anyway. But, if they know your values, the rules, and the reasons behind them, more likely than not they will follow your rule.

Nurturance means that you take time out to spend with kids. No matter how old kids are, they need to know they have some special time with you as an adult, as somebody who loves and cares about them and listens. If you go to the movies with your children but rarely have any one-on-one time to talk and listen to each other, time with your children is not as valuable as it could be. Going to the movies together is better than nothing at all, but taking time to talk about what is going on in their lives and how they feel is important for people to feel valued.

Feeling valued translates into healthy families. Mark Laaser contrasts unhealthy and healthy families in his book *Faithful and True: Sexual Integrity in a Fallen World*. As you review the characteristics of healthy and unhealthy families in the next paragraph, think about the values you were raised with and have operated with as an addict and co-addict and see what you want to change.

In unhealthy families boundaries are either very rigid or nonexistent. In healthy families boundaries are firm but flexible. Parents care and nurture each other and their children. There is personal respect for boundaries. In unhealthy families, the rules are centered around keeping the secret, so people are not to acknowledge what is going on. It is the "don't ask, don't tell" rule so you just don't talk. With that rule comes the injunction not to feel anything, to blame others for your problems, to minimize and deny that problems even exist unless it will get you something. Children in these families take on roles that are rigid and defined.

In healthy families, children's roles are more flexible, but the parents stay in the adult position so children have a chance to grow and mature over time. People take personal responsibility for their actions, and honesty is rewarded. People talk and feel, and accept that problems are inevitable in life and can be dealt with, and these folks can ask for help. People listen to each other, individuality and teamwork are both supported and encouraged, and feelings are accepted. Physical self-care is modeled and taught, children feel safe and know that they can always come home. Basic needs are provided for. Healthy families learn to cope with and express a full range of emotional states. Spirituality plays an important role in daily living.

As shown in some research in the area of prevention education, some basic characteristics are consistently seen in children who do well in the world. This should help you shape your parenting plan. (If you need to re-parent yourself, if you focus on these areas and stick with them, you will find life is easier.)

Children who are successful as adults (and during childhood) have high emotional intelligence. Daniel Goleman, author of *Emotional Intelligence*, describes people with high emotional IQ as having five specific abilities:

- The ability to recognize a feeling when it happens

- The ability to handle feelings in appropriate or self-enhancing ways

- The ability to motivate self to delay gratification and stifle impulses

- The ability to recognize emotional states of others (having empathy)

- The ability to respond rather than react to emotional states of others

Researchers are finding that these skills can be taught to children (and adults), who then improve in many areas of their lives. In fact, children who have good impulse control (ability #3) are less likely to become addicts. It makes sense when you think about how addicts are so impulsive with their actions.

Another characteristic found in youngsters who do well is the ability to set reachable goals. Additionally, these children have the feeling that they know who they are—they have a sense of self-worth and self-identity. These young people report being able to talk to their parents about anything (including sex) and talk with them often. In fact, talking is encouraged in these families and the family members report feeling heard.

Finally, these kids know their family's values and can articulate them. Think about how much easier it is for a kid to set boundaries with other children when he knows why you value boundaries and he has practiced with you how to set and keep a boundary.

Because we are speaking about sexual issues, it is also important to mention what happens in sexually healthy families. Parents consider sexuality education as important as all other types of values-based education. Parents are "askable"—children feel safe in asking. Parents utilize "teachable" moments rather than waiting for children to ask questions. They are aware that actions speak louder than words. Parents in these families know the difference between childhood and adult sexuality. Are you prepared to do these things?

Children in sexually healthy families feel good about their bodies, and understand the concept of privacy with regard to boundaries. They are prepared for puberty and feel comfortable asking their parents questions. They are able to make *age-appropriate* decisions.

So what does this have to do with disclosing to your children? This forms the foundation by which you will continue to talk about sexuality in your family. Disclosure to children means assuming responsibility for how your sexual acting out, drug abuse, compulsive gambling, or other addictions, or your codependent behaviors, have interfered with parenting your children. The discussions that follow are critical to rebuilding family and to help your child grow up thinking differently about sexual and other behaviors (and relationships) than you did.

Basic Repair Work

In preparing to disclose:

1. Think about what you want to say about the values you violated by your acting out rather than the details of what you did. In other words, how you failed your child is what you want to be accountable for. Your child is not interested in how many affairs you had or how much money you lost. She is interested in the fact that you lied to her, that you are sorry about it, and that she did not do anything to cause this. It is important to admit that you lied to her mother many times and lost her trust, and that she will probably be angry and sad about it for a while, but that is okay. It makes sense that she'd be angry and that your child would be angry that you lied, too. She might remember that you are serious when you admit that you spent money on things you did not need and that the money should have gone into her college fund or something for the family and you were selfish and for that you are sorry. List those values you violated here:

    _____

    _____

    _____

    _____

    _____

    _____

    _____

2. Discuss with your partner what information you both think needs to remain private between you as adults and marriage partners. (Some information may be okay for adult children to hear.) If it is not information that is crucial for children to make sound decisions about their own lives, then it can remain private between the two of you.

_____

_____

_____

_____

_____

3. Discuss with your mate the differences between the old values you were living by and the new ones you are trying to live by now. Describe those here:

_____

_____

_____

_____

_____

_____

_____

4. Prepare to admit where you made mistakes and encourage your child to talk about how he feels about what you've said.

5. If you are using the letter format, write it now. Sometimes, with younger children, people have made picture stories to tell the "story." (Age-appropriate language and format should be remembered in the preparation.) Others have made videotapes, especially if the addict is unable to disclose in person to the child. One of these formats is good since it allows the child to have something he can hold onto, review, think about, and then respond to. This document is a hopeful "security blanket" for getting a new parent back for the child, so it should be a good incentive for you to stay in recovery to honor this rebuilding with your child.

6. You should read the letter or tell the story to your child. Both parents should be present and in agreement about what is going to be shared. Because it is a highly emotionally charged time for most people, it is safer for children to see both parents being involved in the process. But the addict is responsible for disclosing his behavior.

(Co-addict partners often are aware that their behavior has been hurtful to the children, too. The same process works, just at a different time.)

7. Ask her what she has heard or already knows and if she has any questions.

8. Remind him that he is free to ask you questions, and that you understand that this is hard for some people to talk about, so you are going to bring it up again from time to time.

What Kids Don't Want to Know:

•   The specific details of your acting out

•   How angry you are at your spouse

•   How sex is between you and your spouse

What Kids Want to Know, By Age:

•   It is not necessary or appropriate to disclose to very young children.

•   Preschool (ages 3–5): These children have often been witness to fighting or have heard that you are an addict and don't know what is happening:
    •   Are you going to die or leave me?
    •   Am I in trouble?
    •   Do you love me?
    •   They need guidelines about their genital touching. Too often sex-addicted families get hypervigilant and worry about a child's normal sexual exploration and genital stimulation. (See Debra Haffner's *From Diapers to Dating* for excellent information about what is normal.)

•   Early elementary (ages 5–6):
    •   Is this my fault?
    •   Will something bad happen? (divorce fear)
    •   Who are you now? You are now very different and this child has learned to adapt to deprivation.

- Upper elementary/middle school (ages 9–13)
    - Am I normal?
    - Will I get this addiction because I have sexual feelings?
    - Am I going to end up a drug addict because you are?
    - What will happen to me if you get divorced?

- Teen/Adult years
    - How could you do this to Mom? To the family?
    - How does this specifically relate to me? (You've ruined my life!)

Other Ongoing Repair Work

- Look for moments that are teachable opportunities—for example, a cybersex story on TV.

- Focus more on the positive part of recovery—everyone working to have a balanced life.

- Spend time doing fun things together, to balance the "heavy" conversations you're having with your children. Children (especially early in recovery) need fun time, too.

- If your child is angry and wants time apart from you, give him some space. However, do not forget the job of a parent is to provide structure and guidance. Encouraging your child to write you a letter about his anger is appropriate. Letting him hit you or allowing him to ignore house rules just because you didn't follow them is not okay. If the anger persists, then family therapy is in order.

- Discuss more about healthy sexuality rather than just rehashing the old information about the disclosure.

- Be available. Be patient. Be proud that you are making every effort to be a different kind of parent. It will be worth it.

Despite the problems between you, you and your partner will want to show your children a united front in the fight against addiction in the way you disclose to them and in discussions after the disclosure. If they see you together even though the addict discloses, it can help them to feel less anxious about the future and your role with them.

If a separation or divorce is the best solution for you, then co-parent your children in ways that show them that people can end one type of relationship and transition to another that is still respectful.

In families in which parents end up separating, the losses for children are multiple, so their needs are compounded by grief, fear, anger, and sadness.

Disclosure is not just a matter of having one little talk and it's over. Rather, it becomes an ongoing process requiring many discussions. You have to think through what you will do if you find your daughter on the Internet chatting with some guy several years older than she and you find out it is she who is trying to talk him into meeting for sex. Or what you will do if you find a well-worn *Penthouse* under your son's mattress, or if you walk into your 12-year-old's room with a stack of laundry and find him or her masturbating. Or how you handle if you are watching a television program with your seven-year-old and a female character makes a sexually aggressive comment to a male character. Yes, disclosure is but the first of many opportunities to talk about sexual health, healthy relationships, and developing into a responsible, authentic person. Your job is to keep coming back, offering to talk, listening, writing notes, being there for serious and fun times—but be there. Be as genuine as possible. Don't lose your sense of humor. Have integrity about what you say and do with your children and you can survive almost anything.

Disclosure and discussing addiction are serious business, so limit the time you spend talking about the disease and expand the time you spend with your children talking about what they want to discuss, having fun, and having a positive attitude about the future.

See the Appendix A for the most frequently asked questions pertaining to children.

References

Carnes, Patrick. *The Betrayal Bond: Breaking Free of Exploitive Relationships*. Deerfield Beach, Fla.: Health Communications, Inc, 1997.

Carnes, Patrick. *Out of the Shadows*. New York: Bantam, 1991.

Fossum, Merle & Marilyn Mason. *Facing Shame: Families in Recovery*. New York: Norton, 1986.

Goleman, Daniel. *Emotional Intelligence.* New York: Bantam, 1994.

Haffner, Debra. *From Diapers to Dating: A Parent's Guide to Raising Sexually Healthy Children*. New York: Newmarket Press, 1999.

Laaser, Mark. *Faithful and True: Sexual Integrity in a Fallen World*. Grand Rapids, Mich.: Zondervan Publishing, 1996.

CHAPTER SEVEN: The Other Disclosures

Previous chapters have described secrets, lies, and the initial disclosures involving interactions between a married or committed couple. But this is not the only kind of secret-keeping that you may have to face. This chapter describes several real-life situations in which people have to decide whether to hold a secret or to reveal it, and, if the latter, to whom. Let's begin with the story of the Malik family—Michael, his wife Martha, and their daughter Marjorie. Michael's cybersex addiction affected his entire family.

Michael, a 38-year-old married computer programmer, had a long history of compulsive masturbation. Early in his marriage there had been a crisis when he had spent too much money on pornographic magazines. He had thrown out the collection and promised his wife Martha to reform. Since then, he'd still masturbated frequently and had a small stash of porn pictures, but he managed to keep the situation under control. Martha suspected that Michael's habit had not disappeared, and kept an eye out for pornography in their home.

When Michael discovered the Internet, however, within months his addiction was again in full swing. He spent hours holed up in his study at night, viewing online pornography, engaged in sex talk with other women in chat rooms, and eventually having real-time sex with women online using video streaming. Of course, he kept all of this a secret from Martha. Michael was thrilled that with cybersex, the secret was easier to keep because there was no longer a paper trail. Martha knew that Michael's interest in sex with her had diminished, but he explained that it was because he was working so hard and was too tired.

Late one evening, 13-year-old Marjorie walked into her father's study without knocking and found him masturbating while his digital camera transmitted pictures of him to someone at the other side of the computer screen. Appalled, she yelled that she was going to get her mother. Michael quickly collected himself, rearranged his clothing, and begged Marjorie to first talk with him. Michael reminded Marjorie of how depressed her mother had been recently. He reminded her that he hadn't really had sex with another person, and implored her to keep the secret, for to tell would only hurt Martha. He told Marjorie that revealing the secret might result in breakup of the family, or even in a suicide attempt by Martha. In the end, he swore her to secrecy and promised to stop the behavior.

As we mentioned in Chapter Six, situations like this put the child in an impossible loyalty conflict for which there seems to be no way out. It guarantees that the child will feel guilty toward the unknowing parent. Her relationship with her father and siblings will also be altered—she is now in a position to blackmail her father in various ways, and will also now feel a barrier between herself and her siblings, from whom she also has to keep the secret. To ask a child to hold a major secret from a parent is to do the child a grave disservice.

Learning about a person's sexual secret from a child—or for that matter from any source other than the person—without a doubt increases the betrayal that a partner feels. If you recognize that you are about to be "outed," your best defense is to arrange to promptly disclose your secret yourself. Returning to the story of the Malik family, Michael's effort to persuade his daughter Marjorie to collude with him in keeping the secret from his wife was the worst possible thing he could have done. First, he has put his daughter in an impossible situation, causing harm that may require future therapy to undo. Marjorie is now in a double bind—by doing what she believes is best for one of her parents, she is being disloyal to the other. Whichever choice she makes, she will be hurting one of her parents. In addition, Michael has undermined his ability to be an effective parent to

Marjorie, who is now in a position to pressure him to get preferential treatment compared to her siblings. Depending on her personality, Marjorie may feel a loss of respect for her mother and a sense of superiority to her, since she is now in possession of information that her mother doesn't have.

Second, when Martha eventually learns, as she is likely to, of both the cybersex behavior and the cover-up effort involving daughter Marjorie, she is likely to be so angry that reconciliation may be impossible.

In addition to problems involving children and secrets, another difficult scenario is the initially incomplete disclosure that results in sequential or staggered revelations. This situation, usually due to an effort to evade the consequences of one's behaviors, was discussed in detail in Chapter Three. Our recommendation is to avoid this problem by initially disclosing the outline of *all* the secrets, while avoiding details. Do not omit a significant part of the acting out; it will only make things worse in the long run.

Several other situations involving secret-keeping will be discussed in this chapter. These include:

- When a slip or relapse has occurred, so that additional disclosure is necessary

- When one member of a couple has acquired a sexually transmitted disease or has a health problem due to the addict's sharing dirty needles

- When one partner has already decided to leave

- When there is a secret no one else knows

- When long-ago secrets have not been revealed; timing of disclosure

- When the secret involves a friend, neighbor, or colleague

In this chapter we will discuss good and bad ways of handing the above situations.

Exercise:

Examine the list on the previous page and see what other disclosures you need to address. Have you had a slip or relapse that you have not revealed? Anything else? List all the possible "other disclosures" that you need to make. Identify what will be the hardest part of these disclosures for you.

_____

_____

_____

_____

_____

_____

_____

_____

How Can I Possibly Tell Him/Her About My Relapse?

Sometimes staggered or sequential disclosures occur, not because the addict is deliberately hiding some information or has forgotten some events, but rather because a slip or relapse has occurred. Now there are new secrets to uncover, new lies to reveal.

As mentioned in Chapter Five, we recommend determining at the time of the first disclosure how much information the partner wants to hear. After the initial disclosure is worked through, the addict and partner need to determine what information the partner wants on an on-going basis. Some partners want to know when someone has a slip and what the addict is doing to get his recovery back in line. Others want the addict to take that information to their sponsor or therapist, but do want to know if the addict has relapsed in ways that will harm the partner.

Unfortunately, the partner is often so in shock or angry and hurt that it takes a while to get clear about what to share. Revisiting what the partner wants to be told several times during the first couple of years of recovery is important.

It is not easy to be honest in this situation. Perhaps your partner has told you, "If you ever use again, you're history." Or perhaps you and your partner have spent months rebuilding trust, and you believe that learning about your slip or relapse will set your partner's level of trust back to zero. Perhaps you feel so much shame at your "failure" that you cannot bring yourself to confess what happened.

Understand that this is a common experience. Addiction is a disease of relapse. Over half the addicts in our survey reported at least one slip or relapse since the initial disclosure; most had more than one. When this happens, a decision about a new disclosure must be made. Below are the reactions of several spouses to hearing about a partner's relapse:

A woman who decided to stay with her husband after he had another affair wrote,

> I was very upset. He had had such great sobriety. I thought we had beaten his addiction and that it was "history." I shared about the effects of the relapse on me at my COSA meetings and had other people to talk to. I knew the behavior was about him, not me, but still I was really disappointed. We had been separated for two years while he was acting out, but this time I didn't even consider another separation. We wouldn't put our son through that again. As I saw it, we could each continue working on our individual recovery, or we could divorce if we felt there was nothing to work on.

Another woman reported she has learned a lot from her husband's relapses:

When my husband had his first relapse just after his first birthday in the program, I was totally shocked; he was one of the stars of the program. I was angry, hurt, and scared. When three months later there was another relapse, I wasn't very shocked, and experienced much less anger. The second time I didn't process as much anger with him—instead I processed with S-Anon and Al-Anon people and in my journal. I have grown a tremendous amount as a result of the two relapses. I have moved from dependence on him to dependence on myself and on being a "big" person.

Yet another woman is considering divorce after learning of several relapses:

When I finally was told the truth about his relapse I chose to accept that as an addict, he fell off the wagon, just like taking one more drink or drug. That allowed me to be at peace and accepting of him. After two years and two more relapses, I realize that this is a process and that nothing is black or white. I am, though, at a point in my life where my tolerance for "gray" has worn as thin as it can. I am considering divorce.

In each of the cases above, the spouse was knowledgeable about the disease of addiction and aware that relapse is always a possibility. Each spouse had had experience with a Twelve-Step program for information and support. Each one was able to separate the addict's behavior from herself and not "take it personally," and could rationally consider her choices rather than respond out of neediness and fear of being alone. In the last case, because the relapses were continuing, the wife was considering an end to the marriage.

The partner's response might have been very different if she were not herself in recovery and if she did not understand the nature of addictive disorders and the need to detach from the behaviors. In such a situation, her fear might be greater and her tolerance for a less-than-perfect recovery lesser. She would most likely believe that the addict's problem had been "cured" and would be less likely to accept the relapsing nature of the disorder.

A relapse involving another person is likely to be more threatening to the partner and to be considered a more serious betrayal than is behavior involving only the addict. For example, if a sex addict masturbated or accessed pornography on the Internet, the disclosure would be less threatening to a partner than if he'd visited a prostitute. Or if an alcoholic left the bar after one drink rather than getting drunk and driving drunk with his children in the car, the partner would be more able to view the relapse as less serious.

Addict Exercise:

Because slips and relapses are the most common "other disclosures" addicts face, you will want to complete this exercise. When you are considering how and when to disclose a slip or relapse to your partner, there are several factors to consider. Below are listed some questions that will prepare you to make a disclosure:

- List the changes you have made in response to the slip or relapse (for example, increasing your Twelve-Step involvement, getting a new sponsor, making your environment safer, beginning or resuming therapy, etc.). You are likely to have a more positive and understanding reaction to your disclosure if you are taking steps to learn from the relapse and prevent it from happening again. If you have made NO changes, then identify the changes you need to make and start making those immediately.

_____

_____

_____

_____

_____

_____

_____

_____

_____

_____

_____

- Write out the exact nature of the slip. You may even want to do what is called a "relapse autopsy." This is where you not only describe the exact nature of the relapse, you also identify everything that contributed to the "death" of your recovery efforts. What were the triggers that occurred? Did you find yourself in such an emotional situation in a high risk environment that it "just happened" before you were even aware that you were acting out? Did you make seemingly unimportant decisions that contributed to getting in that wrong environment? For example, you decide to go on the Internet just to find out what movies are showing to surprise your wife by inviting her to the movies this weekend (when you know that using the Internet when alone is dangerous for you). Did the acting out put you (and therefore) your spouse at risk of a sexually transmitted or other type of disease? If so, an early disclosure is more urgent—set up a time for that now. Additionally, since you are taking that kind of risk for your health as well as your spouse, perhaps intensifying therapy or going to residential treatment is the next step to really getting a handle on the problem. If you are continuing to put your partner and yourself in harm's way with the knowledge you have about addiction and recovery, the problem needs to be addressed more seriously.

_____

_____

_____

_____

_____

_____

_____

_____

_____

_____

- Is your spouse or partner involved in her own recovery program and/or in counseling? A spouse who is not working on herself is likely to be more frightened of a slip or relapse, more likely to continue perceiving herself as a victim, and less likely to be empathetic to the addict's struggles. Sometimes when the partner has not been in a recovery program herself, she remains caught in her anger and resentment. This is the partner who also fears intimacy and uses the addict's behavior as a way to obtain distance and derive energy from the drama. This partner does not do well when hearing about slips, much less relapses. The information becomes fuel for the fire of anger. In such a case, it would be helpful to disclose within a therapy session.

_____

_____

_____

_____

_____

_____

_____

_____

_____

_____

- Do you and your partner have a supportive environment in which to carry out the disclosure? The ideal setting is in a therapy session, after you have had a chance to discuss the relapse with the therapist. Twelve-Step sponsors, or another couple in recovery, are other possible resources.

_____

_____

_____

_____

_____

- Is a slip (a minor relapse) of a sufficiently serious nature as to (a) interfere with your maintaining a "program of rigorous honesty" in your recovery, or (b) likely to affect your primary relationship more adversely if it is revealed than if it is not? Revealing all slips is not always in the best interest of the relationship. For example, if you fantasized about another woman while making love with your wife last night, will it really benefit your marriage to reveal this? If this event was a break in your recovery plan, it might be more appropriate to discuss this with a sponsor or therapist rather than your wife. Determine what must be told versus what is better revealed to another support system and steps taken to make changes in thoughts and actions.

_____

_____

_____

_____

_____

_____

_____

_____

_____

_____

I've Exposed Her/Him to a Health Risk. What Now?

Most of the time the addict has some time to consider exactly when and how to disclose painful information to the partner. However, in certain cases there is pressure to disclose immediately. One such situation was discussed above—if your child, your boss, or the law has information that you believe they will soon reveal to your partner. The consensus among partners we have worked with is that it is far better for them to hear the information from you than from other people.

Another situation requiring urgent action is when you have caught or possibly been infected with a virus or other infection as a result of unprotected sexual interactions or sharing needles. (Any activity with another person that involves sharing even the smallest bit of bodily fluid can be the route of a virus or other infection.) Not all viruses or infections show symptoms immediately, so thinking you can wait for the results of medical tests puts you and your partner at risk. Your spouse may need to visit a doctor for evaluation and possible treatment. At the very least, you will need to begin using condoms or to abstain from sex or other activities that might spread the infection to your partner. In both cases, your partner will need an explanation, and the sooner the better. We know of several wives who chose to leave the marriage because they felt that the biggest betrayal they'd experienced was that their spouse continued to expose them to health risks. One of them told us,

> He had shared needles and had unprotected sex with other men, and then he'd have sex with me. We have two young children. He put his own pleasure above my life and potentially, that of our children! He was willing to expose me to a fatal disease. When I finally found out, all I wanted to do was put as much distance as possible between us. We are now divorced. Thank heavens I didn't catch anything from him.

Painful and risky though it may be to admit to your spouse that she is at risk for an STD or other health problem, it shows caring, and the spouse will eventually recognize this. On the flip side, the message a partner gets when the addict repeatedly exposes her to HIV, hepatitis, chlamydia, and other diseases is that he just doesn't care. Postponing this disclosure makes it far more likely that the eventual outcome will be the end of the relationship.

The Secret No One Else Knows

Not all secrets include two or more people. A person can hold onto a secret that no one else knows about. Think about the lesbian teenager who has never told anyone how she feels or thinks about her sexual orientation. The impact on her as an individual intensifies when her parents begin to pressure her during college about when is she going to get married and give them some grandchildren. If this young woman continues to maintain that internal secret, and fakes attraction to the man she then marries in order to please her parents, not only is her life affected, but so is that of her husband and child. She might become one of the many gay men and women who don't come out until middle age, at which time they are faced with painful choices about leaving their spouse and children to begin a new life. Perhaps if she had been able to disclose the secret to her parents and receive support, she would have been able to begin the coming out process many years earlier and might have made different choices about her life partner.

When Long-Ago Secrets Have Not Been Revealed

Jay had been in recovery from his sex addiction for two years when he and Monica had dinner out with friends one evening. In a conversation about "the old days," Jay recalled how three years earlier, he and Monica had had a fight and she backed out of accompanying him out of town on a business trip. Upset with her, he'd phoned a stripper to visit him in his hotel room. Monica clearly remembered what Jay had told her at the time to explain the charge on his credit card, and she now chimed into the conversation: "and when he actually saw the stripper, she was so unattractive that Jay paid her and sent her away." Jay looked at her as though she must be insane.

"I would never have done that!" He readily admitted that they'd had sex. Monica was livid. Once they were alone in the parking lot, she angrily confronted him.

"You lied to me! You told me you'd sent her away! How could you have done this? How can I ever trust you?"

Jay sighed and looked at her wearily, "Monica, before I got into recovery I told you so many lies that I no longer remember what I did say. Lying was so much a part of my life back then that I lied even when I didn't have to. I'm sorry about this particular lie, but I'm sure that there will be other occasions when you will realize I lied in the past. All I can say is I haven't lied to you once since I got into recovery two years ago, and I intend to continue being honest with you. That's the best I can say."

Monica realized that what he said made sense, and that she would have to accept the possibility of other lies without getting upset all over again. For two years Jay had given her no reason to doubt his word. She would have to draw a line between the "bad old days" and the time in recovery, and judge them differently. She would have to forgive the past, meaning she'd have to be able to hear about it without getting upset all over again. Part of the task of doing this turned out to be a period of grieving the loss of the past as she had previously perceived it. Instead, she had to accept that her life with Jay had been a web of lies and deceptions, not the great marriage she thought she had.

Partner Exercise:

If you are the recipient of a disclosure of a long-ago secret—for example, an affair that ended years ago or finding out about the loss of the bonus check your mate received that you never saw because it was gambled away. Grieve the difference between the reality and what you thought you had, and let it go. Tell yourself, "It is frightening to be reminded of what happened and it makes me sad and angry that it happened, but I like my life now and I feel good about how I am in our relationship now; I am letting go of that past anger and fear." Then focus on what has happened in your relationship more recently. List ways your partner is being trustworthy. Describe ways you feel secure in your relationship with a trusted friend. If you find evidence that your partner is being trustworthy, examine why you feel stuck and seek to correct your thinking errors. You may want to do several thoughts–feelings journals (see p. 82) to help you. Then forgive the past and remain in the present.

When the Secret Involves a Neighbor or Friend

On May 21, 2001, in the Dear Abby newspaper column (*Arizona Daily Star, May 21, 2001, p E5*), a reader described her dilemma regarding disclosure. She'd caught her next-door neighbor peeping into the bedroom window of a neighbor across the street. "When I confronted him, he begged me not to tell his wife, giving all kinds of psychological reasons for his behavior, including his upbringing." Seven years earlier the writer had caught him peeping into her bedroom, but it wasn't until now that she realized it was this same man. "Now he claims that being caught has completely changed him. He has promised it will never happen again. Somehow I don't buy it."

Her question was, "Should I tell his wife what I know?" Abby told her to immediately tell the neighbor who was being spied on "so she can take steps to protect her privacy. Your local police should be informed so they can keep an eye on the man. . . . but, I see no reason to tell his wife. That information should come from her husband or the authorities."

It can be inferred from the letter that the man in question is a sex addict, a compulsive voyeur who has been peeping in windows for many years. His wife may or may not be aware of his activities. Should the letter writer disclose his behavior, and if so, to whom—the police, the wife, the latest victim?

To find out what experts in the field would recommend, we emailed about 30 of our professional colleagues. Apparently this was an interesting ethical problem for most of them to consider. Within a few days nearly all of them replied. On notifying the police, most who mentioned the police said yes, while a few were uncertain. The reasons for notifying the police were:

- Addicts/sex offenders need to be held accountable for their behavior and reported for illegal actions.

- The man needs help and he isn't going to get it by being shamed and "putting his wife in charge." Police involvement will really catch his attention and make it more likely he will get help.

- The police probably won't do anything, but at least they'll have a record of the incident, and once they have another incident they are more likely to act.

- The police will immediately contact the man and his wife, and the letter writer will thereby be spared the embarrassment of interacting directly with the wife.

- The only reason to notify the police is to find out if he has prior arrests for similar issues and better assess his dangerousness. No way can they really "keep an eye" on him.

One person who was unsure about notifying the police felt that, at least in some states, this would be a permanent serious legal mark against the man that would stigmatize him forever, and that this should be the last resort. This therapist favored first discussing it with the wife. The therapist who would not notify the police didn't specifically rule it out, but said "I would get professional healers involved before the police; the police are not known for bringing about a positive outcome to these cases."

Interestingly, the group was split 3:2 in favor of notifying the wife. Those who said yes gave the following reasons:

- The man is sick and needs an intervention, and the wife is the one who is most likely to arrange it or to pressure him into treatment. "The person with the most leverage is likely to be the wife."

- The wife most likely wants to be told; she probably is already aware of the behavior or suspects it.

- If he is reported through other means and caught by the police, it will most likely have severe consequences that will adversely affect the wife. She deserves to know.

- If the man dreads his wife being told, then the most likely reason is it will result in consequences for him that will lead to his having to stop the behavior, a desirable outcome.

- Chances are that the man is engaging in other compulsive sexual behaviors, which might be risking the wife's health.

The experts who recommended against telling the wife said:

- It's not the neighbor's responsibility to tell the wife. Why should she get further entangled? She has already been victimized by him in the past, and now has caught him a second time; she has her own issues to work on.

- The wife may not appreciate another woman calling her and telling her that her husband is a voyeur. She may become angry and threatening. She might deny the problem and blame the messenger. It would damage the relationship between the letter writer and the man's wife. The message would carry more weight if it came from the police. "It would be no different than reporting a burglar to police. One wouldn't call the burglar's relatives."

- The wife may well be aware of the voyeur's activities and has had no luck in getting him to get help. It might be very shaming for her to have some woman who lives in the neighborhood, especially one she may not know well, confront her with the message. She would then feel it was her responsibility to get him to do something that she already knows is futile.

Some respondents mentioned that telling the wife would depend on the relationship between the two women. If they were friends, the wife would more likely want her friend to alert her to the situation, and the letter writer would be more comfortable telling her and less fearful of retaliation. One expert advised informing the police and also telling the man about this and advising him to tell his wife; whether to tell the wife herself as well would depend on the relationship between the two women.

Only a few therapists mentioned the neighbor who had been the latest victim, and all said they would notify her as well. The reasons were:

- The neighbor was the victim—she needs to know so she can decide whether to notify the police.

- The neighbor should know so she can protect herself in the future.

Finally, let's check in with wives who've been in exactly the same situation as in the Dear Abby letter. On June 19, 2001, Abby published the reactions of two wives of voyeurs. The first wife said, "As the wife of a peeping Tom, let me tell you the kindest thing they could do would be to tell her. With therapy, the couple may be able to salvage their marriage and his self-respect. But, like all addictions, only when he reaches bottom will he get the help he needs. Please reconsider and suggest that they tell the wife."

The second woman, whose marriage to the voyeur ended 25 years earlier, wrote, "Your advice was 100% correct… He lied so convincingly about why he was late—and even when he was eventually arrested—I not only believed him, but most people other than the police did too." After her husband was arrested 3 times over a 12-year period, "I finally had to face facts. When I did, I had a nervous breakdown… Perhaps you are not sure what your values are or you may want to change or "improve" your values. Here are a few questions to get you started. I remember the shame and disbelief as if it were yesterday. (*Arizona Daily Star*, 6/19/01, p. E5).

The variety of responses by professionals to this ethical dilemma, and the different responses of the two wives, shows that there is often no one right answer. No wonder it is difficult for the average person to decide what to disclose, how much, to whom, and when! One solution is to gather more information. For example, if we knew more about the relationship between the voyeur's wife and the neighbor who discovered him in action, it might be easier to advise her whether to disclose to the wife as well as to the police. The role of the couple counselor is precisely to help solve such dilemmas for couples.

When You Learn That a Friend's Spouse Is Having an Affair, Using Drugs, or Gambling Compulsively

A closely related, and more common, ethical dilemma is what to do if you learn that the spouse of your close friend is having an affair or exhibiting any other addictive behavior. Do you tell your close friend? Dr. Shirley Glass, a psychologist specializing in infidelity, usually advises confronting the offending person first and advising that person to tell the partner; if not, then **you** will do it. The reason is that otherwise the friendship is ruined because it is too uncomfortable to be carrying those kinds of secrets. In her experience, Dr. Glass related, "When the betrayed partner later found out that other people knew, they were very hurt and angry. In many cases, the relationships were permanently severed because they focused their feelings of betrayal on the colluder who could be a potential informant." (personal communication with Dr. Glass, May 28, 2001)

Interestingly, in Dr. Glass's experience, when someone does eventually tell the betrayed partner about the affair, it is most commonly the affair partner, who presumably wanted to drive a further wedge between her lover and his spouse. "It usually backfired because the crisis it evoked was a catalyst to stop the affair and rebuild the marriage."

We have known sex-addicted women involved in affairs with married men who tell the wife as an external intervention for themselves. The sex-addicted women knew that telling the wife would likely end the affair when the addict was not able to.

The stories in this chapter represent some real-life situations. The correct approach is not always clear; gray areas abound. As we have seen, determining the best course involves, above all, communication. If you are uncertain about whether to disclose or keep a secret, about whether telling will help or hurt your partner, your recovery, and/or your relationship, consult others. Talk with a sponsor, a counselor, or a friend. Sometimes the uncertainty remains. You may need to follow your heart and take the risk of opening your heart to your partner, even if the outcome is uncertain.

When You Really Want to Leave

After years of struggling in his troubled marriage, 50-year-old Arthur was ready to call it quits with Angie. He progressively distanced himself emotionally, and finally got involved in an affair with a younger woman he'd met at the company where he was doing some consulting work. Perhaps on some level Arthur wanted Angie to find out; perhaps he was hoping that if she caught him, Angie would demand a divorce, so that he wouldn't have to take the initiative himself. At any rate, he left enough clues around that it didn't take Angie long to figure out what was happening.

Her response, however, was not what he'd been expecting. Instead of announcing the end of the marriage, Angie took all the blame on herself and insisted on going to counseling to try to save the relationship. Not wanting to hurt her even more, Arthur couldn't face telling Angie directly that he wanted to leave, so he reluctantly assented to joint counseling.

In preliminary individual sessions, the counselor learned that Arthur had emotionally left the marriage years earlier. He explained to Arthur that couple counseling is likely to be effective only if both partners have the same goal. Hearing of this case, Dr. Shirley Glass (personal communication, 2/9/02) commented that the lack of investment in their marriage is a significant part of the problem for persons who say they've been out of the marriage emotionally for years. She would counsel such people to put some energy into working on the relationship; sometimes they start to feel a bond again. This is particularly true, according to Dr. Glass, if they have detached for their own reasons rather than because their partner was negligent or abusive. In Arthur's case, however, he was not amenable to working on the marriage; his only desire was to get out. The individual counseling sessions clarified for him that he was only prolonging and postponing the pain that Angie would inevitably feel at learning the truth. The counselor then persuaded Arthur to disclose to Angie in a joint session that, for him, the marriage was irretrievably broken.

Disclosing a painful secret can be made less painful for the partner if it is accompanied by a declaration of a commitment to the relationship. If you and your partner have a long history, memories of many good times, and perhaps children, it may be very difficult to disclose that the marriage has ended for you, especially if you believe that this will be devastating for your partner.

As you will see in Chapter Nine, however, for those whose marriage ends, there **is** life after divorce, even for the one who still feels committed to the marriage. Although at first, life without you may indeed seem to be hardly worth living, soon enough your former partner will reclaim herself or himself and realize that life has much to offer. People who are in a recovery program can call on the support of their Twelve-Step program, program friends, counselor, and the tools of the program and can indeed become contented and fulfilled. Although we do caution against acting too quickly about the future of a marriage after a disclosure, if your marriage has been over for some time, tell your partner and let him or her begin to heal from the loss.

References

"Dear Abby," *Arizona Daily Star*, 5/21/01, p. E5.

"Dear Abby," *Arizona Daily Star*, 6/19/01, p. E5.

Glass, Shirley. *Personal communication with Dr. Glass*, 5/28/01.

Glass, Shirley, P*ersonal communication with Dr. Glass*, 2/9/02.

CHAPTER EIGHT: Special Issues
Lies Influence Relationships, and Relationships Influence Lies

Disclosing to your spouse and children is extremely difficult for everyone involved. The addict who discloses usually experiences an immediate sense of relief. The experiences for the spouse and children are varied. Matters are further complicated when one has to decide what to say at work, with family members and friends, or within your faith community.

Family Members

Depending on your relationship with your parents, siblings, and other extended family members, most addicts and partners want family members to have some information. If you are estranged from family members, then you may decide to keep private the information about the addiction. However, if family members provide emotional support for you, it is important that they have general knowledge of what is going on in your life. There may be other members of your family who are dealing with similar problems or have dealt with them and can be of help to you. Some addicts can identify generations of other family members who have struggled with addictions:

I come from a family of drinkers, lots of depression, and abuse of prescription drugs. My great-grandfather made "white lightning" and sold it during the Depression. He was known to be able to drink the stuff and it not affect him. My own father was depressed and drank heavily, which did not help matters. Then he crushed his hand in an accident at work. He was on pain medication and had disability. The longer he could show he was in pain, the longer he got to stay on disability. Before long, he was addicted to the pills—which he drank alcohol with. It is a wonder it did not kill him. Then I come along and do about the same thing—just without the alcohol. I am recovering from addiction to prescription drugs (Xanax and hydrocodone). Now my son is in treatment for addiction to marijuana and alcohol. It's scary. I wonder if it will ever end.

Being exposed to addictive behavior happens in a variety of ways:

I found my Dad's pornography collection when I was 8. He was a drinker and I was pretty sure he had sex with other women because I saw him once with a woman, not my mother, downtown. My Mom would accuse him and they'd yell and he'd be out the door. It wasn't long before I was using those images from that porn, masturbating to shut out my whole lousy life—their fights, being smaller than other guys my age, never measuring up. I am sure pornography and masturbation were my introduction to sex addiction. It worked like magic—felt so good, let me fantasize that I was *somebody*. It took me away from my problems but I didn't stop there. I used the pornography to make friends with other guys. It wasn't long before I was introduced to sex by an older neighborhood boy. When I went to treatment and talked to my Dad, he admitted that he had problems with affairs and pornography too. He said his grandfather was known as a lady's man—I never knew him but wonder if he was a sex addict, too.

If you are not lucky enough to be able to disclose in a treatment center with staff guiding you, the same principles apply for telling close family members as do for telling your spouse. Provide only general information that may be educational as well, but leave out the details. It is also helpful at this juncture to apologize for any ways your behavior may have hurt them. You and your partner need to decide what you will disclose and what you want to keep private between the two of you. The addict should disclose about his behavior and addiction, the co-addict about her behavior and addictions, if applicable.

Here is a sample letter of what might be said to parents who are supportive and with whom the addict and partner feel close:

Dad and Mom:

I want to thank you for meeting me. What I have to say is very important and it is important to me that you are willing to do this. The purpose of this meeting is not to blame anyone for anything—what I have done is my responsibility alone. My purpose is to let you know what has been going on with me and Susan and what I plan to do about it.

You may not know that Susan and I have been having problems. We are pretty good at keeping secrets. I have been very good at keeping secrets, not only from Susan, but from everyone.

For many years I have been using sex like a drug—like a drug addict would, to make me feel better when I feel anxious, or depressed, sad, or mad. Sometimes I use it when I feel good because I don't know how to deal with feeling good either. The point is, I don't know how to handle how I feel and I learned early in life that one way to do it is through a sexual release. Some people call this sex addiction, so I now call myself a sex addict.

I don't want to tell you all the details of what I do because that is something I deal with in therapy and with Susan. I am also in a Twelve-Step program much like Alcoholics Anonymous and it is helping me learn how to handle my feelings. In therapy I am learning more how to have confidence in myself, and Susan and I are working on how to be healthy together.

> I want to say again, I am not blaming you or anyone for how I am. Lots of people hear that someone becomes a sex addict because of something that happened in their childhood. I have come to believe that lots of things from my childhood influenced how I saw the world and responded to it, but now I am an adult and can make adult choices in responsible ways. I am grateful to you for all you have done for me. I know you did the best you could to raise me well.
>
> There are lots of books you can read to find out more about sex addiction. I can recommend a few and I am willing to answer some questions. The only questions I won't respond to are those that Susan and I want to keep between us.
>
> I need your support and love now. I am sorry for the hardship this has caused everyone involved and for the worry I have caused you. I am better and have great hope for the future.
>
> I love you. Your son, Al.

Then ask them—Do you have any questions now?

Exercise:

If you want to disclose to your parents, use this space to write your first draft of a disclosure letter to them.

Many addicts and partners have been the victims of sexual trauma within their families of origin, and are in a delicate position with regard to disclosing. However, disclosure can provide freedom from shame and help a survivor move forward in his/her recovery.

If a part of your addiction or co-addiction history is that you are a survivor of sexual trauma, you may want to talk with your therapist about how to handle resolution of those issues as part of the disclosure process. If those issues have been addressed in your family of origin and you feel safe within that family system, a disclosure is appropriate. Ending the family secrets is an important step to stopping the multigenerational transmission of these traits.

Often survivors are tempted to blame parents for the sexual abuse the survivor endured. It is important to obtain therapy for childhood sexual trauma. Remember, *the therapy for holding the victimizer accountable is different from disclosure. Disclosure is important in order for you to be accountable for your behavior.* It is appropriate, nonetheless, for survivors to include, as part of their disclosure, the boundaries they need to make public. Here is an example:

Dad:

The purpose of this letter and our meeting is for me to explain what I have been doing that is very unhealthy for me. I also want to talk about what I have learned about myself in therapy, what I am doing to help myself, and what I would like you to do to help me with this.

I learned early in my life that I could make men do things for me by having sex with them. Having sex with men made me feel powerful and like I had control over them. This may be related to the sexual interactions between you and me, but I am not blaming you for my behavior. I am responsible for what I have done and the choices I have made. I started using sex like a drug and my life got out of control because I took more and more chances to feel powerful and to cover how bad I felt about myself inside. I am a sex and love addict. I've hurt my kids, my husband, the people who are important to me in my life, and mostly, I have hurt myself.

But I am doing better now. I am going to Twelve-Step meetings, therapy, and even though Bob and I are getting divorced, I am getting along better with him, too. I am learning to be a better mom.

To help me with my recovery, I have a couple of requests. First, when we are together, I need to have more space. I get anxious when you want to put your arms around me all the time. I also get uncomfortable when you talk about your girlfriends and about having sex with them. I'd like us to focus on talking about the kids, work, the weather, movies, or things like that. If you have some problem with me, then it is okay to tell me about it and I will do the same with you. Then we both can make decisions like adults about what to do next. In the past, I've made matters worse when we disagreed by yelling at you and then at my kids. For now, I'd like no touching until we are about to leave, then a brief hug is okay.

I appreciate that you have listened and that you came to talk to me today. Do you have any questions?

Setting boundaries to help you maintain your recovery is important. This is an appropriate time for the survivor to do it.

Exercise:

If you are a survivor and have determined it is right for you to disclose and/or set boundaries, write that draft letter here:

_____

_____

A New Love Relationship

When an addict begins a new relationship, many people are not clear when or if to tell the new person in their life about their addiction. All addicts are at risk for relapse, no matter how long they have been sober. Informing a potential mate is important. But when to tell is determined by the type of addiction, any legal issues involved, and the seriousness of the relationship.

Many addicts say that they are not going to disclose until they are sure this person is "the one." Unfortunately this can backfire because a potential mate will take it as a lack of trust and, in some instances, a form of dishonesty that you did not disclose before the relationship became serious.

Certainly, it is not wise to tell anyone new in your life all your story, but after a few dates, beginning to "test the waters" about how someone will respond to the knowledge that you attend Twelve-Step meetings or that you go to a group to work on learning better ways of coping can open the door for further discussions.

Most people are pretty accepting of drug addiction or gambling and food issues; people are less likely to respond positively and are more likely to jump to conclusions when it comes to sex addiction. Preparation of a disclosure letter is a good idea, including information about addiction in general. As indicated above, sharing general information about your addiction first is safest. If you are still in the early stages of recovery (first couple of years), a new love relationship is probably premature and it's best to slow down. New relationships cause people to feel more energy and excitement, but that energy is due to the chemicals your brain makes. Realistically, these relationships take a great deal of energy and time— sometimes compromising your recovery.

If you are in a new relationship and believe you are ready to become more serious, a conversation about the desire to move to the next level is a good way to start. State that one of your values is that people in intimate friendships should have enough trust in each other to tell each other the truth and not keep secrets. Indicate that the relationship has grown to a degree that you believe it is time to disclose information that for the most part is private in your life. Then give general information about your addiction and the type of acting out that you do. This is easier if you are a drug addict or some other behavioral addict; accept that sexual information of any kind just makes people nervous.

Latoya was a gambling addict. Although she had abused alcohol and had smoked cigarettes during her years of gambling, gambling was her main route to escape her feelings of inadequacy and her fear of her first husband's temper. She gambled in isolation and secrecy. Her first marriage had ended in divorce. It took her seven years to get her gambling under control and her finances back in order. Dating was long in coming and she was very careful while early in recovery to go to social events with a group of friends. Eventually she met a man close to her age, Washington, who was also divorced and who had two children. Initially she accepted invitations to accompany Washington to church and then other activities that included his children. After Washington started to ask her to dinner and the movies without the children, Latoya was convinced that Washington was getting as serious as she felt. This is what she shared with him about her addiction:

> Washington, I am so fond of you and your children. You have done such a wonderful job of raising them. I am feeling like our relationship is getting pretty serious and feel like I owe you much. Part of what I owe you is the truth about me. If we are going to have some type of commitment to each other in the future, I think you deserve to know this about me.

> I am a gambling addict. That is why I go to meetings at the church on Wednesday and Saturdays—I go to meetings for my addiction then. I also used to drink heavily when I gambled, and I smoked. That is why I don't drink now and was attracted to you because you don't smoke. My first marriage was rough and I used gambling to escape my feelings. I was not able to face my fear of my husband and in the end I only made him angrier because I forced us into such debt. Even after we divorced, when I had basically nothing, I stole money from him and continued to write checks on our old account. I was just lucky I did not get into trouble legally. I had to file bankruptcy and am just now beginning to get my credit reestablished.

I have seven years of solid recovery with no relapses, but I know as an addict I will never be totally free of this disease. That is why I still go to meetings after all these years—they help me stay grounded, help others, and remind me of where I have been. I hope this doesn't change things between us—you mean the world to me and I would hate for our friendship to end.

Latoya and Washington were married about a year later. Washington supports Latoya in her efforts to sponsor other addicts as well as tell her story in the church where they attend services.

George had a more difficult task with Evelyn. George had been an alcohol and sex addict for as long as he could remember. He stopped drinking many years before but despite three attempts at sex addiction treatment, he struggled for almost 15 years of regular relapses. During this process he had met a wonderful woman from his church. Both devout Catholics, they discovered they loved many of the same things. Because they were Catholic, they had taken a vow of celibacy but spoke often of marriage. Determined not to lose Evelyn, George gave her a beautiful two-carat diamond engagement ring when he asked her to marry him. Evelyn was very excited and wanted to marry soon, but George kept finding ways to postpone the ceremony because he had not been able to go more than five weeks without a relapse on Internet pornography and masturbation or engaging in anonymous sex with masseurs. Finally, through the support of individual therapy, his men's group, and medication for his depression and intrusive thinking, he experienced several months of sobriety. He agreed to set a date for marriage but was determined to not disclose to Evelyn his sex addiction.

It was in his men's group that he became convinced that he had to tell Evelyn. He had had sex with others while engaged to her. Not only that, but he'd had unsafe sex while acting out. All seven men in his group agreed that continued secret-keeping would not help his recovery nor be fair to Evelyn. One of his peers in group commented, "If you cared as much for Evelyn as you have been saying for over a year now, I can't imagine how you could demonstrate that more than by giving her a chance to choose you as you are—addict and all." He knew then that it was the right thing to do and the only way he could remain sober. Keeping secrets was against everything he wanted in this marriage. With so much at risk, this is what he wrote in a disclosure letter to her:

Evelyn,

You have been a great sunshine in my life, a great gift of joy, a wonderful companion, the woman I love, with whom I want to spend the rest of my life. There are some things you need to know about me about my life. Some of them happened a long time ago. Some happened in the recent past.

The decision about which I have the greatest regret is that I agreed to abort a child when my first wife became pregnant. Next to the abortion, the act of which I am most ashamed is that when I was 12 and my sister was 6, I molested her. It was a single episode that involved only masturbation, but it greatly influenced my relationship with her. I was so ashamed of what I had done that I wanted my sister to disappear, simply to cease existing. So just seeing her was a reminder of my own guilt and shame. This caused the great damage in my relationship with my sister and underlies my present difficulties with her.

You should also know that once, about eight years ago, I was arrested for indecent exposure. I was masturbating in a booth that showed pornographic videos when a police officer opened the door to the booth and saw me. I was convicted of the crime, but received deferred adjudication and was on probation for six months. Finally, you should know that I have had sex with men. I do not believe that I am a homosexual. My addiction has grown out of extensive childhood sexual abuse by men and imprinting of that abuse has led me to be sexual with men.

I have been in recovery for my alcohol and sex addiction for over 15 years. This has involved attending thousands of meetings, years of therapy, and three separate stays at treatment facilities. It cannot be said that my efforts have been half-hearted. But whereas I long ago left my drinking behind me, my recovery from sex addiction, unfortunately, has been more difficult. I have not been perfect in my attempts to remain celibate. It is this lack of perfection during the time that we've been dating that I want to talk to you about today.

While we have been dating, I have continued to have sexual activity beyond the activity between us. Most of this activity has been masturbation, often combined with using pornography on the Internet.

My greatest single problem has been Internet pornography. To combat this problem I have put blocking software on all my computers. Not all of my sexual activity, however, has been by myself. I have had sexual contact with men, mostly with masseurs who have masturbated me. On two occasions I have received oral sex from men. It was immediately after the most recent of these two events, in January two years ago, that in desperation I sought out my therapist and began therapy with her and joined her group. Most recently, on two occasions while we were dating, I had sex with women, once about 2 1/2 years ago with a woman whom I contacted on a phone chat-line and once about a year ago with the woman to whom I went for a massage. I do not know the names of either of these women and would not know how to contact either one of them.

I am willing and fully prepared to let you know anything you want to know about my past sexual behavior beyond what I have spoken of. After I finish reading this prepared statement, I will answer any questions that you have.

You certainly must be asking yourself: how can he have done these things, these things he knew what hurt me deeply, these things so contrary to his faith and mine? How could he have done these things if he in fact loved me? Please do not doubt for a moment the depth of my love for you. I have not loved any person as deeply and thoroughly as I love you. I hope you have seen that love in my behavior, in the ways that you have seen that I have changed myself while I have been dating you. No, it is not a lack of love for you that leads to my addiction. Nor is it a lack of faith. My faith is deep and my faith is wide. It is the core of my life and the compass of my daily actions.

What you must understand is the power of my addiction. It is relentless, and it is pitiless. It rises in my soul like Satan himself, once the most powerful and glorious of the Angels, now the most dishonored, the source of all evil. I have struggled with my addiction for years and sometimes lost. I do not ask you to understand these battles, I ask only for you to believe that those battles have indeed been fought and that I despair when I have lost those battles, when I have given in to my addiction.

I think you've come to understand that my sex addiction is a means to relieve tension, stress, fear, and all manner of pain. While I have been dating you, the single most powerful factor in keeping me in my addiction has been the pain of knowing that I was keeping secrets from you. Nothing has caused me so much fear—the fear that if you knew the truth of my life, you would leave me—a loss I felt I could not bear. Today you know the truth, the deceit has ended, and the engine driving my addiction is stilled.

Other sex addicts in recovery have told me that once they were completely honest with their spouses and lovers they were able to build a sounder, deeper love based on complete honesty. I hope that will be true for us as well. Believe me when I tell you that my willingness to tell you the truth, the willingness to risk losing you, is the greatest manifestation of my love for you. If you can return that love, your help and under-standing can be invaluable to me and my recovery. Many of my friends have told me what a great help their supportive wives have been to them. Up to now my best friend has been in the dark about what is going on with me. That is no longer true.

My therapist will tell you the distance I have come with her and my men's group, moved by my love for you. She will tell you that she has seen many men overcome sex addiction on a daily basis and that she sees that I am on the path to recovery. She will tell you that now that I have disclosed the extent of my addiction to you, I should have all the pieces in place that can lead to lifelong sobriety. She will tell you that there are no guarantees, that my recovery can never be more than daily reprieve contingent on the maintenance of my spiritual condition. I hope that she will tell you that she thinks that I am a pretty good bet. Yes, surely a bet, but a good one.

All my love, George

Evelyn was shocked and deeply moved by George's disclosure. Despite their long courtship, this took her some time to get over. At first, she was very disturbed and angry about his acting out during their engagement. It took her several therapy sessions to clarify the impact this disclosure had on her and the relationship. She was not as disturbed by the homosexual encounters as she was about the intercourse with a woman during their engagement. Evelyn reported being hurt more by the secret keeping than anything else. Because of the infidelity in her first marriage she quickly concluded that this relationship would end the same way. However, after she had had an opportunity to voice her anger at the betrayal, and have her feelings validated as normal, she began to have more compassion for George and how difficult the disease had been for him to manage. It helped her to know about addiction and began to see his behavior as a result of the disease instead of thinking something was wrong with her. She gained hope from the full year of sobriety he had when he disclosed and she began to understand that he had waited until he could actually report at least a year of recovery before he disclosed. Evelyn was grateful that George valued her enough to tell her before they were married so she could make an informed choice. She said if he had waited until after the wedding, she would have had the marriage annulled immediately. Through more couples counseling and a great deal of discussion with their priest, this couple was able to move ahead with their marriage plans within a year of the disclosure.

When You Are Not Sure You Are Really in Love

When an addict is actively in addiction, sometimes he thinks he is in love with his partner but then when he gets sober he is no longer so certain. If this has happened to you, rather than just going along as if you are in love, it is better to speak about this ambiguity. Here, a gay addict speaks to his partner about his feelings about love and what he proposes. This was part of his disclosure process.

> I care deeply for you. I am learning how to feel love and love myself and others. I am working hard to honor my feelings and accurately identify them. I am not sure that what I feel for you is love or friendship or respect or some combination of them. I would like to stay together to clarify what my feelings are now that I am in a sober state and in recovery. I hope you will give me the opportunity to develop a relationship with you based on honest sharing, genuine caring, and love.

Friends

Sometimes it is easier to disclose to close friends than to family. Again, the disclosure needs to reflect the closeness of the friendship, and how the friend may have been hurt during periods of acting out. If the addict has a relationship with a friend of his partner, the addict may want to disclose to the friend. However, in most cases, the partner discloses what she feels comfortable disclosing with the friend and uses the friendship as a means of support for her. Some partners unload all the details of the addict's behavior to the friend, who then aligns with the partner and becomes protective toward the partner and angry with the addict. As the partner, be clear with your friend the role you want her to play. Your friend should be there to listen, reflect, and then ask questions or remind you of what you have said you want to do to change. If you want your friend to fight the battle for you, you will not learn.

Besides disclosing, tell your friend how he/she can help you. Be specific. Sometimes it is unclear to friends whether you are seeking support for leaving or you just want to vent. Let her know that venting helps you, but that you are not ready to give up the relationship with your addict spouse (unless you are) and that all you need is for her to acknowledge what awareness you have gained and validate how difficult it is for you. If you have been out-of-control in your co-addiction and she has been a victim of your behavior, apologize for that and encourage her to remind you if she again sees you engaging in that type of behavior.

For the addict, friends are critical to recovery. If you have been acting out with friends but wish to continue seeing them now that you are in recovery, then you must disclose your addiction and the need to not engage in those behaviors when you are together. Sometimes disclosure includes telling "using" friends that you can't see them anymore. This is a loss that requires grieving. (In fact, it is part of grieving the loss of your addiction.) Use the disclosure as a means to set a boundary and even say goodbye to "using" friends. In Raphael's case, he had to tell Luke they could no longer be friends. This is what he said:

> Luke, hey man, it's good to see you. I'm glad we had this chance to talk because I have something that is very important to me to share with you. I have really been evaluating my life and how I've been doing stuff that is

hurting my wife, my kids—me. It is even affecting my work. I had some great fun with you, going to bars, talking—but the drug use and even smoking—well, it really isn't who I want to be. I am pretty sure I am a drug addict and for sure addicted to cigarettes. But no matter if I am or am not, I know I have to stop doing that stuff. So it means I have to stop hanging around with you. I want you to know that this is not about you—I am not judging you. You've been there for me, but I can't take the chance that you'd want to do those things and then maybe I would too, so I wanted to tell you face to face because you've been my friend. I won't be calling and hope that you won't call me—unless you are interested in going to a Twelve-Step meeting with me for drug addicts! Good luck man. I'll keep hoping the best for you. Bye now.

Exercise:

List the friends you must leave behind because association with them is too high risk for your recovery. Write the basic disclosure and good–bye letter here:

_____

_____

_____

_____

_____

_____

For friends who can provide support for you, disclosure is important so that they know what you are dealing with. If you have hurt them with your behavior or have been keeping secrets within the friendship or have lied, then it is appropriate to admit and apologize for that kind of behavior. The level of friendship should dictate how much you tell. Some friends can hear the details and be supportive. Others cannot. Your best bet is to start slowly with general information, what you are doing to care for yourself, and what they can do to help. If you are willing to answer questions, report so.

Exercise:

List the friends who can provide support here. Then write each a disclosure letter and arrange for a meeting to share. After the disclosure follow up with a note of thanks. If it doesn't go well, still thank them for the times you've shared and keep the door open for a future time when they feel they can trust you enough to try the friendship again.

_____

_____

_____

_____

_____

_____

_____

Disclosure After an Arrest

There are certain circumstances in which one is forced to decide how to handle situations when other people find out. This may be because an arrest is made and a sheriff or police officer comes to your home or place of work and arrests you. Sometimes notification of the arrest is printed in the newspaper. If the arrest seems newsworthy, the media may get involved. Each of these situations prompts worry and curiosity by family members, neighbors, and co-workers.

If you're arrested, telling the truth to your partner is important, but the usual order of business is to get an attorney. Of course, tell your attorney everything. You are protected by attorney–client privilege, so what you say cannot be repeated without your permission. This can pose a problem with a partner who is unsure what is going on. Let your attorney guide you in these instances about your legal risks—but your recovery remains a priority, so try to work with your attorney about what you need for your recovery. If you act out while out on bond or on probation your case may be pretty much a sunk ship!

When legal cases have not been settled, often you have to tell those who are important to you that you cannot speak about the case per the attorney's advice, but that you need their support. Look for ways people can help—respite care for the children, cooking a meal, providing a shoulder to cry on.

Sometimes enough information is already in the public that you are forced to say something. If your "case" has been publicized through the media, and they are approaching you, your family, or your neighbors, decide what you are going to say to the media with your partner and run it by your attorney. Frequently a "no comment" stance or "you can speak with my attorney" is useful. Helping your kids be ready with a "no comment" is helpful. We are so tempted to give the media the true story—imagining that fair-minded people can make sense of your addiction and will quickly forgive you or be less angry with you. Wrong! In too many cases the media will distort the truth, omit crucial details, or slant the story in ways that will make you regret you said anything.

But make it possible for your children to play with their playmates, providing them with language to use to talk about the situation. For example, a 6- to 8-year-old child might say to a friend, "Some people said that my

Daddy did some bad stuff. I don't know what happened and I don't want to talk about it. I love my Daddy and I don't want to talk about it. OK? If you keep talking about it, I have to go home."

Be supportive of your spouse and children but allow them opportunities to vent their feelings. Listen, admit you have been wrong or agree that the media are not being fair or nice, and ask what you can do *today* to help them feel better. Even if your family members are not able to manage their own feelings during these times, manage your own emotional state in healthy ways. Vent your anger and sadness with your recovery peers and with your therapist, and develop ways to stay focused on helping your family in these high stress times.

Telling Neighbors or Members of Your Faith Community

Once the court situation is over, depending on the age of your children and following the tips in Chapter Six, be prepared to disclose and then provide ongoing information to help your youngsters cope with the situation. Decide on a need-to-know basis what to tell specific neighbors and those outside your immediate circle of family and best friends.

Exercise:

Ask yourself:

- What do these people need to know to be able to interact with us without it being a problem?

- Will they hold this against my family? Will they let their children come over? Should their children be here, given your offense?

- What do you want to say about this disease, your behavior then and now, and the risk you are putting others in by being near them.

- If you have probation or parole requirements, what do the neighbors or others need to know about that to feel safer around you and your family?

• If the neighbors are being supportive, let them know what they can do to help. Inviting your children to their home for a fun activity or a sleepover can help your children feel some sense of normalcy. Perhaps they can sit with the children while you and your partner have an evening out or go for a walk together.

Sex Offender Registry

When an addict is listed on a sex offender registry, various types of disclosures are required. Most of the public believes that only pedophiles and rapists are listed on the registry. That is not true. A conviction of any sex offense can result in being placed on the registry, often with a legal description of the offense that is unclear about the behavior. For example, "sexual production with a minor" represents dozens of things, one of which might be what you did (such as made a video of yourself and a 17-year-old you thought was 21), but your neighbors don't know that. In some states, judges even require sex offenders to put signs in their yards stating "Danger! A convicted sex offender lives here!" Preparing for being listed and handling people's reactions is important for the addict, partner, children, family, neighbors, and community.

Not every community is ready to support you if you or your mate has committed a sexual offense, but you may be surprised how people will support you if you are doing everything in your effort to stop your offending behavior and keep yourself and your community safe.

If you are on a registry or are going to be, it is only a matter of time until someone finds out. First and foremost, your partner and children need to know how to handle the anger and fear of others. Excluding small children, everyone in the family needs to talk about the possibility of violence by uninformed, fearful, and angry people. You need to have your internal voice remind yourself that you are not bad (even if you or your partner or parent did bad things) and you need to come from a place of strength, knowing that you have a right to be in your home, your yard. Still, it is important to be wise about what you do. Until you have a group in your community who knows some of your story and is supportive of your efforts to be healthy, it is wise to go places together. Being alone draws suspicion, and a single person makes a better target than two or more.

If you have been friendly with your neighbors in the past and none of them have been a victim of the offense, it is likely they will listen to what you have to say. What has worked best in these cases is to select one or two people or couples who are most likely to listen, learn, and be supportive. Ask those people to meet you in your home. When they are present tell them you have something very important you want to tell them and hope they will hear you out before making a judgment. A letter format works well here, too, because people usually will let you finish the letter before reacting or asking questions and getting distracted by their own confusion or fear. Of course, the addict should read this letter and the partner should be present. If teenaged children are in the household, they can be present if they want the neighbors to know that they know and the family is working on this together. The letter should:

1. Tell the purpose of the meeting.

2. Admit that you are guilty of the offense and that you will be listed or are already listed on the sex offender registry.

3. Admit that your actions were wrong and that you are sorry for hurting the victim, your family, them, and the community.

4. Declare that you are in therapy for the problem and are providing financial support for the victim to get therapy (if you are). If you are on probation, indicate that you have listed your probation officer's name and number on a card (that you give to them) should they want to report anything of concern or want to ask questions. (Check with your PO to determine that it is acceptable for them to receive these types of inquiries. They generally want neighbors to report anything suspicious.) Let them know the conditions of your probation (such as can't drink alcohol or be with minors unsupervised).

5. Tell them that you want their support of your family. If you have children, indicate you don't want your children to be punished because of your behavior and want your children to be able to socialize with their children at their home. If it means that you can't participate in driving children to swim practice, admit you know it will mean more work for them, but you need their help to make sure your children aren't singled out to feel badly about something that was not their fault.

6. If they have children the same age as yours, indicate your willingness to discuss what to say to their kids about what has happened so the children are safe and not scared. Even when your offense doesn't involve children, people are afraid that you will progress to that. This is where sharing limited information about the nature of your offense is important. Outline what you are doing to make sure that you are not alone with children.

7. Again repeat that you are sorry for your actions and hope, after they think about it a while, they will be supportive of your children and your partner. At this point, if your partner and children want to, they may talk about how as a family everyone is working together to deal with this challenging time. Then ask if they have any questions or want to say anything.

8. If they are supportive, be grateful and agree to answer questions they might have. Most people want to be assured that their children are not at risk, so provide information about how that will be accomplished on an on-going basis.

9. If they come down hard on you, agree that you have been wrong and only ask that they not hurt or punish your family because of your issues. Ask them to think about it and suggest that you all meet with your PO or therapist. (Again, seek approval from the PO or therapist prior to making that statement. Offer to pay your therapist for his or her time.)

Sometimes it is helpful to have this first conversation with your minister or rabbi or other religious leaders present in your home.

If you have been very isolated, it is less likely that your neighbors will be supportive. They have no history with you and will be afraid. Each case must be measured within the context of your situation. We do know that people are less likely to reoffend or relapse if they are not isolated. So, whatever you do, find a place where you can share your situation. In most Sex Addicts Anonymous meetings you can talk about these issues.

Here is how the family of one sex offender handled the sex offender registry problem:

When Bill, a junior high school science teacher, was sentenced to 12 years in prison for having a sexual relationship with one of his 14-year-old students, his wife Colleen moved in with her parents in a quiet suburban neighborhood. Her parents helped with childcare of her three daughters while Colleen finished college, then graduate school, and became a successful career woman. Colleen's religion did not support divorce or remarriage, so Colleen decided to wait for her husband's release. Every week for 12 years Colleen and the children visited her husband in prison. She also arranged for a counselor to do joint counseling with the couple during additional prison visits.

Because Bill's arrest and conviction were widely reported in the newspapers, Colleen's neighbors were well aware of her circumstances. Over the years they got to know Colleen and her three daughters and came to admire her for her efforts to keep the family together. When it was time for Bill's release, Colleen visited each of the neighbors, beginning with the ones she knew were most supportive, and talked with them about Bill's approaching arrival, about how he had matured in prison and had spent years making amends to his family and regretting his offenses with the young student, and about the plans the family had to make a new life for themselves. She assured them that their children were not at risk, and asked to hear about any concerns they might have. By the time the neighbors were informed by law enforcement that a sex offender was about to live in their neighborhood, they were sufficiently knowledgeable about the situation that it was not a problem either for them or for Bill.

Colleen had for years dreamed about relocating to a new city, one where nobody had heard of Bill or his history, but she realized she would have the most support from the community if she stayed put. Her decision proved to be a good one.

Work Settings

Jason, a 42-year-old man with seven years of recovery from cocaine and sex addiction, landed a new job as marketing director of a psychiatric hospital. Surrounded as he was by psychotherapists, nurses, and other professionals sympathetic to people with psychological disorders, Jason soon disclosed to his co-workers his history of cocaine binges and anonymous sexual encounters and his Twelve-Step involvement. Unfortunately, the word quickly got up to the administrators of the hospital, who were less than pleased. One of them made Jason feel sufficiently uncomfortable that he soon moved on to another job. In his new position, he chose not to disclose his story.

If your acting out behavior doesn't impact your work setting, other than distracting you, then it is a private matter that is disclosed to others primary in your life. However, if you are at risk of acting out at work or have previously done so on the job, you may need to disclose to someone in the workplace. If you are fairly certain that you will lose your job, then you have to weigh the importance of disclosure versus the impact of job loss on your recovery.

Sometimes the work setting is so filled with triggers that a relapse is likely if you continue to work there. It is not necessary to disclose if you are leaving your current job for one that is better suited for your recovery. What you disclose at work is determined by the likelihood of your boss or co-workers finding out and their need to know.

Addict Exercise:

- How might your relapse prevention plan interfere with work or involve others?

- If you acted out at work, then who has been victimized by your behavior? Are amends in order?

- Is your work environment small enough that everyone needs to have at least some understanding about what you have done? Will that help them understand why you always bring up what you did with your wife over the weekend when an attractive female client enters the room?

- As a result of a higher authority (the court, licensure board, and sometimes your partner) are you required to work only with a certain population or stop working with a certain employee?

- Do new corporate policies and procedures need to be in place to protect the employees and management? What can you share that may help prevent problems in the future?

Now complete a decision-making matrix (see p. 190). In the upper-left corner list positive consequences for disclosing, and in the upper-right corner list negative consequences for disclosing. In the bottom-left corner list positive reasons for not saying anything at work. In the lower-right corner list negative reasons for not disclosing. This should help you decide what to do.

For the most part, we advise that if people at work don't need to know, don't tell—unless it is vital for your recovery.

Partners often want to share information about what has happened to gain support. This type of information is often grist for the rumor mill, so be selective with whom you share. Talk more about your feelings and the impact the addict's behavior has had on you, rather than giving details that may come back to you in an inflated form that makes you look like a fool for staying with the addict.

If you have to take time off because of your own health reasons or to be supportive of the addict or family members, then you may need to give some information to your Human Resources department. The least amount of information necessary is usually a good rule of thumb in these instances. Despite the promise of the Human Resources department to maintain confidentiality, it is likely this type of information will be too much for some people in corporations to keep private. This is a time when you need to be taking care of yourself and do not need to be dealing with other people's judgments.

It is not always easy to balance the "rigorous honesty" of addiction recovery and the reality that disclosure in certain circumstances may have adverse consequences that call for careful planning or for nondisclosure. In this chapter we gave you guidelines for getting through this difficult experience. In the next chapter we will describe how to bring together what you have learned so far as you start your new life after disclosure.

CHAPTER NINE: After Disclosure: What Now?

After disclosure addicts report feeling relief at not having to live the double life, but they are also overwhelmed by the fear of the reactions to the pain they have inflicted. Partners most often report being in shock, hurting beyond belief, and experiencing a wide range of feelings. Some partners are so overwhelmed they become depressed and suicidal, and isolate themselves due to the shame associated with the addict's behavior. Other partners feel threatened and are so angry they cannot tolerate having the addict near them; they often are quick to threaten divorce. The flood of emotions seems overwhelming and couples usually do not know what to do next. A rule of thumb for people early in recovery—do not make any major decisions in the first year.

To prevent further deterioration of the relationship, couples need to formulate a plan to keep the relationship on hold. Initially, it is useful to determine if you want a short separation. The idea is to separate so self-repair can be implemented and a support system can be established. The support system needs to both support you *and* hold you accountable. In volatile situations, having two places to live for a while is optimal.

Unfortunately, not everyone is in a position to do that. Even in situations in which people can manage their anger, sometimes they need a short time apart. Some homes are large enough so that each partner can have their own private space to go to for self-repair. You may want to stay with friends or family for a few days. Learning to ask for help is a useful skill; this is a time to practice. However you decide to get your "space," place a few things there that provide a sense of well-being. Sometimes it is helpful to print statements that represent how you want to think and respond—positive self-talk. This will help in times when you cannot easily remember how you want to respond to situations.

Boundaries and Agreements

To reduce further damage to the relationship, it is important to agree when you will talk with each other and how you will manage yourself during times when you are talking. If you feel that face-to-face discussions are too painful early on, then write notes to each other. If living separately, designate certain times to talk by phone or, if computer use is not an issue, correspond by email. Because this is a cooling-off period, it is appropriate to decide what subject matter is off-limits for now. For example, you may want to postpone intense discussions about the disclosure information until both of you have a support system in place and have had time to reflect about the impact of the addiction and codependency on your marriage, your children and family, and most of all, on you.

It is important to talk about the disclosure information but we recommend you do that in therapy sessions. If that is not possible, delay the conversations until you've had some time to heal and get clear about your feelings and your hopes for the future.

When speaking about day-to-day issues, be careful not to fall into the trap of what John Gottman, Ph.D., who has studied married couples for years, calls the "Four Deadly Horsemen." Too often when couples are hostile with each other, they revert to four destructive styles of interacting. These do not always show up in this order, but generally the conversation starts in a harsh way. One party criticizes the other harshly rather than presenting a complaint. A complaint describes a specific behavior whereas a criticism contains harsh or negative words about your mate's personality, and frequently adds on some criticism from a previous situation that is unrelated to the specific behavior in question.

For example, a complaint might be:

"Len, I am frustrated because you agreed to pick up the kids from school and bring them home by 6:00 P.M., but you are consistently late."

A criticism would sound like this:

"I cannot believe that you can't get this one thing right. What the hell is wrong with you? This is so simple; if you really cared you would get the kids back to me as we agreed. This is just like all the other times you've screwed up—no wonder I can't trust you."

Another negative style is to use contempt when you complain or criticize. Sarcasm and cynicism are passive-aggressive ways to show contempt. They include mocking your partner, using hostile or inappropriate humor, being belligerent, rolling your eyes, and name calling—all of which send the signal that you are disgusted by your partner. Using contempt inevitably leads to more conflict or another "horseman"—stonewalling.

Stonewalling is when the listener gives the talker all the cues that he or she is not listening. There is no eye contact, no head nods, no verbal encouragement—like saying "uh-huh" or asking questions for clarification. The listener sits like a stone wall, and looks down or away the whole time the other person is talking or goes to their room and shuts the door without explanation.

The fourth horseman is defensiveness. Defending your actions is a normal response when you are attacked, but in cases in which someone continues to criticize, defending yourself usually makes matters worse. This is especially true if you are the addict because you are the designated "bad guy" for now. When you defend yourself, you are saying the problem isn't me, it's you. Accountability is the first order of business for the addict during this phase. However, both the addict and co-addict partner have been in a dance of self-destructive behaviors and they *both* have to learn to identify and change those behaviors.

If you catch yourself using any of these styles, call a timeout and tell your mate you need a break for self-repair because you don't like the way you are thinking or behaving. One way to engage in self-repair is to learn to stay grounded internally.

Exercise: Self-Repair through Internal Grounding

A prerequisite for this activity is learning to correct thinking errors through use of thoughts-feelings journals (see p. 82). If you have not completed several days of thoughts-feelings journals, do so, then return to this exercise. In this exercise we refer to your authentic self. This is the person you strive to be—the healthy person in recovery. Your authentic self operates from a set of values that guide your behaviors. If you have not listed those values yet, do so now.

Values That Guide My Behaviors As an Authentic Person

1. A goal of all healthy people is to maintain a clear sense of their authentic selves. This is especially true when the heat gets turned up in a fight or when your brain gets hijacked by old memories. As you work though issues, you and your mate will become more and more important to each other. That makes the threat of losing your mate even more frightening. So when you call a timeout for self-repair, remind yourself who you strive to be as an authentic person. Review your values list again and tell yourself you refuse to return to presenting an inaccurate picture of yourself.

2. Think about your anxieties, limitations, and shortcomings by identifying what is making you anxious or fearful. Determine what you can and cannot do. (Remember the Serenity Prayer—this is a good time to say it!) This will prevent your anxiety from driving your decisions or immobilizing you. I like to say another little prayer when I am stuck. "Help!" or the longer version is "Higher Power, I don't know exactly how to fix this. Please show me the way. If I can't fix it or if it isn't my job to fix it, help me to get through this with integrity and doing no harm."

3. Hold yourself accountable. Identify what you are doing that is not helping the situation. Are you afraid? If so, are they reasonable fears about what is going on, or connected to something from your family of origin? Are you being selfish, trying to manipulate the situation, engaging in behaviors that you know will make things worse? What other options do you have that will make things better? What would you be doing if you really wanted to show your mate that you loved him/her?

4. Acknowledge your projections and thinking errors. Admit when you are wrong—don't wait for your mate to do so first, or ever, for that matter.

5. Tolerate the discomfort. It is the way to grow. Support yourself through positive affirmations. Pray for your mate. Soothe yourself through meditation, humming, or singing; have a special coloring book and color yourself to safety.

If this doesn't work at first, you just need some practice. Eventually you will find that it will work for you. In the meantime, to create a safer playing field for discussions, the following guidelines may help:

*   Be ready to call "timeout for self-repair" if discussions become attack and defend games. Practice self-repair through the steps outlined above. Be sure to agree upon a time to continue talking later.

*   Have an adult third person present to discuss painful issues if you are not able to have these discussions without becoming angry.

*   When discussing, stick to the issues at hand until you get resolution or agree that you are stuck and need to cool off or get help before moving to another topic.

*   Don't blame each other. Talk about feelings first. You may want to use the behavioral change request form in these discussions (see p. 204).

*   If you cannot talk without getting out of control, agree to limit your contact to letters or emails.

*   Set specific hours you can be reached by phone.

If your separation is for more than a few days, establish ground rules for dealing with day-to-day responsibilities. Who will pay which bills? How will your children's needs be met? If one parent is the primary care taker, how will respite and visitation be managed? What are the arrangements for visiting with the pets? Who will take the car to the tire repair shop? Initially, how long is the separation for? When will we meet to decide our readiness to spend more time together?

To determine who should do what, make a list of all the things you were responsible for in day-to-day maintenance in your household. If logistics allow, it may be easier to keep doing what you have done. Otherwise, decide who is best at what. Additionally, if this is an area where the addict can "stretch" to show his commitment by handling new responsibilities, he might volunteer to take those on. Or if the co-addict partner has been an over-functioning partner, she may want to give up some of her responsibilities.

If you have children, agree to treat each other like friends in front of them, no matter how angry or disappointed you are with yourself or your partner. You already know that it's not good for your children to be put in the middle of your pain, and have probably reproached yourself more than once for doing just that. If you can follow this suggestion, you will feel much better about yourself.

Regarding your sexual and emotional connection with your spouse, often the partner has a list of "off-limits" items. This might include not being touched or kissed. Some partners don't want to be told that the addict loves them—others want to hear it and see behaviors that demonstrate this. Obviously, these items are an individual preference.

Allowing the partner to have an "off-limits" list here that the addict has to abide by may seem overly punitive to the addict, but during the first few weeks or months after disclosure, the partner is frequently still in shock. It takes a while to even understand how she feels. The partner needs a chance to get clarity about what the addictive behavior has done to affect her life and its meaning to her. Because she has been lied to so much, it is critical that she get validation that her feelings are normal for this stage of the healing. This can happen in therapy, in Twelve-Step groups or other support groups, with a minister or rabbi, or perhaps with a best friend. The partner will want to know why the addict did what he did—but rarely is any explanation enough to take the pain away. For now accept that he did not do what he did because of you. He did it because he could not handle his emotional states in a healthier way. Now he has a chance to learn how to do just that. He will also learn that his experiences in his family of origin most likely contributed to his inability to manage emotional distress effectively. These lessons help take away his shame and self-blame. It is important for the addict and the co-addict partner to share what they are learning about themselves through recovery, so find a time to do that.

Is there any way to stop the pain and to feel better? The pain is part of the grieving process; there is no way around it unless you stuff your pain, which is not a good idea. It is therapeutic to tell the story of what really happened, so by all means talk about it with program friends and other confidantes.

For several weeks, set aside a time every few days to note what impact the addiction has had on you so that you can share that information with your group, therapist, or close friend. It is through talking about what has happened and listening that we grow, understand, and heal. For partners, it is important to have someone validate that what happened was hurtful, that it was not in your imagination nor are or were you crazy. You are not wrong to be enraged, sad, fearful, and hurt. At first, the only relief comes when the truth (or at least part of it) is out.

Addicts, during the first year it is especially helpful when your partner is complaining or gets caught in her post-traumatic stress by remembering events of the past for you to acknowledge that what you did was wrong. Reassure her that she has every right to feel the way she does. After you acknowledge your past behaviors, you can help your partner stay in the present by asking her what you can do *today* to make things better.

Some partners have a different reaction to the disclosure—they want to push all their thoughts and feelings about the crisis out of their minds and quickly move to forgiveness. This is usually a form of denial. Fear of facing the pain is too frightening. The fear is that if I let myself feel this pain, I won't be able to shut it off. But part of the grieving process requires that you face the reality that much of what you thought was your relationship was a fantasy. Something else has been going on for a long time.

Your Personal Healing

As you can see, the process of disclosure is an opportunity to "grow yourself up" or mature in ways that help you personally and help your relationship. It is your responsibility for your own healing. In times of crisis, we often mismanage our emotions and make matters worse. Someone who is able to manage emotional states is said to have high emotional intelligence. According to Daniel Goleman (1995) that means the person can:

1. Recognize a feeling as it happens.
2. Manage emotions by soothing yourself and bounce back quickly from life's challenges and minor crises.
3. Motivate self to have self-control in order to delay gratification and control impulses.
4. Recognize emotions in others and have empathy for them.
5. Manage your own emotional state when the other person can't manage his or her own emotions.

Emotions that are most often mismanaged are anger, fear, guilt, and power. The emotional state that encourages mismanaged anger the most is shame. Shame is guilt's big brother. Guilt is when you feel awful for having gone too far or for not having done enough. Shame is feeling inadequate for not being worthy enough. Underlying the shame are confusion and a feeling of abandonment. Shame makes us want to either blame someone so we don't have to look at our part in the situation or get revenge for how someone hurt us. But getting revenge doesn't mean getting over what has happened. Also, getting revenge never feels very good for long. Instead, it builds a wall around us that doesn't allow healing love to penetrate.

Anger can be helpful to give us energy, but after a while it gets in the way of healing. Because of the intensity of the feeling, we are seduced into believing that the anger is making us stronger when it actually can diminish our personal power. When we mismanage anger we get caught up in the obsession of the events surrounding the betrayal and we relive the pain of the disclosure over and over. If this goes unchecked we continue to feel powerless. And that is a move right back to addictive and co-addictive behavior.

Partners, if you are having problems with obsessing about what the addict has done or something negative about your own behaviors or reactions, you may want to implement an activity to help yourself reduce those invasive thoughts. An exercise used by many therapists allows your creative side to come out. Susan Forward (1999) describes a version of this and calls the exercise "The Movie in Your Mind."

Exercise:

First, make an imaginary movie using the obsessive, intrusive thoughts and pictures that tromp endlessly through your head. You can use the images you have in your head of your addict acting out in some manner. Make the movie as vivid as other visions you experience in your head most of the time.

Next, become a movie critic. Write a synopsis of the movie as if you were writing it for the *Today* show or some magazine. Then write a review of the movie. Totally trash the movie, being critical of the "actors," the location, and the story line. Make it really scathing, using humor as much as possible. This will start the process of reducing the power of these thoughts in your head.

Next, empower yourself with your remote control. Yes, actually use the remote control you have at home. Carry the remote with you at all times as a symbol of having control over your thoughts (and of the thoughts of the addict that live in your head). When the thoughts invade your mind, push the off button, just as you would if you were turning off the television. Next, see the image fade to black or automatically turn the screen to black. I find it helpful to see the image, then close your eyes and see the black of your closed eyelids—focusing intently on the black screen. Continue to see the black for 30 seconds—in that 30 seconds you are in control.

If you have numerous scenes invading your head, allow yourself to watch your addict partner, tolerating the pain for a few minutes, then turn it off, see the black screen and say to yourself, "I am getting better, I am gaining control over my thoughts and my life. I will heal. No matter what, I will heal." And you will!

Decrease the time you watch the movie and increase the time the screen is black each day. As the "director" of this movie, you can do what you want with the movie. You may have a positive memory of you being with your mate sometime in the past (not a romantic memory), one in which you felt authentic. You can practice changing the channel with your remote from the obsessive acting out movie to a new movie of you being authentic. Start to see something that makes you feel good about yourself. That something may be a beautiful place you've been to with or without your mate. See yourself there, feel what you need to feel, hear what you need to hear, say what you need to say to feel empowered. That's the movie you want to watch. The more you consciously choose to replace the acting out movie with one that empowers you, the sooner you will be able to have your life back. Before long, you'll find that you can go to black or change the scene whenever you want or need to. After all, it is now your movie!

When we mismanage any emotion, it is often related not only to the current situation but some past event as well. For example, most people have experienced some type of childhood trauma. Birth, after all, is traumatic. But even in the best of families, natural events occur: pets die, teachers or coaches can be harsh, in some families children are expected to do far more than is reasonable. Others are sexually or physically abused. Unless a caring adult is around to help a young person make sense of what has happened, the child will make up stories in his or her mind about why and how something happened—usually taking the blame for things going bad. This self-blame then becomes the way the person sees traumatic events that happen in the present. In other words, the events of today are experienced with the eyes and emotions of the child who was traumatized earlier in life. The person stays stuck in the past and mismanages the emotional state of the present.

Exercise: Learn from the Past, Stay in the Present

One way to "grow yourself up" is to learn from the past and stay in the present. In their excellent book *Who's to Blame,* Carmen Berry and Mark Baker show us how to do that; the steps are provided in the following exercise. Anytime you feel that past emotions may be interfering with taking appropriate action in the present, complete this exercise:

1. What am I feeling right now?

   _____

   _____

   _____

   _____

2. What does this remind me of?

   _____

   _____

   _____

   _____

3. What feelings are underneath what I am experiencing now?
   (Under anger we often find fear and sadness.)

   _____

   _____

   _____

   _____

4. How can I best express my feelings to maximize healing and grow?

   _____

   _____

   _____

   _____

5. Do I need to hold someone accountable or am I overreacting
   because this reminds me of the past? (If it is reminding me of the
   past, is there someone from my past I need to hold accountable?)

   _____

   _____

   _____

   _____

6. What is my part in helping to create the situation?

   _____

   _____

   _____

   _____

7. What can I learn from the situation?

   _____

   _____

   _____

   _____

8. How am I powerful in the situation?

_____

_____

_____

_____

9. How do I want to transition to another place in the relationship with my self and my partner?

_____

_____

_____

_____

After you are able to really figure out what is happening in a given situation, you can then take appropriate action. Instead of mismanaging an emotional state to put distance between you, hold yourself and the other person accountable. Remember also that you are most powerful when you can come from love instead of anger or fear.

Exercise: To Hold Another Person Accountable

1. Write a detailed description of the event or situation about which you experience pain, anger, or another powerful feeling.

_____

_____

_____

_____

2. What meaning did you give to the event? How did you interpret your mate's behavior? (This works for people other than your mate and is a great exercise to teach to kids as well—but watch out, they will use it on you!)

_____

_____

_____

_____

3. How did you make matters worse for yourself?

_____

_____

_____

_____

4. What do you want your mate to do today to help you to heal?

_____

_____

_____

_____

Re-read this again and determine if you are calm enough to discuss this with your mate. If so, ask for an appointment to share this important information. Otherwise return to self-soothing activities until you are managing your emotional discomfort.

If your mate has asked you to be accountable and you feel defensive in response, then you will want to do the next exercise, rather than get defensive. Remember, being defensive doesn't work.

Exercise: Holding Myself Accountable

1. Repeat what you heard about what you did that your mate is asking you to be accountable for.
2. Acknowledge that what you did had an impact on your mate. Look for ways in which your mate has a good point and agree with anything you can agree on. (You can always agree that she seems upset and after hearing her description and the meaning to her, you can tell her you understand how she would feel that way.)

3. Humbly state you are sorry and ask for forgiveness.
4. If your mate has requested something of you, tell her whether you can fulfill her request. If not, suggest a few other options you can do.

Sometimes we use the "behavioral change request" activity in the same way. It is a common communication exercise that many therapists recommend, but has a built-in accountability clause for you as well.

Exercise: Behavior Change Request

Use this exercise anytime you need to talk to your mate about a sensitive issue. It holds both of you accountable for your parts in the situation. Until it becomes easy, write the answers to each line; then ask your mate for time to process.

1. I feel frustrated when you _____
2. Other emotions I feel are _____
3. I make matters worse by _____
4. To hide my fear that _____
5. I also feel sad about _____
6. What I really want from you today to make this better is _____
7. What I expect of myself in this situation is _____

Rebuilding Trust

One of the most devastating consequences of disclosure of secrets is the loss of trust experienced by the partner. Of course, it is a mistake to consider the cause of the loss of trust to be the disclosure—that is only the precipitating factor; it is analogous to blaming the messenger for the bad news. The underlying causes of the loss of trust are the addict's *behavior* and the *lies* that were used to cover it up. Words and promises will not do it— *changed behaviors and evidence of honesty* are the keys to rebuilding trust.

The partner has to believe that the addict has the intention to change for her to begin to trust again. More importantly, the partner has to believe the addict has the competency to implement the changes. The partner may believe the addict wants to change but she may not think he can do it. She will not trust him again until she is convinced he has the skill to do what he says he intends to do.

A commonly heard complaint by addicts is, "I've been toeing the line for six weeks, yet my wife says she can't trust me as far as she can throw me. I'm no longer engaging in my addictive behavior, I come home early every day or phone my wife if I'm delayed, I participate in therapy and self-help groups. What more do I have to do?" The answer is, more of the same, for another year or two. It doesn't seem fair, but think about how long you have been acting out. For most addicts, comparatively, a couple of years is not much. Rebuilding trust after disclosure of a serious transgression is a process, one that takes an average of two years according to research on recovering couples (Schneider & Schneider, 2001). At six weeks, the process is only beginning.

Here are steps the addict and partner can take that serve to rebuild trust in the relationship.

For the Addict:

1. Stop the acting out.
2. Be willing to disclose.
3. Be consistently honest, in small and in large matters.
4. Maintain involvement in your individual recovery work.

For the Partner:

1. Participate in your individual recovery work.
2. Explore and acknowledge your own role in the family dysfunction.
3. Be accountable for your slips, too.

Stopping the Activities

When one person discloses painful secrets to his partner and expresses a wish to heal the relationship, one important expectation is that the person will stop the hurtful behaviors. When a couple sees a counselor, the most important questions asked in the initial assessment are whether the addict has stopped using and if the addict is committed to working on the relationship. In order for the partner to be able to feel safe in the relationship, she will need to see evidence of changed behaviors. Over time, she will then let down her guard and increasingly become prepared to trust again.

Sometimes even the beginning of rebuilding trust can be delayed. Here is the story of Rosanne, married 30 years to a cardiologist:

It's been a whole year since I walked in on my husband Richard while he was having sex with his nurse Yvonne on an examining table at his medical clinic. When I found out she was not the only one, I threw him out of the house the next day, even though he apologized profusely, told me he loved me, and insisted he'd do anything to save our marriage. He said that the pain he'd obviously caused me had made him see the light, and that he and Yvonne are through. We're living apart, and he keeps begging me to let him come home.

I don't know what's the matter with me, he's done nothing for a whole year to merit my distrust, but I can't seem to begin trusting him again. I think it has a lot to do with the fact that Yvonne is still working for him. He told me he consulted his lawyer who advised him that if he fired Yvonne he could get sued for sexual harassment. He says she realizes it's an awkward situation and is looking for another job, but she has so much seniority at the clinic that her pay is very high. It's taking her a while to find another equally good job, Richard tells me. I keep wondering if she's really looking for another position. I believe him that they're no longer sleeping together, but how do I know they're not still flirting, or talking about me, or sharing their deepest thoughts?

Creating safety in the marriage is impossible until the acting out has stopped. In the case of sex addiction, if any contact with other people involved in acting out occurs or if the addict continues to act out with his behavior of choice after the disclosure, the addict is not in recovery and then safety and trust are once again destroyed. The addict should develop a list of behaviors in which he will no longer engage. Both the addict and the partner need to know what is on the list. (Addicts often carry that list with them at all times to remind themselves not to engage in that behavior.) It is a good idea for co-addict partners to have their own list of behaviors that they want to avoid. These are called "bottom lines." If either person has crossed a bottom line, they will agree to share that information with the other. Some couples want everything shared in the beginning, just to see how it works. Later, partners often do not want to know every time the addict is triggered, but do want to know generally what has been difficult during the day and what the addict has done to correct the situation. This means telling the partner information about any interaction that is related to the bottom line list, *not* waiting until your partner asks direct questions that you cannot avoid answering without lying.

When there are ongoing problems in the workplace related to the addiction, it makes it very difficult for the co-addict/partner to even begin healing. Rosanne, the partner in the example above, did eventually reconcile with Richard, but only after his nurse Yvonne found employment in another state.

When the addictive behavior has been an affair, the addict may be ambivalent about the end of the affair, and may in fact mourn its ending. The co-addict/partner frequently senses this and remains mistrustful. If the addict is ambivalent, this should be discussed rather than continuing to pretend the addict has both feet in recovery. It is virtually impossible for an addict to stop acting out in the workplace if his "drug of choice" still works there.

In cases where acting out was through obtaining drugs or other behaviors such as use of cybersex at work, then decisions about who should know and how the addict will safeguard the work environment need to be discussed and implemented.

As we described earlier in this chapter, partners of addicts often obsess about the addict's behavior. What they imagine may be far worse than the reality. Because of this, it is helpful to learn the truth. Another reason for answering all the partner's questions is that in the past, the addict was the one to decide what the partner should know or not know. It is empowering to partners for them to be the arbiters of what knowledge they want.

On the other hand, co-addict partners often erroneously believe that the more knowledge they have, the more they can control a situation. Partners may, therefore, seek detailed answers to a thousand questions—answers that might only serve to cause them pain as they are replayed over and over in their heads. How can the need to know be balanced with avoiding the pain of learning the "gory details?"

One technique to help the co-addict/partner clearly decide what is important to know is as follows:

1. Write down all the questions you have for the addict.

2. Next to each question, indicate how you will use the information (for your own safety or to build up your arsenal against the addict?).

3. Sort the questions. Decide what is important to know now versus what you're unsure about (you are not really sure it will help you to have that information). For the questions that you are not sure you want answered or exactly how much you want to know, for now, place them in an envelope and leave them with your therapist to be reviewed at a later date. Then you can determine if you still want those answers.

4. Review the list with your therapist. Then write a letter indicating what you want to know and why. This can first be read to your group to get additional feedback. Then read it to the addict in session with a therapist or at an Recovering Couples Anonymous (RCA) meeting.

Distrust and suspiciousness are to be expected in the early stages after disclosure. Although some therapists may recommend doing some detective work to diminish the fears of the partner, we find this type of behavior often consumes the energy of the co-addict partner and produces a probation officer/offender relationship for the couple. This keeps the addict and co-addict partner on unequal footing, which is often a trigger for both parties to resume old behaviors.

Sometimes the co-addict can't get unstuck from obsessing about the addict's past behaviors and projects them on everything that happens in the present. In rare cases, the addict may offer to set up a fund to hire a detective. More often an addict will offer to take a polygraph test in her presence, if that will help. Sometimes just offering to do this "objective" measure is enough insurance or proof to the co-addict partner that she can move on with her work.

Similarly, the drug addict may be asked to submit to a urine drug screen, which is a test for various drugs of abuse in a urine specimen. This test is routinely used in physician monitoring programs and in other recovery situations. A series of negative results (i.e., no illicit substances are found in the urine) establishes a track record of recovery, and some addicts find it useful to have this outside monitoring until they learn to manage their emotions rather than act out.

Ongoing Honest Behaviors

Addicts become so accustomed to lying that it becomes second nature. You frequently lie, even about matters where there is no reason to lie and no cost to telling the truth. After years of watching you lie, dissemble, stretch, and bend the truth, and cover up various actions, it's not surprising your partner does not trust you. You have to build a new track record to combat the miserable one that your spouse has had much experience observing.

One of the most effective trust-rebuilding strategies for the addict is to adopt a lifestyle of rigorous honesty. For example, if your wife asked you to pick up a carton of milk on the way home and you forgot, your addict's approach upon arrival home might be to tell her, "I got held up at the office and didn't have time," or some other such excuse. Instead, try telling the truth: "I'm so sorry, it just slipped my mind." If the two of you are shopping at the hardware store and the clerk gives you an extra dollar bill in change, give it back. When your partner observes you being honest in the small ways day after day, week after week, she will be more likely to believe that you will be honest in the big ways.

The Addict Should Demonstrate Ongoing Commitment to Individual Recovery

In order to be willing to risk trusting after betrayal, the partner needs evidence of the addict's *actions*, not just words. The most persuasive actions are those that demonstrate commitment to your new lifestyle, a life in recovery. This includes active participation in couple and/or individual therapy and group sessions, completion of therapy homework assignments, attendance at Twelve-Step meetings or other support groups, friendships with other recovering people, and decision-making conducive to recovery efforts. For example, part of your addictive pattern may have been to dress particularly seductively on Friday afternoons, then stop at the local lounge for their Happy Hour after work (after removing your wedding ring) and enjoy yourself flirting with attractive men. Your husband will be happy to see you coming directly home after work.

The same goes for reorganizing your computer involvement if you are recovering from cybersex addiction. Agree to use the computer only when your mate is at home; move the computer out of your home office and into the kitchen or den where there is less privacy. Change Internet service providers to a "family-oriented" ISP that blocks sexually oriented material from your computer. Purchase a software filter that will also block sexual Web sites, gambling sites, and so on. Estimate how much time you need to use the computer at any one time and set an alarm clock for that time. When your partner sees you adhering to measures such as these, he or she will be more likely to agree that you are sincere about your recovery efforts.

The Co-addict Partner Should Acknowledge Her Own Role in the Dysfunction

When the partner accepts some responsibility for the problem, she does not deny that a wrong was done to her, nor does she excuse the addict's behavior. However, what she does is begin to balance the unfortunate parent-child dynamic that is so common in the relationship between an acting-out addict and the partner—a dynamic that says that the addict is the "bad little boy" (or girl) and the partner is the controlling parent, always right.

Accepting some responsibility also functions to get the partner out of the victim role, a stance that implies powerlessness. It is empowering to recognize one's past actions, because it suggests that the partner can take some future actions to help remedy the problem, rather than remaining a helpless victim of the addict's behaviors.

It is not easy to for a partner who is hurting to look at her role, and it takes time and effort. This leads us to the next step.

The Partner Is Actively Involved and Committed to Their Own Individual Recovery

Many co-addict partners are so dependent emotionally on their mate that life without the other person seems unbearable. You may be one of the many people who was blindsided by your spouse's disclosure and was devastated by what you heard. The pain that you felt may still be fresh in your memory. You may be telling yourself, "How could I have missed what was happening? I will *never* let myself be hurt again like that!" One way to avoid another such terrible surprise is to decide never to trust him again. You can continue waiting for the other shoe to drop, while trying to avoid it by questioning his every action, doing endless detective work, and shutting yourself off emotionally.

Alternatively, you can work to become more centered yourself, less dependent, more differentiated. Your goal regarding your relationship is to be able to decide whether to stay or leave on the basis of what is best for you, *not*, as in the past, because life without "him" is a fate worse than death. When you are more your own person, when you can imagine having a good life without your partner, then you will be more willing to risk making a mistake in trusting him again. Even if it should turn out he does not deserve your trust, you will never again be as devastated by the truth as you were the last time. This is why an important part of rebuilding trust is to do your own recovery work, to learn to trust yourself, and to learn how to live with yourself.

Ending the Relationship

When a marriage ends, one or both people go through a grief process similar to the stages of mourning a death described by Elisabeth Kübler-Ross (1968). The well-known stages of shock, denial, anger, bargaining, depression, and acceptance do not necessarily happen in a neat sequence, but tend to overlap and sometimes repeat. Experiencing these stages is normal, and the duration of the process varies, at times lasting several years. As compared with mourning a death, grieving the end of a relationship has its particular challenges, which include the absence of a ritual that involves community support (similar to a funeral) and the lack of finality of the loss. The possibility of a reconciliation may make it harder to emotionally let go of your mate. From his experience counseling widows and widowers, William Worden (1991) formulated four tasks of mourning. These tasks are equally applicable to people who are grieving the ending of a relationship through divorce or separation. They are:

- *To accept the reality of the loss*—It's common in the early period not to believe the loss, to distort its facts, or to deny the meaning of the loss so as to make it less significant than it actually is. Some people remove personal items of the dead person (or the former partner), so they're not reminded of him; others leave his clothes and personal effects untouched for years, as though the dead person were still living there. Some people feel the presence of the dead person near them, and have conversations with him. The task is to accept the reality of the loss.

- *To work through the pain and the anger*—The most common way to avoid this task is to numb out so as not to feel. Some people idealize the dead person (or former spouse) and have only pleasant thoughts of him. Others escape through drugs, frenetic activities, or other addictions. The task is to experience the emotions connected with the loss.

- *To adjust to an environment in which the beloved is missing*—Worden says that many survivors resent having to develop new skills and take on roles themselves that were formerly performed by their partners. This task consists of adapting to the new situation and developing new skills.

- *To emotionally relocate the beloved and move on with life*—The beloved continues to be the central emotional relationship for the survivor. Life may be enjoyed in various ways, but the survivor partner can't imagine falling in love again. The task of this stage is to move the beloved to a place in the survivor's psyche that is still important, but leaves room for others. It includes withdrawing emotional energy from the deceased (or divorced) partner and reinvesting it in another relationship.

Although your mate is not dead, the relationship is, and you still need to go through these steps. Lisa's story illustrates this. As you read it, see if you can identify each stage as she works through it:

Lisa was a middle-aged professional woman who'd been married for 20 years. One day her husband, Brendan, announced that no matter what the consequences to their marriage, he felt compelled to drop everything and fly cross-country to meet Veronique, a young woman he'd been corresponding with on the Internet. Brendan, who years earlier had been very active in sex addiction recovery, had in recent months fallen into spending a lot of time viewing pornography on the Internet as well as chatting with other women in computer chat rooms. Right up until he decided to leave, he kept telling Lisa that his computer activities did not affect his feelings for her and were just an enjoyable outlet. Lisa had spent years in Twelve-Step recovery from her co-addiction, and realized she had no control over Brendan's actions.

Lisa handled Brendan's departure very well, she thought. Several times before he'd been obsessed with someone at work, and he'd gotten over it, so she figured he'd soon be disillusioned with Veronique and would return home. They would then go to couples' counseling, he'd agree to resume his recovery activities, and they would rebuild their relationship. Meanwhile, she went to work, did household chores, had lunch with one or another girl friend several times a week, and basically acted as though Brendan were away on vacation or a business trip. He emailed her occasionally about his activities (naturally omitting any mention of Veronique) and she responded in a friendly fashion.

After a couple of months Lisa began to reframe what was happening to her relationship. She recognized that Brendan's latest obsession was part of an ongoing pattern, which a few years earlier had included a marital separation of six months because of another affair he had. If he did return and she agreed to resume the marriage, there would most likely be yet another affair in the future. A friend told her, "You can't avoid the pain. The only question is, do you want to feel it now or at some time in the future?" She made the difficult decision to end the marriage. Now she was overwhelmed with pain and anguish over the loss of the relationship. She'd come home from work and cry as she looked at Brendan's clothes hanging in the closet or at the beautifully land-scaped yard he'd so carefully tended. She missed him terribly. Work was a welcome distraction, but at home she was desolate. What made it worse was that Brendan had indeed gotten bored with the new relationship, and wanted to come home. Lisa knew she could end her pain at any time by agreeing to let him come back, but she remembered her friend's advice about just postponing the pain. Whenever she felt herself weakening, she'd phone a Twelve-Step friend, who would remind her of the reality of her world.

After several weeks of pain, Lisa began to get in touch with a great deal of anger. How could Brendan put her through this?! She deserved better! The anger was very empowering, and she began to feel better. The fatigue she'd been feeling for weeks resolved, and she decided to make some changes. Lisa packed up Brendan's clothes and other belongings and put them in the garage. An over-flowing water heater made her realize she needed to take more responsibility for her house. She hired a contractor to walk through the house and advise her on necessary repairs and maintenance. She had all the repairs done, and arranged for periodic maintenance of the air conditioner, yard, and the like. Previously, Brendan had been the computer expert of the two, upgrading Lisa's computer and troubleshooting computer problems. Now Lisa found a local technician who made house calls and could solve all her computer problems. She began to feel more com-petent in her role of home owner. Lisa had always enjoyed traveling with Brendan, and had assumed that trips to foreign countries were now a thing of the past. But in the following year she took a couple of vacation trips to exotic places with a woman friend, and found that she could enjoy herself even without Brendan's company.

Around the time her divorce was final, Lisa began to feel that her marriage was indeed in the past. She had many good memories of Brendan, but felt closure about their relationship. For the first time since his departure, the thought of meeting someone new became appealing to her. She signed up for a computer matchmaking service, and cautiously began dating.

Disclosure While Dating

Many recovering addicts and co-addicts find themselves unattached, some because their primary relationship has ended, others because they have not yet chosen not to marry or be in a committed relationship. If you are a single person in recovery from addiction, you may decide at some point to begin dating. This will inevitably bring up the question of when and how to disclose your addiction history and your recovery activities.

What is a good course for a recovering addict to take? Here are a few suggestions to guide you:

- "Rigorous honesty" doesn't mean tell everything on the first date. Early dates are like auditions, opportunities for two people to see if they have enough in common, and enough chemistry, to want to spend more time getting to know each other better. This is not usually the time to talk about your messy divorce and obnoxious ex-wife, your unsympathetic boss, or your addiction history unless you are specifically asked.

- Conversely, don't wait too long to disclose. It is tough to determine when to tell. A good rule of thumb is to have a few dates before you decide anything. Talk to your recovering friends and your sponsor. If you are still feeling good about the budding relationship, and determine that you would like to transition to a more involved, exclusive, or committed relationship, then it is important to disclose the part of your addiction history that would influence the relationship. If you are still actively acting out, then you probably don't need to be dating, but for sure want to inform your date if he or she is being put in harm's way by your addictive behavior.

- If you are asked direct questions, answer honestly. This may be a gateway to disclosure. For example, if you are attending Twelve-Step meetings on a regular basis and are asked, "What are these meetings about?" you can explain. If you are asked, "How come you are so knowledgeable about addiction issues?" it's better to answer honestly.

- If the relationship has progressed to the point where each of you is revealing intimate details about your life to the other, withholding the basic facts about your addiction recovery may be perceived as being dishonest. It's probably time to disclose.

- If you are considering entering into a sexual relationship with someone, it is probably desirable to disclose in advance of having sex with that person.

- When you do begin to disclose, don't start by announcing, "I'm an addict." Most people do not understand what this means. They may be too frightened to really hear what follows. You may be better off having this type of conversation:

  > "In the past I had difficulty with some behaviors. This caused me some problems with my marriage and in fact led to getting a divorce. I went for help, and recognized that my behaviors were compulsive. Looking at them as an addiction has been very helpful to me. I've been in counseling for this, and for the past two years I've been attending a self-help program like Alcoholics Anonymous. I go twice a week. It's taught me tools that have helped keep me away from these behaviors and I feel a lot better about myself."

  > "Wow. What kind of behaviors are you talking about?"

  > "Well, I had several affairs while I was married. I knew it was ruining my marriage, but I just couldn't seem to stop. Now that I've gotten help I am optimistic that I've learned how to stop. I know how to get help if I'm tempted again. This isn't behavior I'm proud of; I really do believe in monogamy in a committed relationship."

Other people have different but equally difficult disclosures to make to potential new romantic partners. For example, herpes is a sexually transmitted disease that typically becomes chronic and can be transmitted to another person during a recurrence. Use of condoms and avoidance of sexual intercourse during outbreaks are important means of preventing the transmission of the disease. If you have a herpes infection, potential sexual partners need to be informed. When to disclose this disease can be a difficult problem for unmarried people with herpes.

On an Internet herpes support group, the mother of a young woman who'd caught a herpes infection from her first boyfriend wrote,

> I've heard a lot of ways that people have told, and one really successful way is to say, "Before we get intimate, I need to tell you something. I have a skin virus, and I will have it for the rest of my life. I take medication to suppress it, but it is contagious, and there is a chance you could contract it. I want to give you the chance to not continue the relationship. However, I would like to educate you about it. It's herpes." Something like that. Before you say the H word, warm him up to the idea. Believe me, there are ways to have a healthy sex life and wonderful relationship, and even keep your partner negative. The most important part is to educate both of you, and to tell him before you are intimate. That way he has no reason to be angry at you.

Similarly, someone with an ongoing psychiatric problem, such as schizophrenia or bipolar illness (manic-depressive illness), may do very well on medications and lead a productive and happy life. Yet there is the potential for relapse, and clearly, a romantic partner needs to be told at some point about the presence of the disease.

Because bi-polar disorder as well as other co-morbid conditions are often present with addiction, this information is important to include in a disclosure if you have these illnesses.

Reconciliation

The rebuilding process is the first stage of reconciliation for the couple, but we want to encourage people to actually date each other again. The courtship rituals that you establish during this time as a renewed, stronger person will lend memories to sustain you in trying times.

Couples often revisit the boundary lists and adapt those to a more trusting relationship. It is important to share experiences with other couples. Try to establish a mix of recovery and non-addicted couple friends. Attend a class together and meet other people.

The last stages of forgiveness continue during this phase. This involves forgiving yourself. In general, you might think about forgiving yourself for thinking you were not good enough and for not asking for what you want and need. Forgive yourself for not believing that you deserve to be happy or loved. Forgive yourself for all you have done or not done in support of these beliefs. Or how about forgiving yourself for judging yourself as weak, or flawed, or not sexy enough, or smart enough, or successful enough. Forgive yourself for not trusting that your authentic self could rally for you and the Divine within you could help you find a way.

Iyanla Vanzant is a remarkable woman who has written numerous books on the power that lies within each of us. In her daily devotional, *Until Today*, she reminds us that we decide how our day is going today. It is so demonstrative of how we can respond when we have grown ourselves up and can truly take care of ourselves, thus freeing us to be in a committed relationship. It is one to use and re-use every day:

> I open my heart and mind to be aware . . . I must make a decision about how my day is going to be.
>
> As soon as *you decide* that you are going to be faith filled, joy filled, peace filled and filled full, you are going to have a good day. The moment you decide that you are not going to be beat down or weighed down, put down or run down, hung up or beat up, upset or set up, pissed off or blown off, you are going to have a good day. When you decide in your own mind that you are going to get grounded, be centered, stay focused, have a vision, accomplish a goal, complete a mission, pursue a dream, live with

a purpose, you are going to have a good day. As soon as you decide to accept yourself, celebrate yourself, correct yourself, authorize yourself, validate yourself, to be who you are, and to love yourself just the way you are, you are going to have a good day.

If you decide to take a moment to get still, to clear your mind, to open your heart, to listen to the sacred voice that guides you, that protects you, that knows you and loves you, you are going to have a good day. And if you find that you are not having a good day, it could be that you have not made the decision or taken the time to do what you know you must do to ensure that your day goes the way you have decided it should. Until today, you may not have been aware that decisions fuel the spirit. You may not have realized that you have the power to decide the direction of your day and your life. Just for today, make a decision about how you want to experience the day. Fuel that decision with a commitment to do what ever it takes to ensure that it happens.

Every day, decide that you are going to have a good day!

Recommitment

After a lot of hard work and self-searching, most couples want to reconcile and recommit to their relationship. This is after caring has been re-established through relationship-enhancing behaviors. This is after you have learned how to hold yourself and your mate accountable. True intimacy starts after you learn how to trust yourself and manage your emotions in healthy ways rather than fall back into old ways of thinking and acting.

Couples who survive the first two years or so of recovery are surprised at how strong they have become as individuals. They are ready to recommit to having a marriage that is realistic and a healthy place to grow as individuals. Research indicates that couples who stay together and report long-term happiness have goals for their relationship in addition to goals for individual growth. They have established caring, commitment, and a process of compassionate communication.

True Friendship

Mature grown-ups have the strength to see and acknowledge their own ambivalence toward their partner at times. They are able to tolerate the discomfort of both loving and hating their mate at the same time and recognize their mate also feels this way. They are willing to experience emotional pain as a pathway to personal and relational growth.

We know how terrible your emotional pain has been. Our hope is that now you are on the way to true friendship.

References

Bader, E. and Pearson, P, *In Quest of The Mythical Mate.* New York: Brunner Mazel, 1988.

Berry, C. and Baker, M. *Who's to Blame? Escape the Victim Trap & Gain Personal Power in Your Relationships.* Colorado Springs: Pinon Press, 1996.

Forward, S. *When Your Lover Is a Liar*, New York: Harper Collins, 1999.

Glass, Shirley. 2001, personal communication

Goleman, D. *Emotional Intelligence.* New York: Bantam Books, 1995.

Gottman, J. *Why Marriages Succeed or Fail.* New York: Simon & Schuster, 1994.

Kübler-Ross, E. *On Death and Dying.* New York: 1968

Schneider, J. and Schneider, B.H. *Sex, Lies, and Forgiveness: Couples*

Speak on Healing from Sex Addiction, Second Edition, Tucson, Ariz.: Recovery Resources Press, 1999.

SIECUS Report, Washington DC: Sex Information and Education Council of the United States, 1995.

Vanzant, Iyanla. *Until Today*. New York: Simon and Schuster, 2000.

Worden, William. *Grief Counseling and Grief Therapy,* Second Edition. New York: Springer, 1991.

CHAPTER TEN: For Helping Professionals

Because disclosure of sexual information tends to be the most difficult for professionals to handle, this chapter refers to working with sexual infidelity. However, the information provided is appropriate to most addictive behaviors.

Relationship distress in couples in which a disclosure or discovery of extramarital behavior has occurred frequently motivates one or both members of the couple to seek professional help. Because this type of disclosure is taken so personally by the partner, we have added this chapter for professionals helping couples deal with disclosure of a sexual nature. The guidelines outlined in this chapter are appropriate for other types of disclosures as well.

There are many similarities between non-addicted and addicted couples seeking help to work through the labyrinth of emotions and decisions. However, there are several special needs of the addict and co-addict. The therapist's actions can be instrumental in helping both the individual and the couple make progress towards healing.

Differences between Addicted and Nonaddicted Couples

Almost all unfaithful mates struggle with disclosure. As with addicts, they do not want to hurt their partners nor get into trouble, so their tendency is to avoid disclosure. Yet, most of the books on surviving infidelity promote honesty about the behavior (mostly affairs). This makes sense because the majority of these books are authored by women who have survived an affair. Most men or women who have had an affair would prefer that they did not have to disclose. Unfortunately, guilt or evidence often prompts the disclosure. In addition to the unfaithful mate's guilt, there exists a wide range of emotions for both people in the relationship.

We have little information about the number of people who get involved in affairs, or go on sexual binges of some type outside the primary relationship and if not caught, do not tell. In the recent past, several prominent political figures have been caught being unfaithful and have made matters worse by denying their involvement with an affair partner or their extensive cybersex or pornography use. In these high-profile cases, it seems that early disclosure would have been the better choice. Still, it is hard to know how many couples survive infidelity because no one disclosed.

Why, then, do we promote disclosure for addicts and their partners? Partly because of the outcome of our research—most addicts and partners agree that telling was useful and in most cases helped them stay sober, gave them enough hope to stay involved in each other's lives in healthy ways, and demonstrated the motivation to change.

Another very important reason is because addictive behaviors are repetitive in nature. Being addicted means that your brain is formatted to seek out situations in which the brain chemistry will be altered enough to ensure an altered mood. The majority of addicts cannot manage to gain any health if they are still sexually involved outside the relationship—they experience too much shame and guilt, which are strong stimuli for relapse. Just as an alcoholic cannot hang out in a bar and expect to abstain from alcohol, sex addicts cannot hang out where their "drug" of choice is, without risking acting out again. Most addicts and co-addict partners find that honesty helps them remain connected to their recovery efforts.

Disclosure seems to offer hope—and almost a form of insurance for the addict and co-addict partner. To lie or continue to lie just fuels the engines that run the addiction and codependent behaviors.

Therefore, we do encourage addicts to disclose to their mates (and vice-versa) in almost all cases. On the other hand, if someone is not an addict, we examine the context and meaning of the infidelity before making any recommendation about disclosure. If a client requests guidance about whether to disclose an affair, some questions worthy of discussion in individual therapy session are:

- Is the affair over?

- Does the client still have any contact with the affair partner, or does his or her spouse?

- Does the client still have strong emotions about the affair partner?

- How did the affair impact the couple's relationship?

- What lies were used to cover up the affair?

- Did the partner suspect, and if so, how much energy and additional lying was necessary to disarm the partner's suspicions? (For example, was the partner accused of imagining things, paranoia, and the like, that perhaps contributed to the partner's loss of self-esteem?)

- Is this the only affair the client has had, or has this been a recurring pattern?

- Does the past affair have any impact on the couple's current relationship?

- How comfortable does the client feel about continuing to conceal the affair?

- What is the meaning for the client of continuing not to disclose, and of disclosing?

- What does the client believe will be the positive as well as negative consequences of disclosing the affair (on himself, on the spouse, on the relationship)?

- What does the client believe will be the positive and negative consequences of continuing *not* to disclose the affair (on himself, on the spouse, on the relationship)?

By clarifying the reasons for the client's consideration of disclosure, you can help him or her decide if it would be the right thing to do. By asking about other affairs, you may be able to identify an addiction problem, in which case disclosure is recommended, and may itself constitute an intervention that will lead to addiction treatment for the unfaithful spouse.

Before even embarking on this discussion, however, we recommend that you ask yourself the following questions:

- Have you (the therapist) had an extramarital affair yourself, or have you been the betrayed partner?

- How does your personal experience about affairs, secrets, and lies affect your feelings and beliefs about the appropriateness of the client's disclosing the affair?

Understanding your own feelings about disclosure will allow you to counsel the client more objectively and more effectively.

The Role of the Therapist

As a therapist, it is not your role to side with either the partner or the addict. It is tempting to side with the partner because the addict has done the betraying. However, this puts the therapist in a triangulated position and allows the couple to focus on blaming or proving their point through the therapist rather than dealing with their own issues within the context of the relationship. Early in therapy, the couple looks to the therapist as the all-knowing expert. Sharing information about what you have learned through the literature, research, and your own clinical experience with couples dealing with addiction can be useful in order to give the couple hope and help them be realistic about what to expect.

The therapist helps to interpret what is happening and discusses the differences between how men and women view and interpret situations. She or he validates each one's reality and the intensity of their feelings. As a coach, the therapist offers strategies to help the couple communicate more effectively (especially the listening and reflecting part of communicating). Incorporating cognitive behavioral exercises will help correct thinking errors and develop skills to build emotional competence. Personal responsibility can be enhanced by teaching the couple skills for holding self and each other accountable.

As the couple progresses you will see them able to move from the attack-defend mode of interacting to productively handling disagreements or difficult issues. Gradually, they will address problems without blaming or bringing up past betrayals. Having moved from interventionist in the early crisis phase, to educator and then coach during the rebuilding stage, the therapist's role near the end of therapy changes to cheerleader, letting the couple practice what they have learned.

How Long in Therapy

Working with these couples is a long-term commitment on everyone's part. It takes between two and five years for recovery to really get integrated into the lives of the couple. Couples therapy helps the relationship grow and sustain the stormy times. We have found that couples most often enter therapy for at least 12 weeks, make progress, and then come back bi-monthly, then monthly for the first year. We typically see couples for monthly maintenance or as crises arise. Couples can benefit from support groups through their local church or synagogue or Recovering Couples Anonymous (see Appendix C).

Crisis Intervention and Early Therapy

Your introduction to a couple often begins with a telephone call from the partner, who reports a crisis—her spouse's infidelity. Ask her when and how she found out, and if there has been an ongoing problem regarding sex in the marriage. If the addict calls, it is usually because the partner has discovered something about his sexual activities, and a major disruption of the marriage has resulted. Ask if the addict thinks he has a serious problem, if he has sought help for the problem, and if so, if he is still in therapy. Determine if he is still acting out. If yes, then schedule an individual session to assess his commitment to getting into recovery.

The partner is usually in a state of shock, either full of rage and anger or devastated and hopeless. She may vacillate between these emotional states, become anxious, and phone you day and night, weekends and holidays. Although listening to her is vital to the process, your ability to model some healthy boundary-setting is equally as important. Assure her that some feelings of desperation and chaos are normal for this period and help her develop a plan for coping with them, including postponing calling you until a designated time. Help her identify a support system by recommending S-Anon or Al-Anon meetings (see Appendix C for support groups) and clarifying with her who may be safe to share this information with.

In the first few sessions (or in those frantic phone calls) it is helpful to reduce her fear by validating her experience and reassuring her that she is not crazy and that self-care is of the utmost importance. Help her establish obtainable goals in these areas.

In our study, most respondents did see a therapist. In fact, most saw more than one. The partners reported that the most important and useful part of seeing a therapist was being supported and feeling heard. Specifically, several partners commented that helpful therapists established a safe atmosphere in which they felt free to ask questions at any time and in which their suspicions were validated. Partners indicated that the therapists allowed them to make choices.

The second valuable type of advice was to take care of themselves and to recognize that the addict's behavior was not the partner's fault. Partners told us it was helpful for them to be told to give yourself time and space to heal, not to make rash decisions, how to set boundaries, and that self-worth comes from inside, not from other people.

In contrast, addicts reported that the most useful advice was what and how to tell. Some (60%) thought that advice to be honest and tell everything was the most useful. Rather than demand the addict disclose, a persistent, gentle coaching to share information with the partner was seen as the most motivating. The therapist discouraged keeping secrets, warning that secrets are destructive and severely damage trust. Therapists also helped addicts make better choices by considering many options. Most often though, respondents reported the most useful advice was that honesty is the best way to rebuild the relationship

Help the addict identify his values and formulate ideas about how honesty can be helpful to him in his relationship with his partner and his recovery. Have him be specific about setting goals for honesty.

Although most people in our study reported their experience with advice from therapists to be satisfactory, those who responded to the question about least helpful advice spoke of the impact and seriousness of disclosure for both the addict and the partner. The primary theme identified for both addict and partner was lack of knowledge and skill by the therapist. This included lack of responsiveness to the emotional condition of the partner. Below are some comments by partners that illustrate the seriousness of the situation for the partner:

> "Another therapist counseled my husband and me, but she didn't know that it was an addiction. Instead, she encouraged me to be a better sexual partner and support his habits."

> "When I found out my husband prefers men or children, I was really devastated. My self-esteem was shaky and that finished it off. I was afraid for my children. I didn't think my husband would stay in our home. Months later my psychiatrist told me he was a pedophile—by then I was so depressed I was planning to kill myself and my children."

> "I was so angry, but isolated. I needed to talk about my feelings, but his behavior was all we could see. Maybe disclosure should follow preparation. This was such a dangerous time for me."

> "The first two therapists did not address my need to ask more. I saw a psychologist for a period of time. He was ill-prepared to help me. He questioned my aversion to knowing the details. It confused me."

"I felt I let my children down enormously by dragging them through all the sordid details. Early, I should have been cautioned about who I disclosed to and advised to connect up with S-Anon groups. I acted inappropriately by making several phone calls to two women he'd been with."

Obviously from these comments, the serious nature of the emotional state of the partners was not enough of a concern for the therapist. Assess the emotional state of the partner before moving forward with further disclosure or before letting the partner leave after a difficult session. Establish a firm goal with her about safety and check for suicidal ideation.

To further assess the case, it can be helpful to give each client a take-home questionnaire at the end of the first session. Questionnaires can be helpful not only to gain information, especially with sexual addiction cases, but as a means of letting each partner "vent." Ask about the type and level of current disruption, abuse during childhood, sexual history including other outside sexual and emotional involvement prior to marriage, sexual behavior and satisfaction within the marriage, other marital satisfaction issues, and how the couple attempts to enhance the relationship. Maintain strict confidentiality about information in the forms. If you determine that some information contained in the questionnaire needs to be shared with the spouse, work with the individual to come to that decision. It is much more useful for the client to come to that conclusion than for you to demand it. If the homework is not completed, it may be a sign of no privacy at home or a lack of commitment to the process by one or both parties.

After trust has been broken, couples often struggle with what to do about the marriage. It is common to see the partner beset with fear that she will be hurt again or will not be able to heal from the betrayal. She is likely to threaten to leave, want him out of the house, leave herself, or become so hyper-vigilant she becomes obsessed by his every move. Reassure couples that their ambivalence and fear about the future of the relationship is normal at this stage. Establish an agreement to not do anything about leaving for three to six months. We recommend waiting a year, but most couples have a difficult time postponing this decision for what seems like such a lengthy time. Couples in early recovery are usually more comfortable agreeing to sit tight for three to six months, and then reassess where they are. At that time, they can recommit to continuing to work on their marriage and perhaps increase their level of commitment to each other. You should also recognize, and advise the couple, that the real recovery takes between two and five years.

Our research and experience indicate that rarely does an addict reveal all during the initial disclosure. He is either afraid of the outcome so only tells what he thinks is enough to get by, or he doesn't remember all his acting out and the lies he told to cover up his actions. Reiterate to the couple that more than one disclosure is probable and set up a system by which past events can be discussed. To deal with the likelihood that the addict will eventually remember more material or may gradually come to recognize the need to disclose additional matters, agree on a schedule of perhaps once per month for the first three to six months for further disclosure of past events and discussion of how the addiction has impacted both their lives.

Addiction is a chronic, relapsing condition; it takes time for the addict to learn to manage it. The partner needs to understand this, and to proactively create a plan for self-care, should a setback take place. If the addict has a slip or relapse, new disclosures should be done as soon as possible. Keeping the information secret will only make the partner trust the addict less. Recognize that despite preparation, any further disclosure is a setback for the partner. Nonetheless, if she can avoid punishing the addict for being honest, this will increase his level of emotional confidence and be empowering for her. If he continues to relapse, she may have to re-evaluate her desire to stay in a marriage in which the person will not use the tools he has been taught to keep himself healthy.

Early on, suggest that the addict clear the home of as many triggers and paraphernalia as possible. Careful attention to this can be a powerful statement to the partner that the addict is serious about changing. For example, if online sexual activities were part of his repertoire before recovery, the addict can move the computer to a public area in the household, purchase software that will block access to sexually oriented Web sites, give the password to a Twelve-Step sponsor or friend, and create accountability by "book-ending" his use of the Internet (that is, phone a program friend or sponsor immediately before and after using the computer).

Most partners want to know why the addict did what he did. Rather than focus on the why, it is more beneficial for the couple to talk about the meaning of the addictive behavior to each of them. How to do a formal disclosure is outlined earlier in the book. Once the anger and fear have subsided, discuss what aspects of the relationship are sources of emotional distresses for the partner or addict. Explore with the couple alternative ways of viewing those situations or other ways to interact during those times. Also make plans for dealing with other high-risk times such as work difficulties, financial hardships, accidents, or illnesses. Be certain the couple recognizes that anniversary dates of the disclosure or discovery or other particularly painful events can be difficult occasions. These anniversaries tend to reignite the partner's anger and the addict's shame and need to be planned for appropriately. The couple needs to increase their ability to cope with emotional distress in general and have firm plans for those anniversary dates.

Inability to manage intimacy is often paradoxically seen after a particularly loving or pleasurable time together. Whichever member of the couple is least able to tolerate closeness will re-establish distance through conflict or by ignoring the other. The resulting confusion creates mismanaged fear, which then becomes a trigger for either addictive or codependent acting out. Resuming sexual intimacy also may trigger flashbacks in the partner. Predict the likelihood of these phenomena and co-create strategies with the couple to help them manage.

More intense flashbacks and other post-traumatic symptoms in the partner can throw the couple into another crisis. Intrusions by a former affair partner, an anniversary date, the discovery of old acting out paraphernalia, or the exposure of a lie about an important event to the partner can trigger obsessive thoughts for the partner. The addict's best defense is to agree his past behavior was wrong, express sorrow, and then ask if there is anything he can do *now* to remedy the situation. It is the therapist's task in session to help her get unstuck. Ask her to identify any additional unanswered questions and to recognize if she is mismanaging an emotional state. Encourage her to express pain without blaming. Advise her to set aside specific times for obsessing, to use a thoughts/feelings journal to help her identify thinking errors, and to develop plans of action. Meditation and prayer are also helpful for most people. Some therapists have found it helpful to use EMDR (eye movement desensitization and reprocessing) to reprocess and extinguish the power of traumatic memories of the betrayal.

It is common for one or both of the parties to have other addictions, depression, or anxiety. Both partners need to address and begin treatment of any other addictive behavior. If severe depression and anxiety are present, consider referral to a psychiatrist for prescription medication. However, remember that some depression and anxiety is normal; it is important for the client to learn to manage those emotional states rather than medicate them away.

If the couple decides to end the marriage, then the goal of therapy is to gain closure and determine what, if any relationship, they want to have with each other. If they share children, help them to negotiate how to manage the responsibilities of co-parenting.

Beginning Repair Work

We have outlined a number of activities for couples to begin the healing process. Encourage the couple to talk about what gives them hope for the future and brainstorm ways in which they can engage in relationship-enhancing behaviors. Most couples can recall some of the early fond memories of their relationship to rekindle these good feelings. Have them talk about how they fell in love in the first place and what attributes attracted each of them to the other. If the couple expresses resistance to this approach, have them focus instead on how they'd like their relationship to be now. Ask them to list the qualities of a best friend and to decide what they want to do differently each day to demonstrate that they are the other's best friend. In Chapter Nine we reviewed several ways to have the addict work toward rebuilding trust. Checklists of how things have improved are very useful.

Most couples have engaged in dysfunctional patterns of attack-defend, pursue-distance, nag-procrastinate, and blame-placate. Children or in-laws are often triangulated into these patterns of interacting that reduce or create homeostasis within the relationship. Couples who learn to relate directly can enhance their time together.

People in recovery often devote so much time and effort on recovery activities that couples forget to go on dates with each other or to spend some alone time together. Encourage them to set aside time to be together to either talk or just to enjoy each other's company. Suggest a homework assignment in which partner and addict alternate in asking for the date, selecting the location, and even driving to and paying for the date.

Encourage open discussion in session of the couple's sexual relationship. As mentioned earlier, this often will provoke flashbacks and difficult times. After a period of hard work, it is particularly useful for the couple to plan a special occasion in which to declare their renewed commitment and trust with each other. Discuss how to optimize sex for both partners. Rather than focus on what behaviors are off-limits, have the partner determine first what affectionate, loving, and sexual behaviors she is open to.

After that time, we recommend that couples schedule "intimacy times." If sex happens, fine. If not, we encourage holding each other, kissing, and other forms of intimacy. These activities can be particularly fulfilling when they are part of the couple's date night.

After couples have been in therapy and recovery for several years, the partner is ready to engage in additional sexual behaviors that both might enjoy, but which may feel more risky to one or the other. Frequently, the addict may hesitate to request a particular sexual act for fear that the partner will think he wants to act out. Encourage couples to dialogue about their sexual desires and to explore whether this is an option. Reading aloud from a recommended book on sexuality is a great way for couples to discuss whether they would want to participate in a behavior or not. However, if the addict has used the partner as a way to act out, these couples need to first process extensively with each other the meaning of sexual expression.

Special Areas of Concern for Therapists

Below we discuss some special areas of concern for therapists who are counseling sex addicts and their partners.

Therapists Who Have Little or No Experience in Dealing with Sex Addiction

In our research with couples dealing with sexual addiction, the primary complaint was that the therapist was unfamiliar with sex addiction and that the therapist's approach prolonged the addict's denial about the extent of the problem. If you have little or no experience with sex addiction, let the couple know and be willing to address their marital problems with a therapist who is familiar with these issues. Some therapists find it useful to get peer supervision from someone familiar with sex addiction diagnosis and treatment.

High-Risk Acting Out

Sex addicts engage in a variety of behaviors that the partner may or may not view as extramarital—for example, collecting pornography, telephone sex, viewing nude dancers, masturbation with another person on the computer, and sexual massage. Most sex addicts, however, do engage in behaviors that involve sexual contact with another person, often without protection from sexually transmitted diseases. This was evident in the results of our survey, which found that of the 100 sex addict responses, 91 percent reported engaging in sexual behavior that included another person.

Involvement with another person presents a different threat or cost to the relationship than solitary sexual activities. For one, it increases the risk that the partner will want to leave the relationship, and therefore makes it more difficult for the addict to disclose the behaviors. For another, involvement with another person risks exposure of the addict— and by extension, the partner—to sexually transmitted diseases. The risk of infection with a sexually transmitted disease, especially HIV, presents an ethical dilemma for the therapist who learns about a concealed affair. Given the ethical stipulation that therapists report to authorities when a person's life is in danger, an HIV-positive addict might be asked by his or her therapist to disclose to the partner. If the addict has not yet been tested, you will want to suggest testing to him.

At times physicians have to deal with very much the same ethical dilemma. Consider the following scenario a doctor might experience:

> Jim, a 43-year-old married businessman who has been your patient for many years, comes in with symptoms that you diagnose as gonorrhea, treatable with penicillin. You explain that state law requires you to report this to the Health Department and that Jim's wife, who is not your patient, must be treated because she has been exposed.

> Jim begs you not to report his case. "I picked up a prostitute a couple of weeks ago when I was at a convention. If you tell Joan, she'll walk out on me. And if you report me to the Health Department, they might call Joan. I swear I've never done anything like this before. Please don't ruin my marriage by telling Joan."

Should you, the doctor:

1. Insist that Jim tell Joan he has gonorrhea and bring her in for treatment. If he doesn't do this within two days, tell him that you will tell her himself.

2. Agree to have Jim tell his wife he has a disease that is *not* sexually transmitted but insist she come in for treatment, or else within two days you will contact her and tell her she needs treatment.

3. Agree to have Jim tell his wife he has a disease that is *not* sexually transmitted, and give him enough medication for her as well as him.

4. Tell Jim he must tell Joan he has gonorrhea, but don't follow up yourself.

5. Tell Jim to tell Joan what he thinks is best.

6. Another option.

This dilemma was actually part of a study reported in 1989 in the *Journal of the American Medical Association* on physicians' attitudes toward using deception to resolve difficult ethical problems (Novack et. al., 1989). What do you think the physician should have done? What do you believe is the physician's responsibility to Jim? To Joan? To their marriage? Give this some thought and then read on.

Here's how 211 physicians actually answered:

1. Tell the truth, doctor will follow up: 19%
2. Deceive the wife, doctor will follow up: 53%
3. Deceive the wife, no physician follow-up: 14%
4. Tell the truth, no physician follow-up: 2%
5. Do what you think is best: 3%
6. Some other option: 9%

Notice that almost 80% of the physicians would agree to help Jim cover up his visit to a prostitute, and almost 30% felt no obligation to be sure she was treated. Also, 22% of the doctors were willing to collude with Jim by not reporting him to the Health Department; another 34% of doctors, who were part of the group who *would* notify the Health Department, said they'd ask the Health Department not to call Joan. The chief reasons given by those doctors who would go along in deceiving Joan were: a one-time affair doesn't warrant the break-up of the marriage; since Jim is the patient, the doctor has an obligation to treat him and respect his privacy in deciding how Joan will be treated; it would be better in the long run for both Jim and Joan. The most common approach, selected by 53% of the doctors, consisted of a combination of helping Jim deceive Joan, along with making sure she was treated. These doctors felt they were making sure Joan's health was preserved, while not putting Jim on the spot.

Notice that Jim tells the doctor that Joan is likely to leave him if she learns of the episode with the prostitute and that most of the physicians in the study apparently accepted this as fact. Do you remember what our survey showed about the likelihood that such a threat will actually be acted on? We found that, despite the fears of the unfaithful partner, much of the time, the relationship does *not* end. Perhaps if the physicians had not assumed that disclosure would inevitably lead to divorce, they might have chosen a different option, one that might have in fact been better in the long run for the marriage.

Other Areas of Safety

If the addict or the partner fears for their physical safety, appropriate steps should be taken to get the couple to separate for a short period of time. If domestic violence has been part of the couple's history, she needs to have a back-up plan for leaving if the situation increases in volatility. Especially when it is the woman who has acted out sexually outside the marriage, the therapist needs to assess the risk of violence before recommending disclosure.

Another area of safety concerns potential victims of sexual offenders. When sex behaviors include victimizing others, the therapist's first priority needs to be to get the client to stop the behaviors. A significant therapist mistake is to focus on getting the addict to understand the sources of the behavior, resolve childhood trauma, etc., without directly addressing the behavior itself. For example, in his book *Therapists Who Have Sex with Their Patients*, Dr. Herbert Strean describes his treatment of a male therapist who over time had had sexual relations with several female clients. He relates how over a four-year period, using psychoanalytic psychotherapy, he was finally able to bring the patient to sufficient mental health that he no longer felt compelled to get his emotional needs met through sexual contact with clients. However, the issue of the trauma done to the clients and the need to immediately stop the behavior was reportedly never directly addressed, and the patient apparently continued the behavior for an extended time period while undergoing therapy. (Sexual relations with a therapy client or patient are so potentially damaging to the patient that it is prohibited by professional associations and licensing bodies throughout the United States and Canada, and is a felony in several states.)

Similarly, when a client relates to a helping professional that her partner disclosed to her some potentially victimizing sexual activities, it is a mistake to underestimate the gravity of the situation. For example, in a survey of partners of cybersex addicts, we heard from a young woman that when she was engaged to be married, her fiancé admitted he was downloading pornographic images of underage girls from the computer. She went to her minister for counseling, to discuss her options. She reported that the minister dismissed her concern, stating that her fiancé was probably "just curious," and that after they were married, his curiosity would undoubtedly be satisfied by having sex with his wife. Unfortunately, the husband's behavior continued long past the marriage, and the wife was now worried about his risk of arrest.

The bottom line is, when disclosure reveals behaviors that are illegal, dangerous, or involve victimizing others, therapists must make it their priority to assure the safety of the addict, spouse, and potential victims.

Mismanaged Anger

In the recent past, partners were encouraged to rage through their anger, hitting mock images of the addict or perpetrator. Research has shown that this approach to helping people express their anger is usually not helpful; instead it keeps the person in a state of rage and connected to their trauma rather than released from it. It is more helpful for the partner to identify what she is angry about, note the level of anger on a scale of 0 to 10, and then make a plan for reducing her anger so that she can think clearly about any action that needs to be taken. Sometimes therapists have partners write anger letters and read them aloud, but it is important that the partner is accountable in that letter about how she contributes to the situation or makes the situation worse for herself. Finally, she should declare what would make things better for her today since nothing can be done about the past.

Premature Diagnosis

When a client presents with a sexual problem, ferreting out its cause may require some detective work. An all-too-common therapist mistake is to diagnose without obtaining an adequate sexual history of both the addict and the partner. For example, a client who complains that her husband is not interested in sex with her may indeed be married to someone who has a sexual aversion disorder or sexual dysphoric disorder (also termed sexual anorexia), but alternatively, he may be an active sex addict who is spending hours every night downloading pornography and masturbating. If a client describes her own loss of interest in sex with her husband, she may have sexual anorexia, but alternatively she may be reacting appropriately to living with a spouse who has disclosed that he spends hours masturbating on the computer, and who, after 10 years of marriage suddenly wants her to participate in unusual sexual practices with which she is uncomfortable. Take the time to ask enough questions to get a full understanding of what is happening in the relationship.

Another type of premature diagnosis is to attribute the cause of any sexual problem to the spouse. For example, years ago a woman wrote to Dr. Ruth Westheimer, who wrote a sex therapy newspaper column, complaining that her husband could hardly wait for her to leave the house so that he could begin watching pornographic videos, and that several times she had returned home early and found him masturbating to a porno movie. Meanwhile, her husband was rarely interested in sex with her. Dr. Ruth's diagnosis was that the wife was sexually boring, and she recommended that the wife become more exciting sexually, to increase her sexual repertoire and her sexual availability. Another therapist, upon hearing a woman's complaints about her husband's interest in pornography, told her that all she needed was a more enlightened attitude about pornography, including joining her husband in viewing the pictures and films. Meanwhile, her husband's *preferred* sexual outlet, one he spent many hours a week doing, was masturbating to pornography. She had, in the past, agreed to experiment with various sexual activities with her husband, but he was not particularly interested in relational sex. In both of the above cases, the husband was a compulsive user of pornography with masturbation.

When a couple has mismatched sexual interests or activities, do not hasten to diagnose the problem as an uptight, sexually uninformed, or prudish partner. Rather than instinctively blaming the wife, get a thorough history.

In other cases, the diagnosis may be correct, but the labeling may be premature. Partners are very sensitive to being labeled along with the addict. Although we have used the term co-addict in this book, codependent is also used in this field for the partner of an addict. However, such labels rarely help the partner begin to see her part in the dance. After the chaos begins to subside, it is easier for the partner to see that some of her behaviors have contributed to the situation with the couple. Early on, let her hear those labels at support group meetings from other partners in similar situations. Introduce the concept, if appropriate, after you (the therapist) understand the context of her situation.

Timing of Disclosure

As we have described earlier, the addict most commonly discloses initially when the partner is about to learn the truth anyway, or when the partner has already learned some incriminating information. Other addicts, however, develop so much guilt that they feel a huge buildup of pressure to disclose. At some point they may disclose everything precipitously, without considering the consequences for the spouse. In both of these cases, the couple probably comes to see you after the initial disclosure, in which case all you can do is support and validate the partner and process the disclosure with the couple. If, however, there is additional material to disclose, doing so in session with you is likely to be most helpful for the partner. If the addict has written a letter to the partner, process that letter in the session. Discourage the addict from disclosing or giving a letter to the partner outside the session or without you first reading it and making comments or recommendations.

Earlier in this book we discussed the adverse consequences of disclosure by an addict during treatment, at a time when the spouse has no support to deal with the effects on her of the disclosure. If the addict is in treatment elsewhere, if the partner is not able to be with him at the center for the initial or for further disclosure, arrange with the treatment center to have him disclose any further information only when she is in session with you.

Use of Outside Monitoring

Some therapists recommend private detectives and polygraph testing to monitor the activities of the addict. Other than baseline verification in the truth-seeking stage early in recovery, we do not recommend this type of monitoring unless the addict agrees that outside monitoring will help *him* remain in recovery. A couple's relationship built on this much distrust is doomed to become a reenactment of unresolved parent-child issues. At some point the partner has to mature enough to tolerate her own discomfort of not being able to be sure of anything but herself.

Saving Face

Often the partner will declare: "If you ever do x, y, z I am leaving you." Then time goes by, the addict does well, and trust is re-established to a great degree. They recommit and everything is going well for a length of time. Then he relapses—usually not to the extent of the original acting out—but he relapses nonetheless. Now the partner is faced with her old threat. All the old memories of the original betrayal resurface as well as the pain. But now it is even harder to leave. The partner has worked hard to make changes herself and has seen changes she has liked in the addict. Now what does she do? We often invite the partner to devise some way that the addict can make restitution by taking certain actions. This may be to have HIV testing done for an extended period of time and wear a condom when they re-engage in sexual activity. Sometimes it is some gift or task he takes on.

While this may seem punitive, when the meaning of the "penance" is reframed through the partner's explanation of "this is what it takes for me to save face with myself for not leaving," the addict often views this in a different light.

Even more powerful is letting the partner discover a new perspective about the addict and herself. With this new perspective, she *can* change her mind.

Countertransference

Since about half of married Americans have had an affair at some point during their marriage, it is quite likely that the therapist has either had an affair or has been in a couple relationship in which an affair happened. It is also common for therapists to have experienced an affair within their own family of origin. If you have not resolved those trust issues, then your countertransference will interfere with being objective in your approach with a couple. Seek assistance from your peer supervisor about these issues and if they persist, refer the couple to another therapist.

Personal Sharing

Although many therapists in recovery disclose some information about their history, it is not advisable to share with couples information about your own affair or sexual acting out history. This type of personal information is private and unless you and your spouse (or former spouse) have gone public with this information, you are betraying the confidentiality of your mate. It is not uncommon for clients who have a less than favorable outcome to then spread stories about you. A client with dependent personality disorder may believe that she or he is your best friend because you have shared such intimate information. It is okay to share less intimate stories that teach skills or demonstrate techniques for resolving problems, but using case examples or metaphors are more appropriate.

Don't Give Up Too Soon

It takes between two and five years for individuals to really get comfortable and do well with recovery. That may translate into many years of couple therapy as well. Couples who stop therapy in fewer than 12 sessions are more likely to separate, and the healing process is replaced with destructive interactions. Unfortunately, this leads to more stress and to increased risk of relapse for both addict and partner. Although most couples do not remain in weekly therapy beyond the first year or so, most who do well return to therapy from time to time for several sessions when additional difficult problems come up.

Be cautious of the couple in which the addict is quickly remorseful and attentive and the partner is swept off her feet into believing all is well. This style of interacting, common in addicted couples, is likely to lead them back to relapse when stress and anxiety return to the relationship. Gently confront the couple in which you see this wishful thinking and unrealistic "flight into health." Explain to them that the path to recovery is lengthy and at times difficult. Encourage the couple to see therapy as a long-term investment in themselves as well as their relationship.

Conclusions

Throughout this book we have emphasized our belief that disclosure is a cornerstone of healing. Most couples who have experienced disclosure agree with this statement, and recommend the process to other recovering couples. We have also pointed out the adverse consequences of disclosure. Clearly, there are some ways of doing disclosure that are better than others. Therapists are in a unique position to facilitate this process for clients, to answer for them questions about the timing of disclosure, about how much to disclose, and to whom, about disclosing to children and to parents, to employers and to TV talk show hosts, about situations when it might be better *not* to disclose, and about the difference between secrecy and privacy. But therapists need to be educated about disclosure, about its benefits and risks for couples, and about how to best facilitate. We hope this chapter has answered some of your questions about this process.

References

Hickson, G. B., Clayton, E. W., Githens, P. B., and Sloan, F.A. "Factors That Prompted Families to File Medical Malpractice Claims Following Perinatal Injuries." *Journal of the American Medical Association* 267: 1359–1363, 1992.

Kraman, Steve S. and Ginny Hamm. "Risk Management: Extreme Honesty May Be the Best Policy." *Annals of Internal Medicine* 131: 963–967, 1999.

Novack, Dennis H., Determing, Barbara J., Arnold, Robert, Forrow, Lachlan, Ladinsky, Morissa, and Pezzulo, John C. "Physicians' Attitudes Toward Using Deception to Resolve Difficult Ethical Problems." *Journal of the American Medical Association* 261: 2980–2985, 1989.

Strean, H. *Therapists Who Have Sex With Their Patients*. New York: Brunner Mazel. 1993.

Witman, A. B., Park, D., and Hardin, S. B. "How Do Patients Want Physicians to Handle Mistakes? A Survey of Internal Medicine Patients in an Academic Setting." *Archives of Internal Medicine* 156: 2565–2569, 1996.

Wu, Albert. "Editorial: Handling Hospital Errors: Is Disclosure the Best Defense?" *Annals of Internal Medicine* 131: 963–967, 1999.

Wu, A. W., Folkman, S., McPhee, S. J., and Lo, B. "Do House Officers Learn from Their Mistakes?" *Journal of the American Medical Association* 265: 2089–2094, 1991.

APPENDIX A: Frequently Asked Questions About Disclosing Sexual Secrets

Although disclosing *any* secrets is difficult, there's no denying that revealing sexual secrets is particularly hard. In our experience, people have the most questions about this type of secret. For that reason, we have prepared a section on the most commonly asked questions we've been asked regarding disclosing information about sexual behaviors. If you have other questions for which you've been unable to get answers, feel free to write to us.

Q: *After three years of "sexual sobriety" from pornography, massage parlors, and prostitutes, I had a slip recently—I got on the Internet and got involved in some interactive cybersex. I told my sponsor and my Twelve-Step group, but not my wife. It took her a long time to trust me again. Should I tell her?*

The short answer is yes. But more importantly, tell her what was going on for you that triggered you to want to medicate with the Internet. If it is merely the ease with which you can access this type of information on the Internet, then also tell her that you must make it harder to access these sites.

Learning all the things that can cause you problems takes time. Be certain that you and your mate have discussed what she wants to know and what she wants you to process with your group members, sponsor, or therapist. We recommend that partners ask to hear about whether you had a bad day and what you are doing to prevent a relapse rather than you disclosing every slip you may have. If she has trouble handling your disclosure, then participate in a few sessions of couple therapy to determine how to manage disclosure of slips without you being punished for your honesty.

Q: *After a lifetime of flirting, intrigues, and several affairs, I recently bottomed out and am beginning recovery in Sex and Love Addicts Anonymous. I haven't said anything to my husband. I don't know if he suspects anything. He's very dependent on me—I guess very codependent—and I think he might get suicidal if I tell him the truth. What should I do?*

If you feel that your mate may be suicidal, you would be wise to begin marital therapy and discuss this with your therapist in an individual session. It is very difficult to hide that you are going to meetings and working a program, so it is likely that it won't be long before he'll know something is going on. Additionally, his codependency needs to be addressed or the dance you both have done in the relationship is likely to start again and put you at risk for relapse.

Q: *In the past few months my husband seems to have lost interest in sex with me. Instead of coming to bed at night, he disappears into his den, where he stays for hours on the computer. He gets angry when I ask him questions, and says he's working hard on some projects, but on occasion when I've walked in on him, he acts very defensive and quickly turns off the computer. I suspect he is involved in cybersex. How can we deal with our marriage problems if he won't tell me what's going on?*

You cannot solve your marital problems alone; even if he doesn't have an addiction problem, your relationship is being affected by the computer use. Try talking to your mate when he is not at the computer, first stating that you miss your relationship with him and would like to get into couple's counseling to see if there is something you can do to improve things. You could also take the direct approach, telling him you are fearful for him and your marriage, that you have heard about Internet addiction and cybersex addiction, and are scared that that may be what is happening to him. Suggest that you both see a counselor familiar with this to determine if there is a problem. Unfortunately, unless he is seriously worried about his use, he will most likely deny any addiction.

In that case, you have to determine if you want to be in a relationship that is consumed with computer use behind closed doors. If not, you may have to play hard ball for him to understand that you are serious— tell him that unless he seeks help with you or unless he starts using the computer in front of you and is willing to show you what he does, then you are leaving. However, *do not* threaten to leave unless you are willing and able to follow through!

Q: *My husband and I have been married for 20 years. Ten years ago, when I was feeling strongly the lack of intimacy between us, I got involved in a brief affair with a coworker. After a month, I realized it wasn't the answer to my problems, and I broke it off. My husband has been in recovery for a year from his sex addiction and I have been in recovery for my codependency. He has disclosed all of his acting-out behaviors to me. Should I tell him about this affair?*

What's good for the goose is also good for the gander. If you expected him to be honest with you about his sexual acting out, then wouldn't he expect you to be honest about yours? If you are both in recovery, you should both practice a program of rigorous honesty.

Q: *I saw my good buddy's wife sitting in a coffee shop with another guy. They were holding hands, and occasionally they kissed. My buddy thinks he has a great marriage. Should I tell him what I saw?*

Would you want to find out from your buddy or from your wife if the situation were reversed? Most people would want to hear this from their mate. Have a chat with his wife. Tell her what you saw and that you think it is her responsibility to be honest with him about the trouble in their marriage. Tell her you hope they can get help and work things out, but you won't keep the secret for her. Let her know you realize that figuring out how and when to tell him isn't easy, but you will tell him in another week unless she does. Remind her that you remain a support for both of them should either of them need someone to talk to after the disclosure.

Q: My wife and I are in marriage counseling. I told my therapist about several affairs I've had over the years. I'm not involved with anyone right now. The therapist says that as long as the last affair is over, there's no point in telling my wife, that we should focus on the present. My wife keeps blaming herself for stuff that's happened between us, which I know is at least in part because I was involved with these other women. Should I tell my wife?

I tend to agree with your therapist. Think about what kinds of things you did to create distance or give you an excuse to get out of the house. Take responsibility for your actions during the times she is blaming herself for the trouble between you. You can acknowledge what you did that contributed to the distress between you during that period, such as blaming her or criticizing her to create distance. On the other hand, if your mate has made it clear that she wants honesty between you about the past and the present, it would be useful to tell her. Most people in marital therapy who are not dealing with addiction are encouraged to focus on the present and not hold on to old history to create chaos now.

I notice that you haven't said you are through with affairs, just that there's no one else now. I would encourage you to look a little further with your therapist into your history of several affairs. Perhaps you are indeed dealing with an addiction, in which case you need to take additional steps for your own recovery. Those steps would include eventually sharing your past with your wife.

Q: The other day I caught my 12-year-old son looking at Internet pornography on his computer. He doesn't know about my own problem with cybersex addiction, and I was horrified to think that he's already involved in the same behavior that almost cost me my marriage. I know that kids, especially boys, are very curious about sex, so hopefully this is just normal behavior for his age. I don't want to make a mountain out of a molehill. How do I talk to him about this without making it so forbidden that it becomes all the more desirable for him?

Think about your values. What do you want your son to know about treating women with dignity rather than making them an object? What would you say if your 12-year-old was experimenting with alcohol? Many men in recovery speak to their adolescent sons about this issue. First they explain how people can be addicted to behaviors as well as drugs; some then disclose their own addiction. (At some point you need to discuss your addiction because your children have your genes, thus increasing their propensity toward addiction.) Second, they acknowledge that it is normal to be curious about women's bodies and sex, but that pornography is not the best way to learn. Then they give the adolescent a few age-appropriate sexuality books such as *Changing Bodies, Changing Lives.* Additionally, they remind the young men that the woman in the picture is someone's sister or daughter and ask if they would want someone looking at and having sexual thoughts or masturbating to images of their sister or daughter. This leaves the door open to further discussions of healthy masturbation, sex within a committed relationship, or any other issues that may come up.

Even if you do not disclose your addiction, it is important to tell your son that although you viewed pornography earlier in your life, you are no longer going to do it because it interferes with your relationship with his mother and because it shows disrespect to women. And be sure to tell him that you do not want him to view pornography on the computer or elsewhere in your home.

Q: When I was 15 I got pregnant and gave up the child for adoption. I've felt a lot of shame over the years about my early sexual behavior, and never told my husband. My daughter is now 21, and I'd very much like to try to find her. Should I tell my husband? I think my husband would forgive me for my behavior, but I also think he'd be very angry about my keeping this from him all these years. I hesitate to rock the boat when we have a very good marriage.

If you plan to try to find your daughter, most likely you will need your husband's help. If you find her and she wants to reconcile, you will undoubtedly want to share that celebration with him. You need to tell him so that he can share in your desire to find her. It sounds like you have a solid relationship. Your husband may be mad or disappointed, but if he gets to hear about your shame and fear as a teen, it seems probable that he will soon be by your side in this goal.

Q: My parents don't know about my husband's sex addiction or his recovery program. As for my own co-addict recovery, I told them I'm going to a "women's support group," which they think is just an opportunity for women to complain about their husbands. I'd like to be able to tell them more, but my husband is sure they'd be very judgmental and negative about him, and he's probably right. Should I keep them in the dark?

This is an issue that is between you and your husband. If your parents have been judgmental in the past, it may be best not to tell them. For now, this information seems to be a private matter between you and your mate.

Q: My husband knows about my affairs up to a year ago, when I got honest with him and started counseling. At the time he told me if I were ever unfaithful again, he'd leave me and file for custody of our two children. Since then, I've had an affair with a guy from a chat room. I'm getting help from my therapist and sponsor in SAA, but it would really hurt him and ultimately our children if I told him. Don't you think this is what the 9th step is for—to make amends except when it would hurt others?

Men are more likely than women to leave relationships after disclosure, but in general, most partners do not leave after a relapse despite the threat to do so. It sounds like you are responding more to your shame and fear of losing him than the actual fear of hurting him and your kids—otherwise hurting them would have been a deterrent to relapse. Also, don't forget, people grow from pain and disappointment if given the opportunity. Do you want him to stay in the relationship based on misinformation, or by choice? What will be the impact if you don't tell and he finds out later? Can you remain in recovery if you do not tell him? (Clearly you were not able to remain in recovery as a result of telling and his threat!) Our experience is that if you hold onto this secret, it will fuel the rationalizations that you will later use to give yourself permission to act out. Then you are back where you started.

Q: I've been involved with prostitutes as part of my sex addiction—I just had an HIV test and it was negative. I'd rather not upset my wife unnecessarily. Should I tell her? She knows about my addiction but thinks it is pornography and go-go bars.

Despite your negative HIV test, if you have had sex with a prostitute you may have infected your wife with some other type of sexually transmitted disease such as chlamydia (which often has few symptoms until it is very progressed). She deserves to know so that she can protect her own health. Additionally, telling one lie to cover another lie is an invitation for relapse. She will be even more upset if she finds she has a sexually transmitted disease or some other evidence that you have not been honest with her.

Q: *What's the best way to tell our 15-year-old daughter and 17-year-old son about my sex addiction? I've been sober for three years and my wife goes to S-Anon.*

Your children are old enough to know about both addiction and sexuality and are at the age in which kids are talking about both and experimenting a lot. Ask them for a block of uninterrupted time for a serious talk. Both you and your wife should be present. Tell them that you want to share information that is hard for you to talk about and you realize they may not want to hear. (Most kids do not want to have this sensitive information. At the same time, they want some explanation about various things that have happened connected to your behaviors.) Because there may be a genetic link to addiction, and because most addictive behavior begins in adolescence, they need to know so that they can be aware of the warning signs of any addiction. Remind them that people can become addicted to behaviors as well as substances. Disclose that you are a recovering addict and that your drug of choice has been sex. Tell them that you've been honest with their Mom about what you have done in your sex addiction. Often in first conversations, specific information is omitted, especially with younger children. However, if you and your wife agree on the content, you may give teenagers more information, leaving out specific details. For example: "I got involved with viewing pornography and compulsive masturbation. Although masturbation is healthy for some people, for me, it was a way to escape and to avoid feeling anything."

Here is a chance for you to talk about the values that guide your recovery: "I also want to say that I now feel strongly that most of the time pornography objectifies women and does not provide any real opportunity for learning how to be with other people much less solve problems. I feel bad about how I used it. It took me away from Mom and caused problems in our relationship."

Mom might chime in here about her codependent part. It may be useful to say that experimental use of certain "adult" behaviors or drugs to alter your mood is common among young people, but kids who have addiction in their background need to be careful not to fall into the trap of believing this is a solution to their problems.

Now ask if they have any questions or want to say anything. Be quiet and give them a chance to get beyond the discomfort of speaking about this. To end, tell them if they ever have any questions to let you or their Mom know. Tell them that you love them. Do take opportunities to bring this up again so it becomes easier for everyone to talk about.

Q: *I've been sober from my bottom-line of cybersex for six months, but I haven't been able to stop the masturbation yet. Do I need to tell my wife every time I masturbate?*

After your initial disclosure, it is important for couples to decide what to share. Early on, partners usually do want to know when someone has had a slip and what the addict is trying to do to stay in recovery. It is important that she not measure her self worth by your ability to remain sober. (A period of abstinence from masturbation is useful and important for you as an addict. Some addicts, but not all, are able to return to a healthy form of masturbation at a later date.) You must also discuss how you can be honest and not get punished for your honesty. Everyone must learn to deal with their own anxiety in the early stages of recovery from addiction and co-addiction.

Q: *My boss is beginning to give me heat because I leave so often to go to counseling and psychiatric appointments. How much should I tell him about my sex addiction?*

Unless you have a close working relationship with your boss, telling is risky. Telling anyone at work has to be weighed against the odds that the information will be misused or that you may get fired. If you feel your job would be in jeopardy, you may have to adjust your therapy schedule or arrange to work extra hours before or after work. If you are a valued employee and you feel you have a good working relationship with your boss, then disclose only general information and the need to continue in therapy. If you can be specific about how much time you will need off, that is usually helpful to your boss.

Q: *I'm caught between wanting and not wanting to tell my minister about my sex addiction. He keeps requesting that I volunteer for Youth Group work. I have an attraction to teenage girls but haven't acted on any of those fantasies. What would be the best way to handle this?*

If you have been part of the congregation for some time and feel that you have a good relationship with the minister, then disclosure will help you be firm in your boundaries and may help educate the minister, who is in a position to help others. On the other hand, if few people know you and this is your first community service, request some other type of volunteer position until you are better known and you get to know the minister better. He should be bound to confidentiality, but in the event any teen made a complaint, you will probably be the first to be blamed.

Q: *I am gay and my sponsor says the only sobriety is to be abstinent. I am not okay with this. Should I change sponsors or is he right? My Twelve-Step group agrees that abstinence is sobriety.*

Some Twelve-Step groups do believe that unless you are married, abstinence is the only way to recovery. However, same-sex marriages are illegal in most states, so marriage cannot determine sobriety for same-sex couples. Some period of abstinence is important for all recovering addicts. Most gay men determine that after a period of recovery, they want to develop a set of guidelines for healthy sexual experimentation and expression. This might include having sex only in a committed relationship, or no sex with strangers and no use of any type of mood-altering drug or alcohol during sex. You must decide for yourself what is healthy gay behavior, but that is very hard to do without input from others early in recovery. Get some advice from other gay men with some lengthy, good recovery about how they have dealt with this. You might be more comfortable in a Twelve-Step sex addiction recovery program whose definition of sobriety doesn't require abstinence for gays. You may also want to find a gay sponsor if possible.

Q: *I just got married. My wife knows about my sex addiction and is very support-ive of my recovery. She does not know my whole past history, especially the cyber-relationship I had with another woman when I was married before. How much does she need to know now?*

Unless you agreed to tell her all about your past, or unless you have already relapsed or slipped or are fearful for your recovery by keeping this from her, what is in the past is not as important as what you share now.

APPENDIX B: Suggested Reading

Understanding and Recovering from Sex Addiction

Augustine Fellowship Staff. *Sex and Love Addicts Anonymous.* Boston: Sex and Love Addicts Anonymous, 1986. The official book of the fellowship of SLAA.

Carnes, Patrick. *Don't Call It Love: Recovery From Sexual Addiction.* New York: Bantam, 1991. Results of research on more than 1,000 sex addicts.

Carnes, Patrick. *Out of the Shadows: Understanding Sexual Addiction.* Minneapolis: CompCare, 1983. The groundbreaking book that explains sex addiction in easily understood terms.

————. *Sexual Anorexia: Overcoming Sexual Self-Hatred.* Center City, Minn.: Hazelden, 1997. The flip side of excessive sexual activities is avoiding sex while obsessing about it.

————, David L. Delmonico, and Elizabeth Griffin. *In the Shadows of the Net: Breaking Free of Compulsive Online Sexual Behavior.* Center City, Minn.: Hazelden, 2001. An informative book about cybersex addiction.

Earle, Ralph, and Gregory Crow. *Lonely All the Time: Recognizing, Understanding, and Overcoming Sex Addiction, for Addicts and Codependents.* New York: Pocket Books, 1989. Another easy-to-understand explanation of sex addiction.

Earle, Ralph, and Marcus Earle. *Sex Addiction: Case Studies and Management.* New York: Brunner Mazel, 1995. A good guide for therapists working with sex addicts.

Hope and Recovery: A Twelve Step Guide for Healing from Compulsive Sexual Behavior. Center City, Minn.: Hazelden Education and Publishing, 1987. This recovery guide for sex addicts is modeled after the "Big Book" of Alcoholics Anonymous. It explains the problem and provides many personal stories.

Kasl, Charlotte Davis. *Women, Sex, and Addiction: A Search for Love and Power.* New York: Ticknor and Fields, 1989. About women sex addicts, and women who hook up with sex addicts.

Schneider, Jennifer and Robert Weiss. *Cybersex Exposed: Simple Fantasy or Obsession.* Center City, Minn.: Hazelden Education and Publishing, 2001. Understanding and recovering from cybersex addiction—for addicts and their partners.

Sexaholics Anonymous. *Sexaholics Anonymous.* Simi Valley, Calif.: Sexaholics Anonymous. 1989. The official book of the fellowship of SA.

Understanding and Recovering from Sexual Co-addiction and Codependency

Beattie, Melody. *Codependent No More: How to Stop Controlling Others and Start Caring for Yourself.* Center City, Minn.: Hazelden, 1987. The classic book for those who want to understand and recover from codependency.

Carnes, Patrick. *The Betrayal Bond: Breaking Free of Exploitive Relationships.* Deerfield Beach, Fla.: Health Communications, 1997. This book shows how childhood trauma influences adult relationships.

Larsen, Earnie. *Stage II Relationships: Love Beyond Addiction.* San Francisco: Harper & Row, 1987. This book shows the importance of rebuilding relationships after Stage I recovery.

Norwood, Robin. *Women Who Love too Much: When You Keep Wishing and Hoping He'll Change.* Los Angeles: Jeremy Tarcher, Inc., 1985. The classic book about women who get involved with addicts and how they can heal.

———. *Letters from Women Who Love too Much*. New York: Pocket Books, 1988. More on healing from codependency.

Schaef, Anne Wilson. *Escape from Intimacy: The Pseudo-Relationship Addictions: Untangling the "Love" Addictions: Sex, Romance, Relationships*. San Francisco: Harper San Francisco, 1990. Explains the differences among these related but different addictions.

———. *Codependence: Misunderstood/Mistreated*. Minneapolis: Winston Press, 1986.

Schaeffer, Brenda. *Is It Love or Is It Addiction?*, 2nd ed. Center City, Minn.: Hazelden, 1997. Useful for understanding healthy versus unhealthy relationships.

Schneider, Jennifer. *Back from Betrayal: Recovering from His Affairs*, 2nd ed. Tucson, Ariz.: Recovery Resources Press, 2001. The classic guide for women involved with sex-addicted men.

Schneider, Jennifer, and Burt Schneider. *Sex, Lies, and Forgiveness: Couples Speak on Healing from Sex Addiction*, 2nd ed. Tucson, Ariz.: Recovery Resources Press, 1999. A guide for couples who seek to rebuild their relationship.

———. *Rebuilding Trust: For Couples Committed to Recovery*. Center City, Minn.: Hazelden Education and Publishing, 1989. (Available from Recovery Resources Press, Tucson, Ariz.) Guidelines, in pamphlet form, for couples.

Weiss, Douglas, and Diane DeBusk. *Women Who Love Sex Addicts: Help for Healing from the Effects of a Relationship with a Sex Addict*. Fort Worth, Tex.: Discovery Press, 1993. A book for partners of sex addicts.

Relationships, Infidelity, and Affairs

Bader, Ellyn, and Peter T. Pearson. *In Quest of the Mythical Mate*. New York: Brunner/Mazel, 1988.

———. *Tell Me No Lies: How to Face the Truth and Build a Loving Marriage*. New York: St. Martin's Press, 2000.

Berzon, Betty. *Permanent Partners: Building Gay and Lesbian Relationships That Last*. New York: E. P. Dutton, 1988.

Brown, Emily. *Patterns of Infidelity and Their Treatment.* New York: Brunner/Mazel, 1991.

Ford, Charles. *Lies, Lies, Lies: The Psychology of Deception.* Washington, D.C.: The American Psychiatric Press, 1996.

Forward, Susan. *When Your Lover Is a Liar.* New York: HarperCollins, 1999.

Hendrix, Harville. *Getting the Love You Want. A Guide For Couples.* New York: Pocket Books. 1990.

————. *Keeping the Love You Find.* New York: Pocket Books. 1992.

Imber-Black, Evan. *The Secret Life of Families: Truth-Telling, Privacy, and Reconcilliation in a Tell-All Society.* New York: Bantam Books. 1998.

Lawson, Annette. *Adultery: An Analysis of Love and Betrayal.* New York: Basic Books, 1988.

Levine, Stephen and Ondrea Levine. *Embracing the Beloved: Relationship As a Path of Awakening.* New York: Anchor Books, 1995.

Moultrop, D. J. *Husbands, Wives, and Lovers: The Emotional System of the Extramarital Affair.* New York: Guilford, 1990.

Nelson, Mariah Burton. *The Unburdened Heart.* San Francisco: HarperCollins, 2000.

Pittman, Frank. *Private Lies: Infidelity and the Betrayal of Intimacy.* New York: W. W. Norton, 1989.

Scarff, Maggie. *Intimate Partners.* New York: Random House, 1987.

Schnarch, David. *Passionate Marriage.* New York: Holt and Company, 1997.

Spring, Janis Abraham. *After the Affair: Healing the Pain and Rebuilding Trust When a Partner Has Been Unfaithful.* New York: HarperCollins, 1996. No matter what the cause of the affair, this book describes how each party feels and how to recover.

Subotnik, Rona, and Gloria Harris. *Surviving Infidelity: Making Decisions, Recovering from the Pain.* Holbrook, Mass.: Adams Publishing, 1994. A cognitive-behavioral approach to understanding and recovering from infidelity.

Vaughn, Peggy. *Beyond Affairs.* New York: Bantam Books, 1981.

———. *The Monogamy Myth.* New York: Newmarket Press, 1989.

Healthy Sexuality

Barbach, Lonnie Garfield. *For Each Other: Sharing Sexual Intimacy.* Garden City, N.J.: Anchor Press, 1982. Practical advice for couples.

Blumstein, Philip, and Pepper Schwartz. *American Couples: Money, Work, Sex.* New York: William Morrow, 1983. This research-based book describes behavior norms for American couples.

Canning-Fulton, Maureen. *Reclaiming Intimacy: Moving from Sexual Addiction to Healthy Sexuality.* Gentle Path Press, 2002. Interactive workbook designed for individuals beginning sexual addiction recovery.

Gochros, Jean: *When Husbands Come Out of the Closet.* New York: Harrington Park Press, 1989. How wives deal with their husbands' homosexuality.

Hunter, Mic. *Joyous Sexuality.* Minneapolis: CompCare Publications, 1992. Simple but clear description of healthy sexuality.

Maltz, Wendy. *Passionate Hearts: The Poetry of Sexual Love.* New York: New World Library, 2000.

———. *The Sexual Healing Journey: A Guide for Survivors of Sexual Abuse.* San Francisco: HarperCollins, 1991.

Moore, Thomas. *The Soul of Sex: Cultivating Life As an Act of Love.* New York: HarperCollins, 1998.

APPENDIX C: Recovery Resources

Addresses of Twelve-Step Programs for
Sex Addiction

For the Addict:

Sexaholics Anonymous (SA)
P.O. Box 111910
Nashville, TN 37222-1910
(615) 331-6230
Email: **saico@sa.org**
Web site: **www.sa.org**

Sex Addicts Anonymous (SAA)
P.O. Box 70949
Houston, TX 77270
(713) 869-4902
Email: **info@saa-recovery.org**
Web site: **www.sexaa.org**

Sex and Love Addicts Anonymous (SLAA)
P.O. Box 650010
West Newton, MA 02165-0010
(781) 255-8825
Email: **slaafws@aol.com**
Web site: **www.slaafws.org**

Sexual Compulsives Anonymous (SCA)
Old Chelsea Station, P.O. Box 1585
New York, NY 10013-0935
(310) 859-5585
Web site: **www.sca-recovery.org**

In Canada:
P.O. Box 72044
Burnaby, BC V5H 4PQ
Canada
(604) 290-9382

For the Partner or Family Member:

Codependents of Sex Addicts (COSA)
P.O. Box 14537
Minneapolis, MN 55414
(612) 537-6904
Email: **info@cosa-recovery.org**
Web site: **www.cosa-recovery.org**

S-Anon International Family Groups
P.O. Box 111242
Nashville, TN 37222-1242
(615) 833-3152
Email: **sanon@sanon.org**
Web site: **www.sanon.org**

For the Teenage Family Members of Sexual Addicts:

S-Ateen
S-Anon International Family Groups
P.O. Box 111242
Nashville, TN 37222-1242
(615) 833-3152
Email: **sanon@sanon.org**
Web site: **www.sanon.org/Teenchk.htm**

For Couples:

Recovering Couples Anonymous (RCA)
P.O. Box 11872
St. Louis, MO 63105
(314) 830-2600
Email: **RCAWSO@iname.com**
Web site: **www.recovering-couples.org**

For Sexual Trauma Survivors:

Survivors of Incest Anonymous (SIA)
P.O. Box 21817
Baltimore, MD 21222
(410) 282-3400

Incest Survivors Anonymous (ISA)
P.O. Box 17245
Long Beach, CA 90807

For Sex Workers:

Prostitutes Anonymous (PA)
PO Box 131
Kennard, NE 68034
(800) 537-7681

Other Resources

National Council on Sexual Addiction and Compulsivity (NCSAC)
P.O. Box 725544
Atlanta, GA 31139
(770) 541-9912
Email: ncsac@ncsac.org
Web site: **www.ncsac.org**

Dr. Patrick Carnes' Web site, with information on various aspects of sex addiction: **www.sexhelp.com**

Jennifer Schneider's Web site, with articles and available books on sex addiction: **www.jenniferschneider.com**

Web site dedicated to information on cybersex addiction: **www.cybersexualaddiction.com**

APPENDIX D: Our Research Results

In this appendix, we provide you with additional information regarding the survey we did of sex addicts and partners (or former partners) about their experiences with disclosing secrets. Although the survey was specifically about issues of sexual acting out, we believe the results will be of use to other addicts as well. The detailed results were previously published (Schneider, J. P., Irons, R. R., and Corley, M. D., Disclosure of extramarital sexual activities by sexually exploitative professionals and other persons with addictive or compulsive sexual disorders. *Journal of Sex Education and Therapy* 24:177–187, 1999; and Schneider, J. P., Corley, M. D., and Irons, R. R., Surviving disclosure of infidelity: Results of an international survey of 164 recovering sex addicts and their partners. *Sexual Addiction and Compulsivity* 5:189–217, 1998).

The survey was done in two parts. Initially, we sought couples for whom sex addiction had been an issue. However, because we were seeking only couples, we recognized that our survey was deficient in people whose relationship had permanently ended, so we subsequently added a second sample of formerly married sex addicts and co-addicts. Because this project preceded the Internet explosion, hard copies of the surveys were distributed, and they were returned by regular mail. Altogether we received surveys from 102 sex addicts (89% male) and 94 partners or former partners (95% female). The mean recovery time from sex addiction was 3.4 years, with a range of 2 months to 14 years.

Tables D.1 and D.2 show some of our results. They are further discussed throughout this book.

Table D.1   Occupations of Respondents (N = 191)

Licensed helping professionals	46 (24%)
Other regulated professionals	40 (21%)
Other employed (CEOs, trades, etc.)	82 (43%)
Non-wage earners	23 (12%)

Table D.2   Outcomes of Threats to Leave (N = 47)

Never left:	**34 (75.6%)**
Partner didn't follow through with threat	17 (37.8%)
Addict and/or partner got help	17 (37.8%)
Left:	**11 (25%)**
Reconciled	7 (15.5%)
Divorced or still separated	4 (8.8%)

Rightness of Disclosure

The survey asked addicts and partners whether they felt *at the time* that disclosure was the right thing to do, and how they feel about it *now*. The findings are summarized in Tables D.3 and D.4.

Table D.3   Addicts' Perspectives on the Rightness of Disclosure (N = 76)

It was definitely probably right	44 (57.9%)	73 (96.1%)
I'm not sure	23 (30.3%)	1 (1.3%)
Probably/certainly wrong	9 (11.8%)	1 (1.3%)

Table D.4   Partners' Perspectives on the Rightness of Disclosure

It was definitely/probably right	61 (81.3%)	66 (93.0%)
I'm not sure	12 (16.0%)	4 (5.6%)
Probably/certainly wrong	2 (2.6%)	1 (1.3%)

Recommendations to Other Couples

When asked, "Would you recommend disclosure to other couples?" a majority of the respondents said yes. Their responses are summarized in Table D.5.

Table D.5   Would You Recommend Disclosure to Other Couples?

Definitely or probably yes	54 (69%)	62 (82.7%)
Uncertain	17 (22%)	11 (14.7%)
Probably or definitely no	7 (8.9%)	2 (2.6%)

Dealing with Slips and Relapses

Because addiction is a chronic disorder, significant slips and relapses may occur. Even when sex addicts do not violate significant boundaries, many deal with recurrent or occasional additive sexual thoughts or minor behaviors (for example, flirting, viewing pornography, or masturbation). We asked addicts, "What types of information are you likely to disclose to your partner about your *current* addictive sexual thoughts, feelings, and behaviors?" Their responses are listed in Table D.6.

Table D.6   What Addicts Disclose About Their Current Status (N = 78)

When I'm at risk for relapse	34 (44%)
My thoughts and fantasies	14 (18%)
Nothing	13 (17%)
Everything	13 (17%)
How I'm doing in general	11 (14%)
When there is health risk to partner	6 (8%)
When the relationship is affected	4 (5%)

We also asked partners from our original sample, "What type of information do you currently want to know about your partner's addictive sexual thoughts, feelings, and behaviors?" The results are shown in Table D.7.

Table D.7   What Information Partners Currently Seek About Addicts' Status (N=82)

Disclosed Behavior	Number Wanting Disclosure
Some specific information	31 (38%)
General status of addict's recovery	27 (33%)
Nothing	10 (12%)
Everything	6 (7%)
It varies, depending on partner's state of mind	3 (4%)
No answer/divorced	5 (6%)

Note: It is common in quantitative research for a participant not to answer all parts of a question or all questions. For example, 76 of the addicts reported what they thought at the time of disclosure but only 75 reported how they felt now. The reported data in the tables reflects actual responses, so totals do not always equal 100%.

EXERCISE FORMS

Y ou may want to make several copies of the following Journal and Decision Matrix worksheets, so that you can use them frequently.

Thoughts-Feelings Journal

Date:_____

1. Event or Situation

What happened? Who was there? When and where?

_____

_____

_____

_____

_____

_____

_____

_____

_____

2. Thoughts

What thoughts were going through your head just before the event, during the event, and immediately after the event? Circle the thoughts that may be related to your core beliefs about yourself.

_____

_____

_____

_____

_____

_____

_____

_____

_____

_____

3. Emotions

What emotions or feelings did you feel? Underline the strongest two feelings. Circle feelings that are triggers for you to want to act out.

_____

_____

_____

_____

_____

_____

_____

_____

_____

4. Body Sensations

Often the body gives us a signal that something is going on before we are really aware that we may be in a bad place. Listen to your body. Describe any body sensations you felt during the process. What does your body do when you get angry or sad? How does it tell you that you are having a strong emotional feeling or reaction?

_____

_____

_____

_____

_____

_____

_____

_____

_____

_____

5. What I Did Well

When we've gotten into a highly emotional situation that we mismanaged, we think we made a mess of everything. This section is to remind you that you did do something right (usually). Think about what part of the situation you handled well or did not make worse. Note those items here.

_____

_____

_____

_____

_____

_____

_____

_____

_____

_____

_____

6. How I Made Things Worse

In this section, list the ways you made the situation worse.

_____

_____

_____

_____

_____

_____

_____

_____

_____

_____

7. Thinking Errors

Look at your thoughts from Section 2. Are any of those thoughts thinking errors? Actively search for information or evidence that contradicts the thoughts or supports the thoughts.

_____

_____

_____

_____

_____

_____

_____

_____

_____

_____

_____

_____

_____

_____

8. Plan of Action

This is what you plan to do to help this situation and plan for next time.

_____

_____

_____

_____

_____

_____

_____

_____

Decision Making Matrix

Date: _____